"This is an incredibly useful book, written v
compassion. Within these pages you'll find a
and practical tips for those 'heated moments' in therapy sessions. An essential addition to the bookcase of any therapist interested in mindfulness-based approaches to psychotherapy."

—Russ Harris, MD, best-selling author of *The Happiness Trap*

"For all therapists who have a 'difficult' client in their caseload, this well-written and personable book is a must-read. Dr. Abblett challenges us to 'lean in,' or move toward, our behaviorally difficult clients, to be mindful of our emotional reactions to them, and to use what we learn to improve our therapy. Replete with terrific exercises that place us in session with these clients, both novice and seasoned professional can benefit from not just reading this volume, but from working through it."

—Phillip M. Kleespies, PhD, Assistant Clinical Professor of Psychiatry, Boston University School of Medicine/ VA Boston Health Care System

"Mitch Abblett has created an invaluable and much-needed tool for clinicians, young and seasoned alike, who are tested daily by difficult clients. With refreshing frankness, empathy, and no small degree of humor he explains how to negotiate the trickiest of therapeutic territory, bringing us face to face with the single most challenging aspect of our work: ourselves."

—Bobby Hermesch, Milieu Director, The Manville School

"*The Heat of the Moment in Treatment* should be required reading for all graduate students in psychotherapy and their professors. Dr. Abblett offers a warm, compassionate, humorous, humble, and human approach to dealing with challenging clients that is also downright practical in its exercises and reflections. This wonderful book is a gift not only to therapists, but also to teachers, medical professionals, clergy members, and anyone in the helping professions."

—Christopher Willard, PsyD; Author, *Child's Mind: Mindfulness Practices to Help Our Children Be More Focused, Calm, and Relaxed*

The Heat of the Moment in Treatment

A NORTON PROFESSIONAL BOOK

The Heat of the Moment in Treatment

Mindful Management of Difficult Clients

Mitch Abblett

W. W. Norton & Company

New York • London

Previous edition published under the title DROPPING THE ROPE: A Clinician's Skill-Building Workbook

Manufacturing by R. R. Donnelley-Harrisonburg
Production manager: Leeann Graham

Library of Congress Cataloging-in-Publication Data

Abblett, Mitch.
[Dropping the rope]
The heat of the moment in treatment : mindful management of difficult clients / Mitch Abblett.
pages cm. — (A Norton professional book)
Revised edition of: Dropping the rope / Mitch Abblett. 2012.
Includes bibliographical references and index.
ISBN 978-0-393-70831-8 (pbk.)
1. Interpersonal psychotherapy. 2. Psychotherapist and patient. I. Title.
RC489.I55A23 2013
616.89'14—dc23 2013001704

ISBN: 978-0-393-70831-8 (pbk.)

W. W. Norton & Company, Inc., 500 Fifth Avenue, New York, N.Y. 10110
www.wwnorton.com
W. W. Norton & Company Ltd., Castle House, 75/76 Wells Street, London W1T 3QT

1 2 3 4 5 6 7 8 9 0

For my wife, Lisa
You teach me every day by example
what it means to focus on others

Contents

Acknowledgments

As a lover of metaphors, I'm going to "bookend" those deserving of my thanks during the process of researching, writing, editing, marketing, and occasional hair-pulling this thing together. On the one end of the shelf, and most important, are my wife, parents, brother and sister, my in-laws, and even my two-year-old daughter, Celia. In your multifaceted and diverse ways, you have been there for me, encouraging, distracting, and sometimes propping me up when things got tough. Just when I thought I had nothing "difficult" to write about, I had *that* interaction with each of you at some point to inspire me (just kidding).

In the "middle" of this book process are all the colleagues who either generously reviewed the manuscript and provided their thoughts and wisdom (Phil Kleespies, Chris Willard, Kirk Strosahl, Russ Harris, Bobby Hermesch, Nancy Frumer-Styron), or provided me with some nugget of guidance, input, or support (Lisa Coyne, Chris Germer, John Weisz, Hanna Nowicki, Jim Prince, and all the dedicated staff of the Manville School). Interspersed in this section of the shelf are all the indirect mentors—those whose writings, talks, and presence seeped into the marrow of my practice and writing (Joseph Goldstein, Jack Kornfield, Sylvia Boorstein, His Holiness the Dalai Lama, Thich Nhat Hanh, Chogyam Trungpa, Pema Chodron, Gregory Kramer, Jon Kabat-Zinn).

This book would not have been possible without that initial email inquiry and subsequent diligent professionalism of Deborah Malmud at Norton Professional Books. Deborah—your input and guidance were crucial to making this book a reality. I also want to thank Sophie Hagen, Ben Yarling, and Karen Fisher for all your efforts in polishing and positioning the manuscript.

And then there's the other end of the shelf—the "bookend" of all of my clients across time. Though any of you included in these pages are highly altered and aggregated in order to protect confidentiality, I remember you all as individuals, and your importance in my life cannot be underestimated. You have all been my greatest teachers and I've been humbled by your willingness to allow me to bear witness to the light and dark of your lives. If our time together was ever "difficult," we, not you, made it so. This book, and my ongoing work, are focused on enabling others, both clinicians and clients, to benefit from the "heat" of our struggles together.

Human misery must somewhere have a stop. There is no wind that always blows a storm.

—Euripides, 422 B.C.E.

Every calamity is a spur and valuable hint.

—Ralph Waldo Emerson, 1860

Introduction
Going Inside Out

I'm going to take a leap and share something with you . . . I have hated clients. Call the Board of Psychology if you want. Start a petition to kick me out of the profession. Say what you will, but it's true nonetheless. I've literally loathed some of the individuals who came to me for help.

I've repeatedly proven Isaac Newton's genius. In response to clients' "dysfunctional," button-pressing in-session actions, at times I've found myself pulled toward equally intense, less-than-therapeutic inner (and sometimes outer) reactions. These people, these clients—willing to part with their money, lay themselves bare, and acknowledge their struggles and failings—have sometimes led me to grit my teeth in session out of unbridled distaste. Does this make me a bad therapist, a bad person altogether? Since I'm a clinician, am I not supposed to be unfailingly empathic? There was a time in my not-so-distant professional past when I would have flinched and answered "yes" to the above.

* * *

My client, whom I'll call Sarah, an 11-year-old girl diagnosed with bipolar disorder, was a student in the private therapeutic day school where I work as a clinician. It was her annual school district team meeting, and the 10 or so of us adults sat calmly around a conference table to discuss how to best educate and clinically treat a girl who rarely knew calm—her world was a vortex of angst, anxiety, and anger. I'd seen her try to flip over a table in a fit of rage, and I thought of that as we all shuffled our papers around the table. "Does the team agree Sarah continues to require special education services?" the

cont'd on next page

cont'd from previous page

school district representative asked of all of us (except Sarah, who was elsewhere in the building, doing her best to navigate the tightrope of another school day).

It was the same, pro forma question every year. Expensive special education services had to be justified. Professionals had to show that Sarah's emotional disability blocked her access to an education. Tens of thousands of state education dollars were not to be tossed about lightly. The answer was obvious. The meeting was not just a formality; it was a muted parade of pain. I looked past Sarah's teacher, and the host of other support staff at our school working with her, to Sarah's father. There was an awkward silence needing a sharp jab to move the meeting to a merciful conclusion. "Yes," I said, and others nodded their agreement. Sarah's father stared blankly at the tabletop in front of him.

"How can you love a child like this?" Sarah's dad asked me with his eyes on more than one occasion. I never heard him say it, but the question was telegraphed by his lifeless droning, the void about his eyes and mouth as he listened to me describe her most recent outburst in the classroom or during recess on the playground. An aura of paternal impotence surrounded him, and I could hardly blame him, though at times I found myself tempted to. "If only you would hang in and reach out to him," I'd say to myself as he left the school after one of our appointments. "Don't pull your depressive disappearing act on her again," I'd think in his direction, the irritation bubbling. Over the years I knew him, I struggled with my regard for him as an artist of absence. He had a knack for emotionally disappearing when Sarah seemed most in need. I was certain from some of Sarah's behavior that she was well aware of her father's resentment. "What about me?" her dad told me once during a meeting. "Don't I get to have a life? Everything is for Sarah. I've burned myself up in that kid."

"Of course you have," I thought behind my pensive, caring exterior. The empathic shell of myself was highly practiced and readily conjured during sessions with this parent. "You're her damn father and you're supposed to put her first," I yelled inside.

There were two "difficult" clients in this case—a volatile girl who would often let you know of her suffering less with words than with spitting, swearing, and flailing limbs; and then there was her father. This man, himself struggling with mental health issues, would vacillate between action and inaction. His struggle to do what was "right" or "ideal" as a parent pulled at me, particularly when I saw the implications for Sarah. I experienced inescapable tugging in this work, and I paid a toll in not proactively addressing the inevitable reactions.

* * *

Together, we're going to wonder what it means and what to do when we experience strong reactions in response to our clients—even reactions as unsightly as disgust or hatred. We'll take a journey together in understanding our reactions to difficult client behavior, and look to improve our skills for compassion, perspective, and proactive handling of the most complex and unnerving interactions we encounter during the course of our clinical work.

We all have difficult clients in our caseloads (or have in the recent past). My hope for your experience of this workbook is that, by the end, you'll have expanded your view of what this "difficulty" is really about—that you'll understand and agree that this book's title is a tad off the mark, but it's where we, as clinicians, often begin in addressing our own experience of the toughest aspects of our work. When the going gets the roughest with clients, we often start with a finger pointed firmly in the client's direction. My hope is that, by the end of this book, you'll see *beyond* the client and the challenges they present during your interactions and see the work as a joint, mutually determined enterprise. Marriages, not individuals, end in divorce. The same applies to clinical work. If it ends badly, it is the responsibility of all parties involved.

Care to Play?

Have you ever played an actual game of tug-of-war? I'm talking about gripping a rope and yanking with all your might as the persons on the other side do the same. Have you ever tried to prove yourself by leaning back, gritting your teeth, and heaving with all your might? If so (or just play along and imagine what it would be like if you did pick up said rope), ask yourself: What is the point of this game?

The typical response is "strength." We play in order to prove our superior brute force—that by the bulge of coordinated full-body muscle flexing, our yanking is so much greater than theirs. Our muscles allow us to move the rope a few yards onto our side, onto our territory, and that makes us superior. Hooray!

Seems a bit silly, right? I guess it's fun to watch such feats of strength at a festival, or maybe among athletes who depend on strength for their particular sport, but what about for clinicians? How much are we trying to prove our superior "strength," our dominance, over our clients? Do we really want clients to back up and respect our insight, our empathy—our therapeutic prowess? And yet, ask yourself this as well: How often have I played a version of tug-of-war with clients in my care? What am I trying to prove? What am I hoping to achieve?

I doubt you signed up for clinical work in order to stand over clients as they lie weak and exhausted on the ground, and point a forceful finger at them as you claim your victory. You didn't become a clinician in order to be "right" in emotionally charged discussions, or to angrily withdraw when they don't seem to take your efforts to heart. You didn't become a therapist in order to shove clients toward change, whether they're interested or not. You didn't enter your training hoping for burnout and malaise. You likely walked down this professional path because you felt drawn toward the sense of worth that comes from witnessing another person heal, watching them take hesitant, faltering steps forward toward a better life despite fear and pain. You like the feeling of having an impact, of truly helping and giving of yourself.

And yet, a-yanking you will go. You will sometimes tune out during sessions. You will push solutions onto clients. You will debate them at every turn. You might raise the possibility of a transfer to a new therapist. Why?

It Takes Two

In our relationships, in our basic exchanges with people in daily life, it's tempting to think that we always act from our own choices and free will. We tend to believe that when we decide to ask someone out on a date, or when we assert to a cashier that they've made an error ringing up our order, we do so out of complete control over our actions. We decide what we do, and this other person has nothing to do with it.

LEAN IN

Find a willing partner, an adventurous soul—a family member, friend, or colleague who would be interested in a unique activity. Say it will be painless. In fact the person won't have to do anything, and that's really what you're looking for. Reassure your friend that, at the very least, it will be an interesting change of pace.

Sit facing each other, within 4 or 5 feet. Make eye contact and hold each other's gaze. For approximately 1 minute (perhaps setting a timer), maintain eye contact and keep to the only instruction in this activity: Do NOT communicate anything to the other person. Ready, set, do NOT communicate. . . .

Note your reactions to this activity in the space below. Were you "successful" in this task? What did you experience while trying not to communicate? Pay particular attention to how it felt.

I've conducted this activity numerous times with training audiences and the results are consistent—people fail miserably. They chuckle, they sniff, they make quick glances to the floor, the ceiling. Smiling seems inevitable. And even if you think you were able to avoid communicating anything, I encourage you to check in with your partner—who will likely disagree.

Every interaction is a two-way street. In every conversation or exchange between two (or more) people, there's a lot of mutual influence going on whether you're aware of it or not. Usually, we're not. In learning to become more open and connected to others, it's crucial that we develop deep understanding of the mutuality of relating. We will spend a significant portion of our work together in this book exploring this aspect of the therapist-client relationship.

LEAN IN

As an experiment, become a close observer of your interactions with others for the rest of today. Notice the subtle layers of communication—how you and others tend to react to minute changes in facial expressions, posture, tone of voice, word choice, even the pauses between words. While you don't need to notice everything (and none of us can anyway—our conscious brain can't keep up), consider the mutual back-and-forth flow of every interaction. We dance with one another, even when we're buying milk or paying for dry cleaning.

Can you notice the influence (even if small) that others have on you (and you on them)? What is happening in terms of your emotions and actions when interactions are going particularly well? When they don't go well? Remember, not only do you influence the behavior of your clients, they influence you as well. It is an inevitable fact of our rope-pulling brains.

Letting Your Pet Theories Off the Leash

You may have noticed that I have not used a word that's probably come to mind for you since beginning this Introduction. What is it? I know you've been thinking it. Go ahead and say it out loud. "Why hasn't he talked about *it* yet?" you've been wondering. "How can he claim to be an expert on this if he doesn't even use the word *countertransference*?"

Here's why I had you use this word instead of using it myself—I think it's overdone. It's almost a brand at this point—the clinical equivalent of Kleenex, Velcro, or Coke. Not only is it steeped in history and, to many, confusion, but some of its varying definitions carry assumptions of deep unconscious tethering between therapist and client.

Freud himself seemed a bit confused about countertransference. In his writings he sent mixed messages about it—that the influence of the client's transference on the therapist was to the point of "requiring the physician to recognize and overcome this countertransference in himself" (Freud, 1959a, pp. 144–145), and also that therapists should "take as a model in psychoanalytic treatment the surgeon who puts aside all his own feelings, including that of human sympathy, and concentrates his mind on one single purpose, that of performing the operation as skillfully as possible" (Freud, 1959b, p. 327).

So on the one hand Freud would have us skillfully recognize our countertransference, but then he would also have us cut out the part of us that reacts and makes countertransference possible. As modern researchers and theorists such as Charles Gelso and Jeffrey Hayes (2007) have commented, Freud's ambivalence around countertransference likely led to its relative neglect in the theoretical and research literature for many decades. This is unfortunate because those of us who practice therapy regularly (from whatever theoretical model) have largely learned that we must be far different than a surgeon who is as emotionally cool as a scalpel. We have learned that we must warm to our clients and use the therapy relationship in an authentic way. Modern research into the construct of countertransference has borne this out.

In their meta-analytic review of the countertransference literature, Hayes, Gelso, and Hummel (2011) summarized the various definitions of this concept, and emphasized a modern view that countertransference is universal for therapists. They stated that this is "because all therapists, by virtue of their humanity, have unresolved conflicts, personal vulnerabilities, and unconscious 'soft spots' that are touched upon in one's work" (p. 89). Across a number of studies to date, research suggests that countertransference reactions impact treatment outcome—the more negative countertransference reactions manifest for the therapist, the less likely therapy attains positive results (Hayes et al., 2011). Again, the literature in this area was largely neglected for some time and therefore much work remains to be done in understanding the effects of clinical work on the clinician's own reactions (and the subsequent impact of these reactions on the work). These results are notable nonetheless. Results showing the countertransference–poor outcome link implied that strong therapeutic alliance may reduce the negative effects of countertransference on treatment outcome (Hayes, Riker, & Ingram, 1997).

The literature has been sparse, but highly suggestive. It speaks of how universal countertransference reactions are and how destructive they can be in treatment if neglected or poorly managed. For a sample of therapists in another study (Hayes et al., 1998), 80% of their 127 sessions were self-identified as involving countertransference reactions of some sort. A quote from arguably one of the great theorist-clinicians to follow Freud points (prior to any of the above research) not only to the dangers of countertransference, but also to the need for clinicians to take care in managing their reactions:

> Freud rightly recognized that this bond is of the greatest therapeutic importance in that it gives rise to a mixture composition of the doctor's own mental health and the patient's maladjustment. In Freudian technique the doctor tries to ward off the transference as much as possible—which is understandable enough from the human point of view, though in certain cases it may considerably impair the therapeutic effect. It is inevitable that the doctor should be influenced to a certain extent and even that his nervous health should suffer. (Jung, 1963b, p. 7)

Here's the bottom line from my perspective: Countertransference is indeed universal, and so is confusion and awkwardness around the term itself. Some labels are used with such frequency that they lose the scent of specificity—they become mere projections of whatever the user wants them to mean. So I don't want to use it. I want you to consider a new perspective on the person-to-person exchange of clinical work. I want you to hesitate in making any assumptions based on your training or experience thus far as to what these reactions mean, or what they are "really" saying about the client. It would be nice if we could start conceptually fresh.

So whether you are a psychodynamic clinician, a behaviorist, humanist, cognitive-behaviorist, or *Yo Gabba Gabba*-ist (it used to be my toddler's favorite television show and the bane of my existence), I challenge you to stay informed by your particular orientation and simultaneously check it at the door. Let go of whatever you think you're supposed to understand or do about countertransference, and let's see what you discover throughout this book about reactions to clients. Don't worry, I'll give you your theoretical coat back when you leave. But before leaving this section, here's one more quote from one of the "greats" for you to consider. I do not mean to cast any theoretical aspersions with this book, let alone with this quote. Instead of drawing lines in the sand, maybe we should just step back and look at the "beachlike" beauty of these words about the work we've chosen:

> Certainly one reason why this phenomenon (countertransference) is occurring more frequently in our experience is that as therapists we have become less afraid of our positive (or negative) feelings toward the client. As therapy goes on the therapist's feeling of acceptance and respect for the client tends to change to something approaching awe as he sees the valiant and deep struggle of the person to be himself. There is, I think, within the therapist, a profound experience of the underlying commonality—should we say brotherhood—of man. (Rogers, 1961, p. 82)

The Journey of a Thousand Miles Begins With . . .

To have purchased this workbook, you have already made a commitment: You are willing to understand your contribution to the therapeutic relationship, and you are at least considering making changes to improve your work. This is no small commitment. Our professional endeavors are truly a two-way street. Not only do you and your clients influence each other, both of you are influenced by a whole host of factors, most of which are far outside your awareness. Think about any given session you've conducted during the past week, indeed during your entire career thus far. Can you honestly say that you anticipated every client action, every comment? Could you even say that you "chose" your every thought, feeling, and behavior during any given session? How much did you allow yourself to wonder at all the possible influences on what was happening during your sessions with clients?

Before you can most effectively act to change the lives of your clients, you might want to pause and ask what creates change for a person.

LEAN IN

Imagine you are standing on a busy street corner. You watch as a holy man (a priest, minister, rabbi, monk—anyone officially holy) walks toward you from across the street. Also there on the street corner is a homeless person, lying on the sidewalk, moaning in apparent pain. You watch as the holy man steps over this person and keeps moving down the sidewalk. Ask yourself: What do I think of this holy man? Write your immediate reactions below:

What do you think "caused" this spiritual guide to sidestep someone in clear need? Take a few moments and brainstorm as many possible explanations as you can. What are all the possible factors contributing to why someone like this would act in such a "callous" manner?

Social psychologists John Darley and Daniel Batson (1973) asked this very question in their classic experimental test of the "Good Samaritan" parable from the Bible. They clearly demonstrated that even seminary students, if led to believe they were running late for a talk they were assigned to give, were quite likely to step over an obviously suffering homeless research confederate. When the pressure is on, perhaps many of us clinician-Samaritans might miss our chance to intervene when it arises.

The point here is that there might be many reasons beyond our initial impressions and assumptions as to why a client might be exhibiting difficult behavior, or why the session has taken a wrong turn. There might be many influences beyond our theories and assessments guiding our actions as clinicians. You (like all of us) will watch clients doing the maladaptive things they do (or not doing the adaptive things) and will make all sorts of judgments, draw conclusions, and assign labels. Some may indeed be helpful, but the question here is whether we are capturing the full picture, whether we may be leaving out crucial factors that will really help the client change for the better. In this book, we will take off our perceptual lenses and give them a good scrubbing. We'll look to broaden and deepen our perspective on ourselves, our clients, and the therapeutic task at hand.

Connectivity is the term I use for this sort of contextual, all-inclusive causal thinking. I'm having us look at it right up front in our discussion together because it is central to learning and deepening your potential to work with the most difficult client interactions. Until you make concerted, consistent effort to step back in your mind while working with challenging clients and wonder about all the facets of their experience—all the things, people, events, circumstances, learning, and so on that might be driving their actions—you will tend toward reactivity; you will frame the client as *being* difficult. You will miss opportunities to intervene. In effect, you'll be more likely to sidestep, like the "holy man," these clients altogether. How often have you heard a colleague say (or heard yourself say), "Oh, I don't work with X type of client." How much are we unnecessarily limiting our ability to work effectively with the widest range of people?

Mirror, Mirror . . .

In my own clinical work, I've been tempted by the thought that it is the clients who must be willing to change. That is why they came to me, right? To change. "So-and-so needs to start taking his situation seriously," I've said to myself with a sigh of frustration. "He is a help-rejecter." Can you see the blaming, the labeling, here? Can you feel the distance these simple statements create? I've been guilty on many occasions of talking to myself as if I had no part in the matter; as if I were practicing in a vacuum—delivering therapy to my clients like a pizza or an order of sesame chicken for them to merely consume. My interventions are made to order and are fairly consistent regardless of the customer. It can be difficult to remember that my behaviors, and my emotions, are intimately interwoven in what happens for my clients in therapy. I must be willing to do things differently as well, even if it is hard, and perhaps painful, to do so. As much as I'm clearly willing to influence my clients, I must ask whether I'm willing to be influenced. I must turn and face my emotional experience of them.

LEAN IN

Consider the following statements. Take a moment to figure out if they ring true for you and circle your response for each.

It is important for me to avoid knee-jerk reactions to clients.

Yes No

There have been times when I have struggled against strong, negative feelings about my clients, myself, or my abilities as a clinician.

Yes No

I have reacted to strong, negative feelings during the course of my work and I believe my emotions or behavior got in the way of things.

Yes No

I would like to create a space within myself for proactive responding when faced with difficulties in my work.

Yes No

I would like to model good emotion and self-management skills for my clients.

Yes No

I would like to minimize the risk of burnout and "compassion fatigue" during the course of my clinical work.

Yes No

The more you agreed to the statements above, the more you are entering a process of self-exploration of your own emotional contribution to the working relationship with your clients. Obviously, we want to do the best work possible, and it is not easy to acknowledge when this might not always be the case. While it may not feel good to acknowledge your "unhelpful" (or even nasty) reactions in the past, you should take solace in the knowledge that clinicians who agree to every statement are the norm, not the exception. We all struggle with strong feelings about our clients from time to time, and we all stumble in managing these experiences. It is primarily a lack of attention to managing oneself that is cause for serious concern.

Keeping the Torch Lit: Understanding Burnout, Compassion Fatigue, and Vicarious Traumatization

It is notable that though the clinical literature abounds with concepts describing the negative effects of clinical work on the clinician, there appears to be little empirical data on the rates of these phenomena. Just like countertransference, there has also been confusion about compassion fatigue, burnout, and vicarious traumatization. Though a thorough review is beyond the scope of this book, let alone this Introduction, I will venture some quick definitions provided by experts (Figley, 1995; Freudenberger, 1985; Rothschild, 2006; Wicks, 2008). *Compassion fatigue* is generalized suffering for helpers as a result of their helping efforts. In this sense, it is the most general of the terms (Figley, 1995; Rothschild, 2006). *Vicarious traumatization* is more specific, involving impairment for clinicians who are working with those who have experienced trauma. *Burnout* indicates exhaustion and depletion of one's physical and mental resources as a result of the work (Freudenberger, 1985). Whatever label you use, all point to ill effects of therapeutic work for the clinician.

Even if we accept that truth leans in the direction of high rates of occurrence of these conditions, there is little documentation. A study published in *Child Abuse and Neglect* (Conrad & Kellar-Guenther, 2006) examined the rates of burnout and what is referred to as compassion fatigue among child protection workers in Colorado. Approximately half of the workers suffered from high or very high levels of compassion fatigue in reaction to their work. The literature discussed above has established the prevalence of countertransference reactions for clinicians (good and bad, experienced or not), but has little to say about how bad things can get for clinicians. One idea floating in the ether for me is that perhaps we clinicians are a bit reluctant to admit the far reaches of our negative experience of our work. I've known many colleagues who've spoken in private about symptoms of depression, anxiety, and traumatic effects from their work, but few of us are whispering these things in researchers' ears. Perhaps we should, because, as we'll see in our work together in this book, such disclosure might do us some good.

LEAN IN

In his 2008 book *The Resilient Clinician,* Robert Wicks presented an interesting list of causes of burnout. Though these obviously require more of an empirical stamp of approval before we can view them as definitive, these factors (listed in part below) make sense and put a frame on the need for the skills we'll be building together. As you scan the list, look for glimmers of yourself. Place a check mark by any you recognize.

_____ Inadequate quiet/down time
_____ Vague criteria for success
_____ Guilt over failures and for taking time to nurture one's needs
_____ Unrealistic ideals
_____ Inability to deal with anger or other interpersonal tensions
_____ Extreme need to be liked by others
_____ Neglect of emotional, physical, and spiritual needs
_____ Poor community life and/or unrealistic expectations regarding support from others
_____ Working with others who are burned out
_____ Extreme powerlessness to effect change
_____ Being overburdened with administrative work
_____ Lack of appreciation by colleagues and superiors
_____ Prejudice or discrimination
_____ High conflict in one's personal life
_____ "Savior complex" regarding helping others
_____ Seeing waste in projects that seem to have no relation to helping clients
_____ Not having the freedom or ability to remove oneself from frequent stressful events
_____ Overstimulation, isolation, or alienation

Clinicians working with challenging populations, those whose work challenges their coping, and those whose reactions blunt the effectiveness of their interventions need help beyond admonitions to "take care of themselves" and to seek supervision or personal therapy. The more you notice the sparks of burnout in yourself, the more you experience negative reactions to your clients or toward yourself, the more you need training in specific skills allowing you to move toward the professional satisfaction you desire.

LEAN IN

I'm going to make an assumption that you're a decent, dutiful person (buyers of professional books usually are). Another assumption is that you've already done many things to manage your reactivity to clients. Take a moment and list these activities and strategies here. Also, indicate why, to the best of your understanding, they may not have been sufficient:

Things I've Tried:

____

____

____

Why They've Been Insufficient:

____

____

____

All Aboard

Now that we've surveyed how universal it is for clinicians to have negative reactions to their work, and how you've tried many things to address your reactions, it's time to begin thinking ahead to what we'll be doing together in this book to give you a new set of tools. I'm a big fan of metaphors. They are mental flypaper that ideas can easily stick to. (See? I told you I liked metaphors.) Here's one for us to use throughout the workbook: We are each a freight train. That's right—a big train complete with an engine car, lots of freight cars, and, of course, tracks to roll forward on.

I would love to claim this metaphor as my own, but it comes from an interesting book by Robert Pirsig (1974) with an even more interesting title—*Zen and the Art of Motorcycle Maintenance.* The book is about a father and son on a journey of deep personal meaning, similar to our travels with clients, as well as our trek together in this book. Pirsig suggests that we each haul our "baggage" about in the freight cars—our habits (nasty as they may be), our peccadilloes, the memories that haunt us with shame and regret from time to time. The freight cars hold all that's come from the past—our families and various younger versions of ourselves are often tucked away in there, knocking at the walls, hoping for a chance to grab our attention.

We are powered by the present moment—our engine car. It is the "now" in which we think, feel, and behave. It is where we should spend the most time if we're going to fuel our lives with meaning, and if we're going to drive forward without crashing. It's only here in the engine car that we can lean out the window, let out a hearty yell, and really experience things fully.

And finally, the train is riding on the rails of our values—the deeply held directions in which our lives are heading. Our values lead us into the future and give direction to life.

The problem is that many of our clients, and often us as well, spend too much time either rummaging through the relics of our freight cars, or laying endless miles of track out ahead (perhaps setting ourselves up for a good derailing). Unfortunately, much of what we call disorder as clinicians seems to resemble either too much "freight car" dwelling (aspects of maladaptive guilt, shame, dysfunctional relationships, and depressive symptoms) or too much track pondering (chasing unrealistic, obsessive fantasies, anxiety symptoms). Many clients (and their clinicians) miss out on the true experience of the journey from inside the engine car—inside the never dull (if one truly opens up to it), always powerful, roar of the present moment.

It is only a metaphor, but it's a way to summarize what we'll spend this workbook doing together—learning the skills of harnessing and maximizing the engineer's job at the leading edge of the train. And the more we learn to hang out in the "now," particularly with our most difficult clients, the more they learn to do so as well. And then the train of treatment can really get rolling (sorry—I'm working to tone down my metaphor compulsion).

In this workbook, we delve into the inner world of the helper. What is our own emotional experience, and how might reactive, mismanaged thought and emotion lead us to act in ways that impede the progress of the work? In order to best understand and effectively manage our emotions as helpers, this workbook asks us to consider proactively practicing strategies to disentangle ourselves from our social and emotional patterning, and to ground ourselves fully in our present moment experience. Only when we are not tied down by unhelpful thinking, and when we can allow our emotions to pass through us, can we truly connect with our clients and help them in their journey toward change.

The book is divided into two parts, the first focused on developing your understanding of why and how reactivity emerges in your work, and how to make sense of your unique patterns as well as learn the primary skills for managing them. Chapter 1 establishes the biological underpinnings of the therapy relationship and thereby removes blame from clinicians and opens up possibilities of working to change the brain itself. Chapter 2 helps you examine your basic patterns of reaction to clients and get yourself motivated for change based on a close consideration of your core values as a helping professional. Chapter 3 assists you in shaping a new relationship to your own thoughts as a therapist, decreasing rigid cognitive processes by practicing well-researched skills for greater flexibility in thinking regarding the more challenging aspects of your work. In Chapter 4, you'll apply acceptance-based mindfulness strategies for understanding and gaining more openness in your contact with the tougher emotions arising from your clinical role. With the basic skills of flexible contact with your thoughts and emotions as a therapist under our belts, we'll move into Chapter 5's in-depth exploration of the long-standing conditioned patterns of reaction all of us bring to our work, and we'll begin learning how to sidestep these patterns in order to increase our positive impact on clients. Chapters 6 and 7 focus on creating greater depth of understanding and compassion for your most difficult clients, and also for the most difficult (and extreme) aspects of yourself that emerge and threaten your work and well-being.

Part II explores specific applications of self-management during actual moments of interaction with clients. To this point in our travels, we've created perspective and flexible understanding. Now, our feet are hitting the pavement—we're in session and things are going awry. Chapter 8 provides discussion and practice in managing the timing of clinical intervention using mindfulness-based self-management. Chapter 9 gives you an opportunity to explore means for increasing your authentic engagement of clients in order to lead them through the toughest exchanges in your work together. Chapter 10 puts you in the driver's seat as a clinician. Here you will cultivate skills for using compassionate limit-setting when client behavior threatens to block your ability to move treatment forward. Chapter 11 delves into specific interaction patterns (such as the threatening or "morally repugnant" client) and gives you strategies for managing the more vexing situations a clinician might encounter. With Chapter 12 we'll end by learning to practice what we preach by developing habits of commitment in our self-management of reactivity with an eye toward enhancing our motivation for ongoing self-development and skill refinement.

As you've already noticed, I will introduce a number of exercises and activities for you to try as we move through the material. Other great training workbooks I've seen have prompted readers with the words "exercise," "try," or "try this." I've decided to prompt your hands-on practice of skills with the words "lean in." Throughout the book, this material asks that you develop a willingness to move toward what's most difficult about your work. This is truly a process of "leaning in" toward what we might prefer to pull away from. If you lean in enough, though, you'll find your perspective on "difficult" changing. So you won't simply "try" exercises, you'll practice developing the paradoxical habit of engaging that which often repels, and you'll hopefully break new ground in your professional work.

Note that this willingness to "lean in" and fully engage with the exercises in this book is *crucial.* Simply reading through the text without fully experiencing and applying the material to yourself and your work may have some benefit, but it will likely fall short of what's possible. To the degree you're willing to really lean into the learning (even, and especially, when your impulse might be to turn the other way), you will maximize the benefits for yourself and your work with challenging clients.

As you look out across the landscape of the more unsightly aspects of your caseload, and the jagged, reactive terrain within your own skin, you are indeed beginning a journey. And I'm here to say that I'm on my own as well. There is no ultimate clinician master of self-management. As Zen master Linj is said to have once uttered: "If you meet the Buddha on the road, kill him!" We are all struggling and scraping our way forward. It's important to be willing to take in what can be learned about how to bind our wounds and penetrate the perceptions that get in the way of our very best work on behalf of clients. Our clients might be hard, and so might our feelings be in reaction, but we don't have to break ourselves against them.

The Heat of the Moment in Treatment

PART I

Skills for Understanding and Managing Reactivity to Clinical Work

CHAPTER ONE

The Hitchhiker's Guide to the Interactive Brain

WHEN I WAS IN graduate school, people would speak in hushed tones about one particular course. "Oh geez, I have to take Bio next semester. There goes my GPA!" It was the mandatory course in neuroscience, and for those of us studying to become clinical psychologists, the intricacies of "action potentials" and "calcium channels" and the thought of having to stomach the smell of formaldehyde as we pondered dissected sheep brains was enough to make us cringe. It was tempting to think (with *what,* you might wonder) that budding clinicians had no business delving into the hard-science ins and outs of the brain. It seemed just another in a seemingly endless series of hoops I needed to jump through on my way to a diploma.

Alas, I survived this course (and developed a sense of awe for the intricacies of the brain), though I must admit I was again tying myself up in myelinated layers of apprehension about the complexity of the content, having saved work on this chapter until after most of the rest of this book was written. Old patterns of cringing die hard (as you know as a clinician, and as we'll see in our work together). And yet this chapter needed to come first. In order to understand how to most effectively manage reactivity as a clinician, this stuff about what happens in our brains during tough clinical interactions needed to be front and center. This topic may indeed be complicated and enough to make many a grad student (and practitioner) flinch, yet failing to go inside our 3-pound, bone-encased universe borders on negligence.

So here I am, a non-neuroscientist, giving you, the fellow clinician, a quick primer on what you (in my opinion) ethically must understand about the mechanics of your gray matter. It's the mechanical know-how you need in order to be most effective as a clinician, especially with the clients with whom effectiveness might seem elusive, if not laughable. Here's how I'll bind up my anxiety a bit—I'll give you the distillation of what I've gleaned about the therapeutically relevant aspects of brain science through brief discussions of a series of seven "principles." Consider my (nonexhaustive) list the non-self-help equivalent of the "Seven Brain-Related Habits of Effective (Psychotherapeutic) Self-Managers." So here's the first (and we've already discussed it).

- Habit 1: The self-managing clinician makes friends with the brain.

My belief (and my own experience) is that many clinicians are "afraid" of the hard-science aspect of the biological underpinnings in the brain for our work. It's analogous to how we all flip on light switches every day, and rely on them for effective maintenance of our daily routines, but without much understanding of the physics and engineering happening behind the scenes. We know it's there, and that it's important—we just don't want to be held accountable for knowing much about it.

To the degree that the changes effected by therapy take root with structural modification in the brain (which, as we'll discuss shortly, is indeed the case), then our ignorance born of apprehension has the potential to limit our effectiveness. We may intervene in ways that fail to take into account the way the brain processes information, and end up diminishing our positive impact on clients.

For example, at the therapeutic school where I work, I frequently interact with students who have been diagnosed with Asperger's syndrome. A hallmark feature of Asperger's is difficulty in thinking and acting toward others with a sound "theory of mind" (the brain-based capacity for taking the perspective of others—their thoughts, feelings, and intentions). If I were completely unaware of recent research linking theory of mind difficulties in perspective taking to the functional capacity of specific areas of the prefrontal cerebral cortex, as well as the temporal lobe (Gallagher & Frith, 2003), then I might regard these kids as intentionally disregarding others' feelings. So when that 12-year-old girl diagnosed with Asperger's leaned near me to inspect the contents of my computer screen during a family session with her father, it would have been a tad less than helpful if I'd assumed malice on her part when she chirped, "Your breath smells and . . . [distracted pause] how much RAM does your computer have?"

We don't need to be neuroscientists, but our best interventions ask us clinical folk to do our due diligence when it comes to knowing a bit about the brain. In fact, we should attempt to integrate as much knowledge from other fields relevant to clinical work as possible (e.g., social psychology, neuroscience, sociology, law and policy, medicine), making connections between varying fields of knowledge in order to better our claim on the "truth" of our clinical role. This integrative spirit is neatly summarized by the memorable word *consilience* coined by William Whewell in the 19th century (Brendtro, Mitchell, & McCall, 2009). Himself an architect, theologian, and scientist (evidently he coined *scientist* as well), Whewell nudges us from the distant past to break out of our overly specialized "now" and extend our understanding beyond the narrow perch of our daily professional doings. I'll dip a bit into other fields throughout this book, but for now, I hope I've done a bit of nudging myself. As a clinician, it's important that the brain become your buddy.

- Habit 2: The self-managing clinician knows that the human brain is highly organized for processing of relationships.

Our brains are built for social communication. Research is booming in this area such that authors like Daniel Goleman (2006) have dubbed it the subfield of "social neuroscience." Though an exhaustive review is beyond the scope of this chapter (see Goleman, 2006; Lewis, Amini, & Lannon, 2000), I'll take you on a quick tour of what's been most relevant and helpful to me in my growing understanding of this important (and recent) body of knowledge.

The emerging research is increasingly clear that human brains (in an ideal state of affairs) are wired to create "limbic resonance" with one another (Lewis et al., 2000; Siegel, 2010) where the emotional structures of interacting brains stimulate and focus on one another. Beginning in infancy, we begin doing a "dance" of attachment with caregivers that continues into adulthood with family, friends, colleagues, and yes, clients. Our brains evolved to develop most fully from relating to those who are good at reading us, anticipating our inner worlds, and helping us make sense of emotion and the environment around us. The recent studies have used technology such as functional magnetic resonance imaging, positron emission tomography scans, and EEG data to explore the patterns, location, and communication within the brain during our social exchanges. An attuned interaction of limbic resonance in which interacting partners correctly read each others' emotional experiences and verify and assist in regulating these experiences is thought to be crucial in maximizing neurodevelopment (Lewis et al., 2000).

So what are these parts of the brain involved in our social dances with one another? Again, thorough reviews exist, but in a nutshell, the science points to specific gross structures or areas of the brain that interact with one another to bring in information from the senses during social exchange, detect threats, parse out and label the other person's intentions and feelings, access memory, and prepare and initiate responses. Studies suggest that specific brain structures initiate defensive reactions in response to threat (a pea-sized structure called the amygdala), sense the inner emotional experience of others (insula), direct our attention during social interaction (anterior cingulate cortex), and briefly hold and process the "working memory" aspects of social input (ventromedial prefrontal cortex) (Hanson, 2009).

UCLA's Marco Iacoboni (2008) has been one of the most prolific researchers on the role of cells in the motor cortex called "mirror neurons" that are thought to be critical for social communication. These specialized cells, first discovered in other primates, are housed in the section of our brain that tracks and initiates physical movements—they prompt us to react when we're watching others. Specifically, mirror neurons react to sensing the "intentional" activity of others (ever yawned when someone yawns in your vicinity?). The human brain primes us for reactions to each other. Their mirroring helps us interpret each other and makes our interactions more fluid and meaningful. In a sense, whether you're shy or outgoing, we are all social machines, and we are always projecting our inner world onto others.

Other specialized neurons called "spindle cells" in the cingulate cortex and insula (limbic system structures) have also been linked with social information processing. Specifically, spindle cells are thought to be involved in more sophisticated social processing in primates, and in humans are considered important for complex therapy-sounding phenomena such as empathy and compassion (sound familiar?). Most of us as clinicians entered the field after being "selected" for our empathic communication skills by fellow students, teachers, professors, supervisors, guidance or admissions staff, and maybe our own family members. How often have people told you over the years that you're a "great listener" or that you're "someone to bounce things off of," or that you "really seem to get people." My bet is that if that's the case, your brain has a healthy crop of limbic spindle cells wiring you in tight to the inner experiences of others by giving you a strong "gut" sense of people (your insula is especially focused on reading your body's reactions during interactions).

Author and researcher Daniel Siegel (2010) suggests that mirror neurons serve as social "sponges" of what others are feeling and intending, and that limbic areas (e.g., insula, cingulate cortex, amygdala) act as amplifiers, giving us a sense of the emotional intensity, or valence, in others' social behavior. When clients glare, scoff, or spiral with despair, your body and brain are actively filtering, sorting, and interpreting their facial expressions, voice tone, gestures, word choices, and so on within a span of just a second or two. Long before your training and "expertise" kick in, your brain is doing what it evolved over millennia to do—socially detect and hopefully, connect. The research continues, but the indications are clear that the human brain appears specialized for social and emotional communication—the life blood of our therapeutic endeavors.

- Habit 3: The self-managing clinician is patient with clients since they are fully aware of just how busy the brain is during any given moment of therapeutic interaction.

Imagine the following issuing forth from one of your clients:

"You shrinks are all the same!" (Client frowning, shaking head, glaring at you) . . .

. . . And in the span of just a couple of seconds . . .

. . . Electrochemical impulses from sense receptors in your eyes and ears project to processing centers in your brain (in the occipital lobe for vision and in the temporal lobe for hearing) . . .

. . . Initial sensory impressions are quickly relayed forward in the brain into the cortex of the parietal lobe toward the top of your head and into the motor cortex where . . .

. . . Mirror neurons in your prefrontal cerebral cortex detect the client's "negative" emotion and fire off signals . . .

. . . Which are sent via the anterior insula into subcortical, lower brain structures to "perceive" the client's emotion and intention in his actions . . .

. . . With your amygdala—the alarm center of the brain, which itself now fires lightning bolts of threat throughout the brain . . .

. . . And subcortical layers are also detecting subtle body changes (perhaps your gut tightens a bit) and relaying this internal information back up to the insula and . . .

. . . then to the middle prefrontal cortex (behind your forehead) where your "observing self" checks in with your various forms of memory to label what the client is experiencing and doing. . . .

"This person is defensively projecting their distress onto me" (you perhaps think to yourself) . . .

"I'm noticing that this frustration with me allows us to not be focusing on how your wife just filed for divorce" (you say while sitting back somewhat in your chair, tapping your pen against your legs that you've just crossed and recrossed). . . .

. . . And in not much more time than it takes to snap your fingers, the client's brain flares with signals—prefrontal mirror neurons to insula to subcortical limbic (e.g., amygdala) and lower brain structures and detection of subtle bodily feedback impulses and then back up to limbic, insula, and prefrontal cortex where they come to an even more fixed conclusion that you're a jerk and are just interested in getting paid. . . .

. . . And around and around our brains go, dancing to and fro with mutual stimulation and up/down and back/forth activation.

How does the meager layer of gray matter you're using right now in your frontal cerebral cortex stand a chance against this lightning-fast surging within and between brains? The above is a hypothetical single exchange among the hundreds that occur in any given 50-minute session. Bull riders at least have a full 8 seconds to stay atop their volatile, kicking companions. We have a mere second-long sliver to catch what's happening inside our brains (and the clients'). How can you possibly ride out this wave of brain processing without reacting reflexively?

It is here that we will be spending a great deal of time learning and practicing how to slow the mind in order to shape what's happening in our brains as clinicians, and ultimately what's sparking in the client's. Psychologist and relationship researcher John Gottman (1999) has experimentally demonstrated that when responding to an agitated relationship partner, or engaging around a hot-button issue, it is helpful to use a "slow start-up" approach in which you intentionally ease into difficult content. This is when we let clients know that "when they're ready" we have "something important we need to discuss" versus pouncing on them about their unpaid bill as they take their seat. Such practices help avoid triggering the alarm bells in the sympathetic nervous system/hypothalamic-pituitary-adrenal axis (SNS/HPAA) of the client's brain (Hanson, 2009). Seems intuitive, right?

Remember your answer the next time you react too quickly (and don't worry, I'll do it too) or nudge a client abruptly toward your agenda for the session. We indeed need to do whatever we can to build pathways of patience deep into our brains. Remembering the complexity of one moment of interaction, how current and chemicals are flying around all over the place inside both skulls in the room, will perhaps help us take just one more breath before intervening. A great deal of power resides inside that gap.

- Habit 4: Self-managing clinicians are patient with themselves because they realize that all human brains are cut from the same complex mold.

You might remember the commercial. It was a national campaign sponsored by the Partnership for a Drug-Free America during the Reagan administration (remember, "Just Say No!") in the 1980s. "This is your brain," the narrator stated, the screenshot showing him holding an egg. "This is drugs," he says, pointing to a skillet on a hot stove. "And this is your brain on drugs." And with that, he breaks the egg into the hot pan, where it sizzles on contact. It's common knowledge that if you do hard-core drugs, you are essentially "frying" cells in your brain with repeated use. This seems beyond dispute. And yet we, as clinicians, often place ourselves apart from our clients when we set standards for our own brain-based actions and emotions—thinking that somehow we're different. Drugs "fry" the human brain and all human brains flash with anger—just not the dutiful therapist's. Anger shouldn't surge through us as it does in our clients. We should be strangers to the depths of despair, the roller coaster of obsessive panic, and the highs of hypomanic impulsivity. We should not be so easily distracted or bored with our endeavors.

And yet, despite all our training and experience, when it comes to the mechanics of things, our brains are essentially the same as everyone else's. Brains of the same feather certainly flock together. Your client processes initial sensations of vision in the occipital lobe of the cerebral cortex (and so do you). When sensory input suggests a threat, the same tiny amygdala fires off similar alarm bells in you as it does in clients. Sure, brains vary (particularly in the details of interconnection between neurons), but essentially the gross structures and their functions are universal. Though the brain (as we'll see) is "plastic" and capable of much more change than originally believed, the basic anatomy is the same for all of us. The same subcortical, limbic structures that regulate our "emotions" (bodily responses we evolved to alert us for survival purposes) are distinct in all of us from the frontal lobe cortex cells that process our human experience of "feelings" (mental representations and interpretations of our emotions) (Cappas, Andres-Hyman, & Davidson, 2005).

Think of it this way: You wouldn't travel abroad and expect gravity to no longer apply to you (and therefore take that extra step off the railing of the Eiffel Tower). Though the language, food, and customs of the native French might be different from what you've known, you would still expect gravity to be relevant to your actions. We would do well to remember this about our behavior and our brains. The physical laws that evolved to regulate the flow of electrochemical impulses through the central nervous system apply universally. Your brain is basically the same as mine, as well as your clients', and therefore you should give yourself a break and allow yourself to process emotion, knowing that you will occasionally spark with reactive behavior and will indeed misread stimuli in your environment from time to time.

In addition to understanding the recently discovered social processing circuits in the brain (i.e., mirror neurons and interconnections between frontal cortex, subcortical/limbic, and more distant nervous system components), it is also important for clinicians to remember that the brain is built to do its processing better under some conditions than under others. Brains can become flooded and types of processing can compete and inhibit each other. Often the "errors" and missteps of our clinical actions are, at biological bottom, the result of a neurotransmission traffic jam of sorts.

LEAN IN

While I was a teaching assistant in graduate school, I taught Introduction to Psychology for undergraduates a number of times. I loved having my classes do various demonstrations of psychological principles in order to drive home an experiential understanding of the material. What follows is one of the activities that was helpful in giving students an experience of how the brain is processing information from moment to moment.

Take a dowel stick (about an inch thick and a foot or so long), or perhaps use a large plastic cup (no glass please—you'll see why in a moment). Practice balancing your stick or cup on an index finger for a few minutes, alternating between your right and left hands. When you're ready, you'll run a series of eight timed test trials (have a friend standing by with a timer; four trials for the right hand, four for the left). A trial begins once the dowel or cup is in place on the finger and any support is removed. The trial ends and time is stopped if the dowel or cup falls or touches anything other than your index finger.

Here's the catch. Do half of the trials (two) for each hand while keeping completely silent. Do the other two trials while reading any selected passage aloud (it could be a paragraph from this book, or maybe something more engaging, like that love letter you couldn't bring yourself to send when you were in college).

This activity is an example of a competition task where the brain's use of structures in one area actually competes or interferes with processing also happening in that region. For most people, verbal processing (such as your monologue just now, or psychotherapy for that matter) requires a great deal of activation in the left hemisphere of the brain. The left hemisphere is also primarily responsible for controlling the movements and coordination of the right hand, and therefore you may have noted interference with your ability to balance effectively with your right index finger when reading aloud. The right hemisphere is more heavily involved with processing and reasoning nonverbally (such as with imagery).

This cerebral lateralization effect has been well documented in the literature (Corballis & Beale, 1983; Kinsbourne & Cook, 1971) and suggests the importance of clinicians' consideration of the complexity of social interaction and full, complete processing of the raw material of therapeutic interactions. Attunement and accurate intervention require focus—a brain intent on cleaning the clutter of competing processing. This is perhaps why BD-CBT never took off (ballroom dance cognitive-behavioral therapy). And just when you were about to brush off that old pair of tap shoes sitting in the back of your closet!

LEAN IN

Think back over your work with clients in recent months. Let your mind gravitate to *that* interaction—the one that went particularly awry, or the one in which you believe you were reactive to a client. Perhaps you did something, or perhaps it was more of an internal reaction—select an episode that strikes you with that raw sense of being "not what I intended." Don't think too much. Simply let the memory arise. Where does the "blame" lie for your reaction? Before answering, consider what we've discussed about the human brain's processing of social and emotional information. Assuming your brain is, in terms of basic anatomy and system interconnections, wired much the same as mine (and your clients' for that matter), what does it mean to think of the "fault" behind your reactivity? Write some nonreactive thoughts below:

As we'll explore later in the book, self-compassion is a prerequisite for developing and maintaining compassion for clients, particularly those who poke at us and cause us serious self-doubt. Good therapy is the "ultimate inside job" in that it requires a loosening of clinicians' rigid and reactively held preconceptions about themselves and clients (Lewis et al., 2000, p. 178). Good therapists (especially those who dare to work with the most difficult populations) practice toward increased capacity for allowing their own brain's cognitive and emotional "chatter" to quiet enough to tune into the unique song of each client. The resonance that emerges (again, I like the music metaphor) is itself an important component of the healing process. "Psychotherapy is physiology" through the balanced harmony of brain-to-brain attunement during therapeutic interaction (Lewis et al., 2000, p. 168). Effective clinicians play the instrument of their brains to rewrite the neurological notes of the clients'. If you're blaming yourself or the client for what's going wrong in any given session, the notes are going to fall flat. If you're attacking, withdrawing, or going numb, the brains will fall out of sync.

- Habit 5: Self-managing clinicians take the reins of the therapy relationship by learning to drop the ropes involved in brain-based games of tug-of-war with clients.

Our brains bind us. Genetically established "attachment systems" in the brain play a crucial role in bonding primates (like us) together (Bowlby, 1958). Infants clearly won't survive without "roping in" caregivers—motivating them through emotional expression to meet their basic needs. The tethering of brains to one another does not end in infancy. Attachment systems allowed us to form cooperative groups, increasing our odds of survival and opportunities for reproduction (Brisch, 1999). Back in our cave condo-dwelling days, we were far from the fastest, strongest, toothiest species around. Evolution roped us together, and we've been dominating the planet ever since. Our brain's capacity for forming attachments has clear implications for therapeutic work.

As we've discussed, clinical work is about interaction, about inevitable communication between two thinking, feeling, and behaving human beings (remember the eye contact exercise from the Introduction?). These two people, clinician and client, form a very special, powerful relationship. This relationship, the therapeutic alliance, has consistently been shown by studies to predict the outcome of services better than any other single variable (such as clinician theory, specific techniques, gender, age, or level of training and experience) (Martin, Garske, & Davis, 2000). Make no mistake, the alliance is indeed an attachment, involving the same systems and structures of the brain as any close, important relationship.

Scientists have suggested that the neuromodulator oxytocin in the brain plays a central role when we're forming connections with each other (Fisher, 2004). When we authentically experience and express warmth and empathy for another person, we spark oxytocin's release in the brain, which creates that distinct connected feeling we all seek in our relations with others. Oxytocin is present in our brains when we bond with infants and when we form collaborative connections with our clients. Oxytocin encourages eye contact, enhances feelings of trust, prompts people to move closer (emotionally) to each other, and may help to muffle the alarm bells sounded by the amygdala (Hanson, 2009).

When you authentically engage a client, your brain registers it in emotional expressions—contractions of the face (eyes and mouth in particular) and modifications of aspects of voice (tone, volume). The client (your observer) is immediately and automatically processing your emotional and expressive behavior in structures of his or her brain that are specialized for handling emotional messages, the insula and anterior cingulate cortex in particular. These areas give clients a sense of what you're saying emotionally. To the degree their brain is resonating with positive labeling of your intentions, oxytocin is released, increasing approach tendencies. Mirror neurons in the motor cortex are helping them prepare to respond, perhaps with authenticity themselves. But what about with our trickier clients, particularly with those who are angry, intense, provocative, or difficult in some way—what's happening in the brains of clinician and client when the interaction is heading south?

It is here that the "neuroaxis" of competing brain systems can end up in a version of a game of tug-of-war (Hanson, 2009). It's what Daniel Goleman (2006) refers to as the distinction between the "low" and "high" roads of social and emotional processing in the brain—the body-up-to-brain reactive flaring of the amydala and linked limbic structures and the brain-down-to-body directing, sensory-integrating, attention guiding, and "let's problem-solve this" areas of the anterior cingulate and frontal cortex. The metaphor is obviously oversimplified (and the neuroscience nuances much more intricate in actuality), but if the low road "wins" (i.e., is sufficiently activated and the high road insufficiently so) our tendency will be to react with debate, lecture, harshness, or distance and will unleash a torrent of cortisol-marinated angst in the brain. It can lead to a behavioral domino effect of further reactivity, withdrawal, and less than effective clinical work.

Remember our discussion of Marco Iacoboni's (2008) model of attunement between interacting brains—mirrors reflect whatever stands in front of them, the good, the bad, and . . . (let's leave it at that). Unless you've built up new patterns (and strengthened regulating connections in your frontal lobe areas), what you get from your tougher clients is what you'll give back (in some form or another). Clearly, we all have some work to do.

Being human, we clinicians make mistakes and our clients act out in (or out of) session, which leads to ruptures in the alliance. When we are skillful in managing these ruptures (using strategies we'll discuss and practice in this workbook), the emotional resonance centers of your and your client's brains will get in sync once again. The dance of treatment will continue and things will get back on track (until the next rupture, of course). Mindfulness is thought to contribute to clinicians' ability to detect these ruptures in the first place (an obvious necessity if the rupture is to be addressed) (Bruce, Manber, Shapiro, & Constantino, 2010). Clinicians' attention to repairing ruptures in the alliance when they occur may have a direct impact on improving the outcome of the work of treatment (Foreman & Marmar, 1985; Kivlighan & Shaughnessy, 2000; Stiles et al., 2004; Strauss et al., 2006).

In our exploration together in this book, we'll first take a close look at how we, as clinicians, can learn to self-manage our reactions to the work. We will then turn toward the clients themselves and practice managing the moment-to-moment interactions of the work in order to enhance the alliance and the therapeutic impact of our interventions. Our journey will quickly derail, however, if we neglect a fundamental assumption: that treatment is maximized to the degree that therapists harness the social and emotional messaging within and between the brains in the room. If therapists become skilled at catching, connecting with, and managing their reactions (i.e., self-regulation), clients detect this and, with consistency, become increasingly able to co-regulate their own brains.

Research in the area of "metacognition" (defined as monitoring and control of cognition, or "cognition of cognition"; Flavell, 1979) is relevant since what we're talking about is developing greater self-awareness and tracking of our own thoughts and emotions as clinicians. One writer noted that "metacognition is seen as a sine-qua-non constituent of social interaction and of co-regulation and other-regulation of behavior" (Efklides, 2008, p. 277). Being capable of accurate monitoring of self and other in the midst of interaction is important for the exchange to be productive. "Self-awareness facilitates the interaction of cognition and emotion as well as the cognitive regulation of both cognition and emotion" (Efklides, 2008). This review and theoretical essay suggests that emerging science indicates that our human neocortical "awareness" allows us the unique ability (though, in order to not offend, we should double-check with chimpanzees and dolphins to be sure) to develop skill in thinking about our own thoughts and feelings and to benefit from feedback loops in our interactions with others. We interact, experience ourselves, experience the other, interpret and judge these experiences, and (ideally, and through practice of skills that we'll explore throughout this book) develop skill for better high-road monitoring of these experiences, interpretations, and judgments for future interactions. Let's take a quick look at an example of what we might do to corral our reactive brains in the midst of our work as clinicians.

It was a particularly difficult day. My 9-month-old daughter had a terrible night and left my wife and me with only a handful of hours' sleep. Needless to say, we were slow getting up and out the door that morning. Before we left, my wife and I got into a "discussion" about who should've gotten up with our daughter during the night (we'd been down that road before—the arguments never helped solve the issue, and somehow, we yet again veered that way). We barely spoke in the car the rest of the way to work after we dropped our daughter off at daycare.

And then I was hit by one issue after another once I walked into my office. An upset parent who had left a voicemail urgently needed to talk to me. A clinician needed help dealing with a student in crisis. I needed to chair an important meeting that I'd forgotten to put in my calendar. And worst of all, I must have accidentally used a ladle to scoop sugar into my coffee travel mug that morning.

I sat with my face in my hands at my desk. I was seething with what life had deposited on top of me. My temples were pulsing, and my clock said it was only 9:30. It's safe to say my amygdala was surging with a near-meltdown level of low-road activity. Somehow I remembered what I'd recommended to clients many times, but usually forgot to do myself. It was a nice therapeutic nugget that made sense, but that seemed below me, an experienced therapist: "Name it." Say to yourself and say out loud what negative emotion you're experiencing, as you're experiencing it, in order to begin getting some distance from it. Somehow, as the clinical wisdom goes, simply labeling a difficult emotional experience allows you to take the reins back, if only briefly.

The recommendation comes from a solid foundation. Research has shown that mere verbal labeling of negative emotions can help people recover control. It appears that the brain clicks on its frontal lobe (reasoning and thinking centers) when we name or label our negative emotional experience (Creswell, Way, Eisenberger, & Lieberman, 2007). Mindfully noting "anger" to ourselves when someone cuts us off in line at the grocery store pulls our brain out of its older, deeper emotional centers that correspond with eliciting fight-or-flight–based emotional intensity (i.e., the amygdala and other more evolutionarily ancient regions) (Payer, Baicy, Lieberman, & London, 2012). Acknowledging our emotions as we're having them seems to put them at arm's length. We can see them, and then we can begin to choose. We can choose to act to open ourselves and connect with others, rather than be carried away in a flood of neurochemicals that wash us over the cliff.

LEAN IN

In the coming days, when you find your body and mind hardening with upset (and the more you're aware of exactly how this manifests in you, the better), nudge yourself to attach words to your experience. Often, thinking in terms of the metaphor of your hand in front of your face can be helpful. When you start, you *are* your anger, sadness, fear, whatever. It is your hand over your face. Can't see anything, can you? The emotion is attached to you—it *is* you.

As you progressively label your emotion, creating more and more distance between the raw emotion and yourself, the observer (sparking awake in your brain's prefrontal cortex) begins to see things more clearly—the emotional "hand" moves farther away from your thinking and reasoning mind's eye. In Chapter 3, we'll call this cognitive distancing "defusion" and we'll spend a fair amount of time learning how to apply it to our work with difficult client interactions.

Here's a possible progression of what you might say to yourself:

- Event occurs . . .
- Body stiffens, clenches . . .
- "I can't believe this! / They are so wrong! / This shouldn't be!"
- "I am angry / sad / frustrated / humiliated / and so on."
- "My body is telling me I'm angry, sad, and so on."

- "I'm having thoughts that this is upsetting."
- "I'm telling myself a lot of distorted stuff. . . . I need to get on top of this."

If you want an experience of the effects of affect labeling in your brain right now, try balling up your fists as tightly as possible and holding them fast. Hold the tension until you find it noticeably uncomfortable. Do a quick zero to ten rating of how uncomfortable you feel.

Rest for 20 seconds or so. Now ball your fists again, and this time, label (either silently or aloud) what you are experiencing. Say "pressure," "tension," or "tense" over and over and then after approximately the same duration as in the first trial, make another emotional "thermometer" rating. It's very likely that you experienced the second trial differently (and perhaps less intensely) than the first.

Notice the "distance" that develops as you label your way away from the event and step away from the raw emotion itself. Instead of reacting out of intensity, it becomes a bit more possible (because of the intentional ignition of your prefrontal cerebral cortex) to choose your response. The prefrontal cortex has been linked with management of our "autobiographical self" (Hanson, 2009), and therefore taking a moment to detach from our identification with our emotions loosens the maladaptive grip we have on ourselves. We separate from our anger in response to yet another last-minute cancellation by a client—instead of *being* our anger, we can lightly touch this emotion and watch as it slowly changes form (and ultimately subsides).

Our emotional reflexes run deep (inside the brain), and change comes only with significant practice and patience. Your (and your client's) amygdala will continue to flare during interactions. As I'm hoping you'll discover through consistent practice of the strategies in this book, you can get better at catching the currents in your brain. Labeling emotion is just one method that helps you create the distance for choice to emerge in the midst of interaction. I still have "discussions" with my wife about who should go pick up our crying daughter. I catch my rigid "She's so out of line" thinking more than before, and I put it at arm's length.

For our purposes here, the point is to note to yourself that self-management of reactivity involves intentional action in the here-and-now of our work as clinicians that directs our energy and attention in ways that change the brain's processing. This intentional activity breaks patterns of reactivity that get in the way of our best interventions and helps us engage our clients even when it "feels" hard to do so. In order to get better at brain self-management, it's important to also understand how adept your brain is at fictionalizing emotional intensity. Hollywood should be jealous.

LEAN IN

Close your eyes and gently bring your attention to the sounds around you. Allow your mind to quiet, letting thoughts and sensations pass, as you settle into the hearing. Life is happening all around you. Listen for the pieces of it both near and far. It is all there within the expanse of your mind, simultaneously. Notice how sounds come and go, passing into and out of your awareness. Thoughts and sensations might arise as well, but regard them as mere blips on the immense screen of your awareness. Come back to the hearing. Continue in this way for a time, resting in the sounds appearing and disappearing around you.

Imagine hearing a faint siren in the distance. It is the sound of an emergency vehicle drawing closer, an ambulance. Imagine that this sound is now filling your awareness. With your eyes still closed, imagine that the sound is now piercing, as I'm sure you've heard from actual ambulances in the past. It's right on top of you. It is here because of a severe accident.

Who comes immediately to your awareness? Yourself, loved ones, friends, family—who comes to mind? Take whoever presses most urgently at your mind, and hold that face firmly in your awareness. The emergency is about this person. He or she has been severely injured, and his or her life has changed forever. Hold this person's face in mind. Notice any feelings, thoughts, reactions that appear. Let them rise on their own. Bring yourself back to the face of this person. Allow his or her presence to fill your awareness.

Imagine this person inside the ambulance as it speeds away. The injuries are severe, the damage done, and the pattern of living forever altered. Stay with the awareness of this person. Notice reactions as they arise. And now notice something else . . .

None of this is actually happening in reality. It is all visualization, a movie of sorts—interplay of signals within your brain.

Allow the ambulance to fade away and come back to the sounds that are present where you are now. Find the sounds both near and far. They come and go as they always do, regardless of the concerns of your mind.

When you are ready, allow your eyes to open. Allow yourself to consider the following questions:

- Did you feel any pain or discomfort while visualizing the injury to this person you care about deeply?
- Did it feel real?

Research has shown that the brain uses the same regions and structures to process imagery as it does for perception in response to actual stimulation from the environment (Kreiman, Koch, & Fried, 2000). The pain we create in our minds can be just as nasty (and, I'll argue, nastier at times) than that which happens naturally. Research has used imaging technology to show that the brain uses the same regions to process imagined pain in a loved one as it does for processing of actual physical pain (Cheng, Chen, Ching-Po, Kun-Hsien, & Decety, 2010). Also, there is some indication that the neurotransmitter serotonin (for some people) actually helps to lessen the pain of relationship loss (Lewis et al., 2000). It's no wonder then that modern Western society ingests serotonin agents (e.g., Prozac) with abandon. If we "juice" our circuits correctly with medication, we can loosen the strings plucked by heartache. Though I'm not recommending that every therapist who copes with frequent interpersonal pain from interacting with challenging clients go out and secure their own prescriptions, I am suggesting that we work to harness (naturally) the flow of neurotransmitters in ourselves in order to help others more effectively.

In this book, we make use of these findings by using meditative and visualization techniques to create greater connection and understanding for those clients that seem hardest to connect with or understand. To the degree that you're willing to dig deep during imagined practice to cultivate a new awareness and contact with the pricklier interactions and more trying reactions you experience in your work, the more your brain will be primed to shift toward more compassionate and effective action in actual clinical encounters.

This is no easy task, and there are no quick fixes (sorry!). As a taste of this, take the visualization experience you just completed. Call to mind the pain you experienced, even if only slightly, when you imagined a loved one having suffered an accident. Now imagine that it's the same accident with the same consequences you visualized but the victim is not your loved one—it's that client you've struggled with in some way. The one you've really found distasteful or significantly frustrating to work with. Does your reaction change at all from that of your visualization of a loved one? If you're anything like me, you likely find your reactions to be miles apart. And that would make sense, right? Deep connection prompts deep empathy.

And yet I'm arguing that connection can be cultivated with even the most challenging clients. It does not come easy, but it can come with consistent practice and mastery of what happens nanosecond to nanosecond inside your noggin. Your brain is much more malleable than it might seem. This leads us to our two final "habits."

- Habit 6: Self-managing clinicians build mindful awareness in order to hold their reactions more adaptively and to facilitate more helpful interactions with clients. This consistent habit of mindfulness changes the physical structure of the brain (theirs and the client's).

The past 20 years or so have been a period of dramatic research interest in mindfulness. In particular, studies have repeatedly documented how consistent mindfulness practice (i.e., regular, intentional direction of attention to present-moment awareness) actively sculpts and changes the physical structure of the human brain (Luders et al., 2012). Specifically, by purposively channeling awareness, areas of the brain involved in emotion regulation, learning and memory, attention regulation, and perspective taking (i.e., structures such as the insula, anterior cingulate cortex, hippocampus, and temporoparietal lobe junctions) have been shown through imaging studies to add cells and connections in response to mindfulness practice (Holzel, Carmody, et al., 2011; Holzel, Lazar, et al., 2011).

Another study (Davidson et al., 2003) measured EEG patterns in depressed and anxious patients. Typically, patients with these symptoms would show increased brain activity in the right hemisphere of the brain while resting (with nonsymptomatic participants showing more activity on the left, where verbal processing is generally dominant). The depressed or anxious patients completing an 8-week mindfulness training program showed a "left shift" in brain activity that persisted at a 3-month follow-up after the study. These and other results point toward the brain's ability to change through mindfulness practice. Daniel Siegel (2010) suggested that with this left shift in the physiology of the mindful brain, people are increasingly able to approach difficulty versus withdrawing from it.

What does this mean for the clinician? We will spend the remainder of this book not only discussing the ramifications of this but, more importantly, practicing and demonstrating the possibilities for self-sculpting our cerebral hardware. I'm hoping you're interested in a bit of "left shifting" for yourself. Through development of your own skills for mindful awareness, you can harness the evidence of changes to the brain for yourself, and ultimately for your clients.

- Habit 7: Self-managing clinicians realize that their "mind" is always bigger than their brain.

Your mind is distinct from your brain. "Mind" is an event in the present moment. Show me your mind from April 5 when you were 5 years old—go ahead, I double-dog dare you to track down and touch the exact physical structures in your brain that hold your experience of that day in all respects. Better yet, go ahead and try to recreate that mind right now. You might as well go to your stove and play catch with the steam coming out of your boiling pot (which, to my mom's chagrin, I probably tried to do when I was 5). Our brains can indeed be boiled down to their constituent parts, but our minds cannot—they are irreducible. They are experiential "wholes"—more verb than noun.

But haven't we just spent the entire first chapter of this book exploring the fundamental importance of the brain for our management of therapeutic interaction? And here I am seemingly minimizing our gray matter.

The physical structure of the brain is necessary, but not sufficient, to encompass the marvel of change within therapeutic interaction. Once you pause to put your finger on the physical structure in the brain involved, "mind" has already moved on with its never-ending procession of now. It is an always-moving sliver of space-time-matter that holds incredible power. Mind is where reactivity to clinical work, as well as its antidote, resides. It is the nexus of connection and change. I know, I know—very abstract for a workbook about strategies. I'll let you off the philosophical hook for now with an experience and less words.

Let's end this brief overview of the neuroscientific underpinnings of our work as therapists (and self-managers of reactivity to our work) with a brief meditation, perhaps either recording the instructions and playing them back, or having a friend or colleague read them aloud.

LEAN IN

Sit in a comfortable, yet upright position. Make sure you're in a place where you won't be disturbed for a few minutes. If you're willing, close your eyes, and as you do so, take a deep, full breath—filling your lungs from top to bottom. Inhale and exhale through your nose and allow your belly to expand with the inhalation. Take a few of these slow, deep, relaxing breaths. Notice your surroundings in terms of the feel of your body in your seat and sensations inside, as well as sounds that arise around you. Simply notice whatever shows up, and witness as each thing stays a while, and then passes away.

Once you are in a deep, centered space, allow yourself to notice that you are noticing. . . . Become aware that this wonderful apparatus called your brain appears to house an ever-present witness to your every experience, and to everything in the world around you. Though it's impossible to feel your brain (no nerve endings there), imagine that you are able to see inside, to watch the fireworks of activated neurons as they dance with electric current. At this moment, you are aware of being aware. You are witnessing that which you often assume is all there is. And as you watch the low-voltage light show inside your own brain in this moment, wonder what it means that you are watching all of this. If your brain is where all the action of "you" is, and you're watching your brain, then who (or what) is doing the watching right now? If "you" that is watching is not any specific structure, cell, neurotransmitter, or behavior, emotion, or sense of frustration, burnout, or anger in reaction to clients, then what might this mean? Might you be able to tap into this "higher you" more regularly in order to better understand and manage what's hard in your therapeutic work?

Return to your breath and your body, grounding yourself in the world we all tend to identify with. And when you're ready, open your eyes and get ready for the next chapter's discussion of what really matters about your clinical work. It's hard to take steps to address what's most difficult until you're clear as to why doing so is valuable.

Think of it this way—if your brain and its inner workings were seawater, your mind would be the wave. You can't hold a wave in your hands, but you can certainly "catch" it in the present moment. In this book we're learning to surf the mind waves threatening to overtake us in our work and to teach our clients to "get radical" as well. We shouldn't merely count to 10 when we're upset in the midst of a session—we should learn a bit about "hanging 10" as well.

MAP CHECK

Take a moment and review what we've covered in this chapter. What was one aspect, one piece of content, that resonated with you—sparked your interest, curiosity, or even angst in some way?

____

Why did this matter to you? What makes this worth writing about? Worth your focus and effort? What is the gravity that this carries for you and your work?

____

What is one specific action you can take within the next 24 hours related to this issue that feels as though it would be important and has the potential to move you in the direction of what matters?

____

≺ CHAPTER TWO ≻

Getting Real About Your Work

I AM A FIRM believer in the research indicating that unless there is a concerted effort to apply new concepts or strategies to real-life situations, skills covered during training sessions tend to either sit stale and unused in the meeting room (along with the leftover bagels and muffins) or in the training handouts that are later shoved away in desk drawers. This book asks you to put things into immediate practice.

With actual skill development and more effective clinical work being the goal, it is important for you to choose one specific client to use within this learning laboratory. This client need not be the most vexing, most difficult of your career, but he or she should be representative of the work you've done and will likely do in the future.

LEAN IN

Let your mind go a bit unfocused for a moment now. . . . Let *that* person, the client you will use as your experimental guinea pig (not voodoo doll) come to awareness. Who is that client who has been especially challenging, with whom the interactions have been taxing and difficult in some way? Don't evaluate or scrutinize the person coming to mind. Simply write that client's initials on the line below:

____

In order to readily bring this client to mind in a meaningful way, it will help to pinpoint at least three (more, if desired) concrete and specific details regarding this person. Think of aspects of his or her appearance, gestures, mannerisms, tone of voice, word choices. Does this person interrupt you often? Make too much or too little eye contact? What is the general emotional volume level? Whatever aspects you select will serve as anchors that will allow you to cue this client up quickly and in a vivid, visceral way. And while you may not find yourself looking forward to it now, the more visceral the memory, the better for your practice of new skills.

Take a moment and list your three anchors for your difficult client in the spaces below:

1. ______________________________
2. ______________________________
3. ______________________________

With your attention still focused on this client, close your eyes if it helps, and allow this client to fill your awareness completely. Do this now.

In the space below, answer the following question: What feelings are showing up now regarding this client?

____
____
____
____

What do these feelings "pull" for? What knee-jerk behavioral reactions do they spark in you?

____
____
____

Now, very important, ask yourself the following while still thinking about this difficult client:

1. What have you tried to do to manage your negative reactions to this particular client?

____
____
____

2. What typically happened in your attempts to manage reactivity? How did your self-management work?

____

____

____

3. What was the "cost" of these reactions? Were there any costs, any unhelpful results, from your self-management efforts themselves? What did you, the client, and perhaps others lose as a result? Let yourself think of all possibilities. This step is very important, so be sure to give yourself the time and space to fully consider it.

____

____

____

____

____

____

No matter what the specific situation might be in your work that is difficult, I'm betting it's safe to say that you've put a great deal of effort into doing something to manage it. And regardless of how you evaluate the success of your efforts, it's probably also safe to say that the struggle with your reactions has been taxing and distressing for you. Imagine you are holding one end of a long rope and the other is held by the negativity you experience. When the angst begins pulling at you, what's been your own sense of how feasible it is for you to yank back, to pull in reaction with all your might?

I'm going to go a bit further and bet that the game of tug-of-war against the reactivity you've experienced with this particular client is not turning out well. I'm guessing your experience has been that the struggle is better at creating professional "rope burn" for you than it is at resolving what's stuck in your work with this person. If so, you might be interested in setting aside the struggle—all the efforts to control away what's understandably distasteful about this client—and put your effort into something else, something perhaps a tad more workable.

You might also be thinking: "I usually like to enjoy myself when I read, but I'm not enjoying this workbook right now." If this or any similar thoughts are showing up, you should give yourself a hearty pat on the back. If thinking (and feeling a bit) about one of your more difficult clients is making you feel a bit shaky, and if it's leading you to become more aware of how you react in a less than ideal way, as well as realize not-so-good outcomes as a result, then you're on the right track. This is not supposed to be a summer beach read. This is the hard path of a clinician who hopes to broaden his or her reach. You don't go to the gym expecting a pain-free experience in order to whip your muscles into shape, do you? So of course this trip down Difficult Client Lane won't necessarily be fun.

So if the rope-pulling against what's nasty and not-so-nice in your clinical work with at least this one individual is not panning out, perhaps you're willing to begin understanding a bit more about the patterns of action and reaction in your clinical interactions. In the next section, we take a brief look at a handy rubric for knowing where things are in any given moment of therapeutic interaction—how it might be going awry, and how you might position yourself to get things moving inside yourself (and outside as well) in a more workable direction.

Heat of the Moment Assessment: A Therapeutic Traveler's Tool

Consider the following case vignette:

"He just needs to quit whining and complaining and snap out of it," Sam, a father and therapy client says about his conflict with his teenage son, Jack. I remind him that when he lectures his son, things always escalate.

"Yeah, whatever," says Sam, shaking his head. His voice rises like a thermometer's mercury. "But why can't he just do it? I never got away with whining and slacking off when I was a kid. My old man wouldn't put up with that for one second."

Sam's hands go into a vise lock on the arms of the chair. His fingers

cont'd on next page

cont'd from previous page

are white with the clamping. "Doesn't he realize how disrespectful it is? Doesn't he see that he'll end up a complete loser?"

I let Sam know that this is indeed hard. I quietly say it must be painful to see things so stuck with his son. I ask him what he most wants in his relationship with Jack. He had started to open up, but now stiffens. "That's not the issue, Doc." He glares at me. "This ain't my problem and you know it."

Listen to how this father talks about his son. Pay less attention to what he says and more to how he says it. Imagine the shaking of his head, the reddened face, and the defeated strain in his voice. You have to wonder at the messages this father and son send one another. Over the course of family sessions, I learned that the son, Jack, tended to reach out to his dad in various ways, but Sam focused more on what Jack was not doing (such as homework and chores) than what he was doing and, more importantly, wanting. Jack was indeed a troubled, difficult-to-manage kid, with much that was infuriating and button-pushing about his behavior. He did, however, want a better relationship with his dad. Sam misread the cues and missed opportunities to connect with his son.

Don't just listen to how Sam talks about Jack, but listen to yourself as well. Imagine you are the clinician. How might you feel? What might your impulse be in responding to Sam's behavior? What would it be like to be faced with such behavior over many sessions? What if you repeatedly tried to help this father make the "obvious" connection with his son, only to have your efforts blocked and derailed each time?

How can we begin to piece together the pattern of action and reaction in these sorts of exchanges? What is necessary is a quick, easy-to-digest rubric for understanding the ebb and flow of difficult human interaction. Whether you're a therapist in session with an angry father like Sam, a relapsing substance abusing client, or a boundary-testing client with an Axis II diagnosis, it would be helpful to have a cue for understanding what is happening and what you might do about it—something like what you get when you happen upon a streetlight. In a moment's flashing of color, you can quickly associate to what is about to happen and what your response options are. A simple message can flash to mind that gives you a chance to shift your behavior. Clinicians need a "streetlight" that makes sense and helps improve their chances for better timed, more attuned, and appropriately aimed interventions in heated therapy sessions.

In the Interpersonal Process Grid (Figure 2.1), I've placed social behavior along two primary dimensions, both arguably involved in every interaction between people: How active (externalized) or inactive (internalized) is the person relative to the other, and how emotionally attuned (or disconnected) are they to each other?

These two dimensions, and the variability people can have on each of

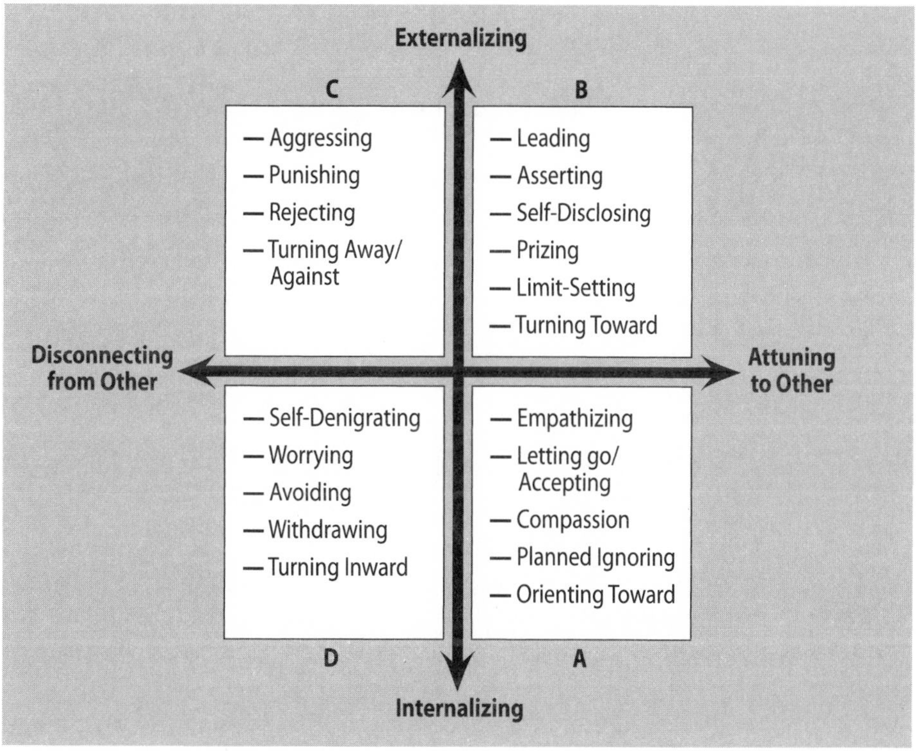

Figure 2.1 Interpersonal Process Grid

them for any particular social behavior, create four quadrants or categories of responses. Descriptive labels are included for each. This simple grid allows you to step back from an interaction and ask, Which quadrant did that behavior fall into? or What side (left or right) was that exchange on?

Take the interaction in session with that father, Sam. Where do Sam's actions, and mine as the therapist, fall on the grid for the sample segment below? Write in the letter of the category or quadrant next to each behavior.

I let Sam know that this is indeed hard. _____
I quietly say it must be painful to see things so stuck with his son. _____
I ask him what he most wants in his relationship with Jack. _____
He had started to open up, but now stiffens. "That's not the issue, Doc." _____
He glares at me. "This ain't my problem and you know it." _____

It would be understandable to feel taken aback by Sam, and find yourself disliking this father while at the same time feeling great empathy for Jack. You might be a bit snappish (C), lecturing Sam on the pitfalls of his parenting (C). You might eventually withdraw and let Sam rant (D). Phone messages from Sam might go unreturned (D). Sessions might begin late (D). It might seem right to allow Sam's session no-shows to go unaddressed, a sigh of relief coming from you (D). You write the words "premature termination" on your final session note, close up the file, and move, thankfully, on.

Sam is a difficult client and, without intending to, you've just finished a game of tug-of-war with him (or more accurately, the negative reactions within yourself). Back and forth, the interactions were a series of misread messages and missed opportunities. A pattern of emotion and behavior developed in you (and between you and Sam) and strengthened until therapy faltered, the strain of it leaving you spent and swirling with negativity. It will be tough for you to see this, let alone acknowledge it. Professionals don't get worked up over this sort of thing, you tell yourself. "I'm better than this."

The Process Grid is a tool for quick, in-session snapshot assessment of what is happening between you and your clients. Are they behaving from the right or the left? Are you leading the interaction by being both active and attuned to the client? Or are you reacting with a D-quadrant withdrawal in response to their own passivity? Whatever the pattern, with a sudden moment of perspective, you as the clinician can make a choice: Where on the grid do I want my response to fall? This book aims to help you create the space to ask such questions, and to feel your way forward even when the impulse of the moment wants to send you in the opposite direction from your client.

Surprise, surprise—your brain is doing quite a bit while you're interacting with your difficult clients. And I'm not talking about how your frontal cortex is crafting genius interpretations or brilliant reframes (though I'm crossing my fingers that this happens)—I'm talking about how the social-emotional circuit is buzzing with activity. And it is all largely automatic and outside your conscious awareness. As we discussed in Chapter 1, evolutionarily ancient structures such as the amygdala, insula, and cingulate cortex are flashing with reaction to your client's provocative rants, relentless bemoaning, or angry finger pointing in your direction. These structures deep in your brain, as well as rapid impulses bouncing up from more remote aspects of your peripheral nervous system (gut feelings, anyone?) are communing with each other for what seems like eons (it's more like a handful of nanoseconds) before your frontal lobe clicks on and begins appraising or "thinking" about what is happening—let alone initiating a therapeutic response. If you're not careful, you may just react in a "left-sided" knee-jerk fashion and your session could go dramatically awry.

As we've discussed, it is important to remember that things are happening rapidly and reflexively in the brain, and they are happening for all of us (assuming these structures and circuits are intact). We all react to emotionally charged behavior in others. It's not that your brain shouldn't process and spark with activity following a client's dropping of an F-bomb in your direction, it's what you will do with your reaction itself over the long expanse of seconds that follows that counts clinically.

Tug-of-war is indeed a silly game, and yet it's so easily and regularly played in our daily social lives. Consider these other difficult client scenarios. Do any look familiar?

- Your client (of about 1 year) has been sober for 3 months. You worked very hard together to make this progress, and now he just entered your office reeking of alcohol. _____ _____
- The victim of domestic violence you have helped to understand her pattern of abuse, and assisted in developing the resolve to move out of the apartment she shared with her violent boyfriend, comes in with new bruises on her arms. She is full of assurances that her boyfriend and she are recommitting to improving their relationship—they are also engaged. "I want you to be happy for us," she says. _____ _____
- The man you've been working with for over 6 months to develop skills to combat his chronic depression has again begun a litany of complaints about everyone in his life who has hurt or failed him. He is no longer willing to discuss use of coping strategies you've agreed have been beneficial. "No one understands what I'm going through," he says. He's crying—again. _____ _____
- A teenager you've spent months building a trusting relationship with, one who has begun talking openly about her self-injurious cutting behavior, seems to have stolen items from your office, including the letter opener from your desk. _____ _____
- An attorney with anger control difficulties is yelling during a session. "I'm so sick of this. Everyone's incompetent! I work with a bunch of morons. And how long have I been coming here? I'm starting to wonder about you!" _____ _____
- A client diagnosed with borderline personality disorder: "If you care about me like you say you do, why can't I call you over the weekends? I don't know if I can make it without someone like you to talk to when it gets really hard. I'm not sure what I might do when my depression gets really bad." _____ _____
- A client struggling in the wake of a fourth divorce: "You're just like every man I've ever known. You bastards have no idea what you put women through." _____ _____
- A client diagnosed with generalized anxiety disorder: You've just given what you believe to be a very important piece of insight to your client—you've really put something together that you think would be beneficial. The client ignores your comment and changes the subject altogether. _____ _____

Think about each of these clients and consult Figure 2.1. Where would these behaviors fall? List the letter of the quadrant in the first space provided next to each scenario.

Now, imagine you are the clinician working with them. How might you feel, and how might you reflexively behave, in the moments following their behavior? Consult the grid and list the quadrant of those reactions in the second space next to each scenario.

Enough About Hypotheticals: Let's Talk About You

Pick the scenario that most closely resembles situations you are currently facing in your work. In the space below, write what the likely outcomes of treatment will be if clients continue acting this way with any consistency, and you react to your emotions with behaviors falling on the left side of the Interpersonal Process Grid. What will be the likely ripple effect of these action-reaction patterns if they continue unchecked?

____

____

____

LEAN IN: TAKE YOUR PET PEEVE FOR A WALK

Think for a moment about what annoys you most about other people. What is your biggest pet peeve regarding others' behavior? What is *that thing* that someone does that really grates on you? List it below:

____

____

____

Imagine being trapped in a situation where you simply could not escape this obnoxious behavior—you're literally up against it for an indefinite amount of time. How much are you up for this? Let's say you did have the option to slide out of this situation. How willing would you be to stay anyway, to press yourself into this annoying state of affairs?

1	2	3	4	5
Not Willing		Somewhat Willing		Very Willing

Stay with this pet peeve in your mind. In the space below, write out what happens in your thoughts and emotions when you lash yourself to it. Try to step back in your mind and simply notice what pops up. Write without analyzing, judging, or censoring—jot down whatever emerges.

____

____

____

____

____

Close your eyes and just stay with the images, thoughts, and reactions, breathing normally and bringing your attention back to this pet peeve if it wanders (or flees). Open your eyes after a couple of minutes and again rate your willingness to hang out with this less-than-ideal behavior from others.

1	2	3	4	5
Not Willing		Somewhat Willing		Very Willing

Maybe your rating has changed, and maybe it hasn't. In our work together in this book, our focus is how to keep our hands on the leash of what's least desirable for us about our clients. We can't just drop our unruly clients off at an animal shelter (nor is it wise to regard them as less-evolved species), and so the question we're concerned with here is whether we can learn to walk with them in a way that works for everyone involved.

Take a moment and give the following questions your full consideration, and record your thoughts in the space below. Don't just think about the one sample client you've selected. Think across all your clients. Yes, you've certainly struggled and you've tried a number of things to manage, and yet here you are, aware at some level that the patterns of thought, feeling, and action remain. Consider all the reactions you've battled with and answer the following:

- How feasible or workable are these patterns for your work? Are they leading to the outcomes you and your clients are hoping for, and in a manner that fits your expectations and theirs? What are these patterns costing you (and your clients)?

- Are you willing to explore these patterns? What concerns might you have about doing so? What obstacles might arise that would make it difficult to take a closer look at this?

If any barriers to doing this work for yourself come to mind (such as your busy schedule, feeling as though the pattern can't really change or that it really isn't something all that problematic), I strongly encourage you to consult a trusted colleague for feedback. Remember, all of us become caught in tug-of-war patterns from time to time. Our brains wouldn't have it any other way. We all benefit from learning to "drop the rope" and create a more helpful, therapeutic interaction with our clients. On occasion, we all need to address our emotions during the course of our work.

If you find any patterns unworkable, what would you prefer to have happen instead? Letting go of any nay-saying objections or doubts your mind might offer, what would the state of affairs be if the pattern with a particular client (perhaps the specific difficult client you envisioned earlier in this chapter) were different and suddenly working? What would this interaction pattern look like? What would you be doing differently?

In our personal lives, we have all experienced tugs-of-war with others (e.g., family, friends, and colleagues). Think of a specific situation in which your emotions were particularly engaged—when you were very charged up and upset in some way. Look for a time when you had that "on the verge" feeling during an interaction with the other person. "I know I'm about to say or do X, and that it will inflame things, but . . ." (and you went ahead and did or said X anyway). In particular, I want you to think of a time when things turned out well, and were resolved in a satisfactory and effective way.

What did you or the other person have to do with your strong reactions in order for this to happen? List your response below.

____
____
____
____

What does this suggest about what you will need to do with your strong reactions to your clients?

____
____
____

As clinicians, we are well aware of what emotions are for. We tell our clients they are merely signals as to what our system needs—that something is important for us to consider or act upon. They are the engine lights on the dashboard of our personal experience. There is nothing inherently invalid about the emotions themselves. They are mere messages. "What will you do with these messages?" we ask our clients. "That's the important question."

With what degree of consistency do we ask this of ourselves? What are we to do with the messages our emotions are giving us during challenging interactions with clients?

Ready, Set . . . Not Quite

When clients push our emotional buttons, it is natural (as we've seen) to experience strong reactions. Emotion surges from deep within the brain.

Our frontal cortex cognitive "appraiser" quickly pieces together judgments we consciously call diagnoses or labels of "poor client motivation." Obviously, not all diagnoses are reactive judgments on our part. Thoughtful diagnosis based on careful assessment can obviously add much to the prospect of positive outcomes for clients. It is, however, a healthy exercise to ask yourself what aspect of you is embedded in every diagnosis you make. More important for our present discussion are the assumptions you make about client motivation for change.

Motivation for change has received considerable research emphasis in recent years. James Prochaska and Carlo DiClemente (1982) developed a model to describe the timing, or sequence, of people's behavioral change efforts. Their Stages of Change model has demonstrated through a great deal of research that as people change things such as substance use, gambling, smoking, weight loss, bulimia, and more generalized changes within psychotherapy, they move through a sequence of stages.

The first stage, Precontemplation, refers to people who, though they may wish things to be different, have no stated desire to change their behavior. If they do make any efforts toward change it is usually at the urging (or coercion) of others. A typical statement from someone at this stage would be: "As far as I can see, I don't need to change anything in my life." The stages progress toward increased commitment to change and increased overt action. Contemplators will say they are aware of the problem with their behavior, but they aren't doing much about it. Action-stage clients are doing just that—taking action and talking from a place of commitment. Those in Maintenance realize they will have to work to prevent relapses of the problem (you can see the heavy influence of addiction literature here). And relapse, whether into problem drinking or poor coping around anxiety or depression, does indeed occur for many, prompting more revolution through the stages (though perhaps with greater clarity and less fallout than before).

Research has linked early (e.g., Precontemplation) stage status with premature termination from treatment and other negative outcomes across different types of problems and clients (Smith, Subich, & Kalonder, 1995). It only makes sense (and the literature supports it) that those who are more committed and active in addressing a problem are actually able to demonstrate and sustain positive changes. But here's a bottom line for you to consider as we wind up this chapter: It is not just the client who needs to develop a greater commitment to change if treatment is to succeed. You must develop motivation for change as well, particularly in working with the more interpersonally difficult clients. If you develop the motivation to understand and address your own role in the unhelpful patterns of exchange during the course of work with clients, then they are much more likely to get motivated to do so as well. They will see the process of change as a two-way street and will be much more available to collaborate in shifting the patterns that block treatment (whatever their presenting issues might be).

Vibrating to Your Own Iron String

So how are you supposed to get motivated for changing your patterns as a clinician? On *Saturday Night Live,* comedian (and now U.S. senator) Al Franken's sweater-wearing therapist character Stuart Smalley got himself pumped up by looking in a mirror and nudging himself with the gentle affirmation, "I'm good enough, smart enough, and gosh-darnit, people like me!" Since sweaters, mirrors, and affirmations alone are unlikely to work, what else might you try as you consider the prospect of working your way through the rest of this book, as you look to shift the powerful currents we all find within us as therapists? It might help to connect with the values guiding your work.

For the purposes of our exploration, *values* refers to the most central desires guiding how we act. They are the "desired global qualities of ongoing action" that set the direction for our lives (Hayes, Bond, Barnes-Holmes, & Austin, 2006, p. 16). They are not the outcomes, the goals that we are so focused on in our professional endeavors (such as symptom reduction, or a client obtaining a job or renovating a relationship). Your values can be thought of as an internal compass that you consult from time to time. The compass gives you a heading, a direction, not an end point. And if you're lost in the woods, the X you've marked as your hike's destination begins to lose its value as the sun is setting and the cold air and unidentifiable stirring sounds descend. Your compass becomes your best friend at this point.

As we journey together in this book, it may behoove you to spend some time connecting with your own compass. Let's pull it out now before the wolves walk into your office once again.

LEAN IN

In order to get a sense of what sits at the center of your professional endeavors, take a few minutes to get yourself centered. Find a quiet place where you won't be disturbed and sit upright, yet comfortably. Close your eyes if you'd like and simply notice your breathing for a minute or two. Just watch your breath coming and going in your body. Notice how the breath moves into the center, the core of you, without much effort on your part.

Once you are settled and centered, imagine the following scene: You're sitting at the head table in a large ballroom. The room is filled with well-dressed folks who have all gathered to hear toasts in your honor. Speakers, people you know and respect as professionals, colleagues, and friends are rising one by one to the podium to give their sincere thoughts on the impact of your body of work. You catch your reflection in the fine silver set before you and note that you are a tad more advanced in age than your present self. It's the sunset of your career. Let go of critique and modesty. What would you most want others to have noticed about your actions as a clinician across sessions, across clients, across the full span of your career?

____

____

____

____

____

____

LEAN IN

You've stepped inside your time machine once again. This time, instead of gray hair and the clink of retirement party china, you're only 10 years old and the clink is the sound of the chain of your bicycle. You've just come in from a ride and you enter your childhood bedroom. On the bed is you—the current "you" with degrees and (if you're like most clinicians) graduate school debt. The young you sits down and the older you begins telling the story of how this clinician gig came about, what it is, and what it might become. What would you want this child to know about what sits at the core? As Ralph Waldo Emerson (1841) wrote, what is the "iron string" within you that you "vibrate" to as a therapist? Again, think of directions, ongoing actions, qualities of being in your professional work.

___

___

___

LEAN IN

One final activity: In the same centered space, imagine yourself sitting with the difficult client you've selected to focus on. Cue up the anchors for this person and render them vividly in your imagination. Imagine it is your planned termination session. What would you be thinking, feeling, saying, and doing during this last session? As an ideal termination session, what would it be like for you?

___

___

___

___

This section may have been difficult for you. This wouldn't be surprising since it is often a challenge to connect clearly with central values. You may have noticed a mental and emotional flinching or tightening within yourself. Perhaps your mind was scoffing at the exercises themselves. "Ha! Time machines and retirement dinners—what silliness!" Maybe you had a hard time staying settled and centered and found yourself distracted. Or maybe you touched something powerful, something vibrating. Whatever happened internally, kindly do one thing for now . . . just notice.

Being Abe Lincoln

I was in graduate school when I happened upon a flier for a literary panel discussion that was to feature some lions of the literary world—among them novelist Kurt Vonnegut (one of my absolute favorites). I sat in the auditorium and listened to the discussion with great interest (at the time, I had my own fantasies of literary greatness), and at the end the moderator allowed members of the audience with burning questions to approach microphones set up in the aisles.

An awkward-looking English Department grad student walked up to the microphone. *I'm way better than him,* I told myself. I knew I could write him into the ground.

"I have a question for you, Mr. Vonnegut," he stammered, clearly nervous. "I've admired your writing for years, and I also want to write satirical novels like yours," he said. The poor guy was embarrassing himself. No one could write like Vonnegut—especially satire. I settled back into my chair with smug satisfaction.

"I was wondering if you might have any advice for me as I move forward."

No question in there anywhere. I felt a wave of condescension for my long-haired friend—this collie of a creative writing student who pushed his glasses up on his nose while waiting for Vonnegut's reply. I wished for a power outage. Maybe someone would faint. Perhaps a fire alarm would rip the room and relieve this guy of further humiliation.

Kurt Vonnegut sat forward slowly. He was thin and looked like he might break in half if he came forward too quickly to the microphone sitting on the table in front of him.

He smiled at the young man, but only a bit. He knew something very powerful, very deep that we could all benefit from. We all waited for his wise, lengthy description of what it took to become truly great as a writer.

"*You will fail,*" he said. And that was it. He sat back and waited for the moderator to move things along.

I watched the wreck that was the aspiring-writer-but-soon-to-be-high-school-English-teacher turn and wander back up the aisle toward his seat in the oblivion section of the auditorium. I couldn't have agreed with Vonnegut more: That guy would surely fail.

Truth be told, I've failed pretty much daily since that day. Some failures have been big (dropping out of law school in my early twenties, broken relationships) and some small (such as the daily tug-of-war with others over the press of fused thinking and emotional patterning). Truth be told, we all fail in big and small ways, and you will do so throughout your exploration of this book. Here's a core question: Are you willing to fail and continue forward in the direction of your values as a clinician?

Abraham Lincoln failed numerous times running for various political offices before he finally landed the job of president of the United States. Thomas Edison failed thousands of times along the way as he toiled toward a rudimentary form of the lightbulbs we take for granted today. The famous examples are endless. The everyday examples are you and me, here and now. I'm sorry to say it, and I hope you'll bear with me and keep plodding along in the book anyway, but you will fail many times with your more difficult client interactions. Even as you head down the path outlined in this book, you will get tense at times. You will become highly frustrated with your clients' behavior, and you will say and do things that make the work less effective. You will continue to wonder from time to time why you are even doing this.

This book uses the journey metaphor quite intentionally. Though you will fail, the skills and strategies we'll discuss will help you to abide it all. You will learn to hold more and more of what's difficult about your clinical work. You will have more wisdom as to the best course of action. Your timing for intervention will improve.

But, at the risk of abuse of deceased horses, let me again use Vonnegut's words: You *will* fail.

LEAN IN

All this talk of failure has led me to remember my own definition of success in my personal and professional lives—it's framed and hanging on the wall behind me here in my office: Emerson's famous quote about success deriving, in part, from striving to "find the best in others . . . to have played and laughed with enthusiasm . . . to know that even one life has breathed easier because I have lived." In my work as a clinician, supervisor, and administrator, this last portion is very important. It helps me to put a comforting, large frame around my efforts. It helps on the darker, failure-draped days. I can't win them all, and some interactions with clients are less than ideally therapeutic, but success so defined helps keep me on track. If you had to (and right now I'm respectfully twisting your arm), how would you, in a single sentence, define success for yourself as a clinician? Remember the values discussion earlier in this chapter and think more in terms of directions and ongoing process and less in terms of specific outcomes or goal posts in your work. This is your work, your life, so how would you summarize what it's really about?

In this chapter, we've discussed and you've explored how clients, and you as a clinician, are fighting natural tendencies toward knee-jerk reactivity. Though the tendencies are natural (thus all the failures), it is possible to learn to drop the rope and train yourself to create small spaces for perspective, understanding, and compassionate, strategic action. Your motivation—your willingness to change—like flint to steel, creates sparks that might also light up the treatment process with even your most challenging clients.

MAP CHECK

Take a moment and review what we've covered in this chapter. What was one aspect, one piece of content, that resonated with you—sparked your interest, curiosity, or even your angst in some way?

Why did this matter to you? What makes this worth writing about? Worth your focus and effort? What is the gravity that this carries for you and your work?

What is one specific action you can take within the next 24 hours related to this issue that feels as though it would be important and has the potential to move you in the direction of what matters?

CHAPTER THREE

Think Stop, and Walk Anyway

Putting Distance Between You and Unhelpful Thinking in Your Clinical Work

WHEN I WAS 8 or 9 years old, I was convinced I would go to hell for merely thinking swear words. I rarely swore out loud, dutifully did my homework, and ate all my green beans at dinner, but somehow I was certain my frequent vile mental graffiti would earn me eternal damnation. Oh, the power of mental chatter! Our rarely quiet, verbal selves have as much capacity to elevate us to declaring our dreams on the steps of the Lincoln Memorial in Washington as they do to depress us on the steps leading down into the basements of our childhood homes. I remember sitting in the stairwell as a boy, worrying about my vulgar self-talk. The intensity of my emotions served as all the evidence of my impending damnation I would ever need.

An important point to remember as you move through this chapter, and for all your clinical work, is that our minds never stop their mumbling, chatting, and sometimes ranting. The mind is churning out thoughts on an ongoing, seemingly ceaseless basis. Though we'll practice methods that often have the effect of slowing thoughts in the next chapter, for now it is crucial to cut yourself (and your clients) some slack around the fact that thinking is ever present, and it does not conform to attempts to will it to stop. In this chapter, we examine the role of our thoughts, our inner chatter, on our work. Are you fully aware of your thought patterns, the filters you use for making judgments, decisions, and impressions of your clients?

A helpful concept for understanding our relationship with our thinking is provided within the acceptance and commitment therapy (or ACT, pronounced as a word, not an acronym) literature (Hayes, Stroshahl, & Wilson, 1999; R. Harris, 2009). "Fusion" is the apparently uniquely human tendency to snag ourselves in our thoughts—to "fuse" with them and give them power over our behavior and our inner experience. Fusion is helpful in many situations where inflexibility of response is actually to our advantage—such as when it comes to putting one's foot on the brake pedal at an intersection when the traffic light is red. Not so helpful is our fusion with thoughts about others and ourselves leading to inflexibility that, in turn, creates suffering and blocks us from taking enriching and enlivening action. Fusion is a natural process that has served us well over the centuries. It kept us out of the jaws of many a saber-toothed tiger. These days, however, tigers loom less frequently, and fusion with our thoughts often restricts our actions and amplifies upset. It can get in the way of our best work as clinicians.

How might we fuse with our thoughts as helpers? Peruse the following and notice if any seem at all familiar:

- "This client has no motivation." (A static, inflexible judgment.)
- "I don't work with borderlines." (A fixed rule regarding one's practice . . . notice any judgment in there as well?)
- "This client is always trying to take advantage of me in session." (Judgment and negatively toned conceptualization rooted in the past and suggestive of the future as well.)
- "He is manipulative." (You can almost imagine yourself a judge rendering a verdict from atop your bench with this one.)
- "I'm not sure I can handle this client—she's too much for me." (What I refer to as "Michelangelo's *Therapist*"—a statue in the form of a rigid helping professional.)

LEAN IN

As you read the statements above, what thoughts of your own popped into mind regarding either your clients, your role as a clinician, or you as a person? In particular, list any rules, judgments, future or past-oriented conclusions, or self-directed proclamations.

Review what you've written. Ask yourself: In this moment (and in my work as a clinician going forward), how helpful will it be if I hold this thought tightly? If I view myself, my clients, and my work with absolute allegiance to this thought? What happens to my experience in this moment?

In case you're beginning to feel a little "less than" for clutching at such thoughts in the course of your work (see how quickly and readily fusion can rear its rigid head?), it's important to note that your mind is simply doing what minds do—generating thoughts, chatting away internally about every aspect of your moment-to-moment experience. Your mind, my mind, all minds, fuse with thoughts from time to time. Adding on an extra couple of years in graduate school, or reading just one more book (even this one) will not erase your mind's fascination with fusion. Remember, what served us well for eons with saber-toothed tigers might not be as helpful when it comes to sidestepping our reactions to *those* clients (even if they do have a slight snarl about them).

Here, we'll work on increasing flexibility in your thinking regarding the most trying, taxing cases by learning to become an adept, dispassionate observer of thoughts that arise in reaction to client behavior (learning to "defuse" such thinking). Instead of viewing the world *from* our thoughts, we can learn to step back and watch our thoughts as mere information, a ticker tape of the mind, for us to do what makes sense based on the directions we're heading (in this case, as clinicians hoping to positively impact our clients' lives). The better you become at merely watching your own thinking in response to clients, the more you will take effective clinical action. Maintaining a flexible relationship with your thinking will be advantageous in every professional interaction.

Monkey See, Monkey Think, Monkey Do

When people in coastal England, France, or Spain looked out over the Atlantic Ocean in the millennia before the 15th century, what did they see?

A flat world, of course, that dropped off into oblivion at the horizon. When we look up at the stars on a clear night, what do we see? The ancients saw gods and mythical creatures. We see stars and galaxies we assume are there. Many are not. As any astronomer will tell you, many have been long dead and, because of the vast distances of interstellar space, their light is only now reaching our eyes. The source is gone, but our eyes see what they see, and our brains make up the rest—flat worlds, gods in the sky, and the snapshot impressions and gut-level reactions we have of our most difficult clients. We take what our senses give us, and the brain fills in gaps and makes up (sometimes woefully inaccurate) shorthand stories. The trick is to learn to let go of our stories in exchange for the most effective clinical practice.

In clinical work, especially with the most challenging clients, it is crucial to remember that we create our worlds—we construct our own sense of reality on a moment-to-moment basis. Have you ever reminisced about a childhood story so many times that you forget what actually happened? Memory, as cognitive scientists have shown, is a construction, always up for amendment with the onslaught of new experiences. Scientists will also tell you that in "reality," there is a small hole in your field of vision—a small gap created by the space taken up by your optic nerve at the center of the back of your eyeball. Of course you don't see these small holes when you look out at the world because your brain fills in the gaps. Our brain tweaks our field of vision, creating a full picture of the world we're looking at.

Recently, I was sitting in my office at the therapeutic school where I work. Our clients are children with severe emotional and behavioral issues—safe to say, interactions with them can be difficult at times. On this particular day, I heard an overhead page for all staff to proceed to the front of the building. This was a sure sign that something significant and perhaps very dangerous was happening. Indeed, a teenage student (who, clinically, faces significant disruption due to trauma, mood, and attachment-related difficulties) was upset and standing on a 15- to 20-foot wall overlooking our building's back parking lot. "I'm going to jump," he said.

I and a couple other staff members who knew this boy well talked to him while a group of others stood nervously below. Kids and teachers were watching from classroom windows at the back of the building. Staff members had run to grab padded mats in the event he jumped (though the potential helpfulness of the mats was questionable from that height). After a few tense minutes, the boy stepped back from the wall and walked inside. I, along with other staff members, sat with the boy in my office and processed what had happened. The boy was able to begin expressing his genuine feelings, and it felt to me as though we connected around the true source of the problem. He appeared safe, was following our directions, and was able to leave my office and head back down to his classroom. I went about my day feeling a little shaken, but overall pleased that we were able to turn things around for this kid. I assumed my perception would be shared by all. I was wrong.

This, along with many other examples I could cite, is a great example of the fundamental role of perception, of our constant creation of the "reality" of what our clients present to us. I felt as though the boy was safe while we were talking to him on the wall, and after he came with us to my office because I was privy to what he was saying. Others who were watching from a greater distance had a completely different perception. From their vantage point, the boy was going to jump at any second, and there was little they could do. These staff members were quite upset that we did not send this boy to the hospital. To them, his behavior was incredibly unsafe (which it was), though my perception was different, due to what I was seeing and hearing, and my own history and training. Perception, as we'll see throughout this chapter, is everything (literally). We will work together on developing skills for not buying so much into the initial thoughts we hold about our most angering, irritating, angst-producing clients.

LEAN IN

Take any difficult client you've worked with recently, either the one you've previously selected anchors for, or another. Any client is fine. Recall a specific time, a specific difficult interaction you had with this client. Do you remember what you thought about the client at the time? If not, imagine what you might have felt. List the thought below.

____

____

Now, imagine watching yourself interact with this client. Maybe you're behind a one-way mirror, or maybe you're invisibly sitting next to the client who is looking over at you in the opposite chair. Does anything shift in your perception of this interaction? Anything at all? Let yourself notice any changes, however slight, and list them below.

____

____

Now ask yourself: What might be some advantages of viewing this client in this way, from this perspective?

____

____

We need to practice what we preach as helpers. Though we often prompt our clients to stand apart from their thoughts and calmly evaluate their validity, we also fail to separate out the impact of our own negative chattering—like most people, we give our thoughts undue weight. The work (as it often does) hits an impasse—our clients balk at change, or emotionally run over us, and we vibrate with reactivity. We feel our way forward in the dark, and in the process, we often move in the opposite direction of offering what is helpful and therapeutic.

The Light at the End of the Tunnel Vision

Suppose it's a bit after dusk on a Friday evening, and you're commuting home in heavy traffic. It's been a long, frustrating week on the job (dealing with difficult clients) and you're rushing toward some downtime at home. The last thing you want is to watch the flickering of the brake lights of the car ahead. On, off. On, off. Every pulse a reminder of the delay of your weekend. You've come to know every nuance of this car in front of you in the last 30 minutes, every scratch, the dent in the bumper, the ridiculous vanity license plate, "GR8LOVR."

Imagine it's quiet in the car. You are lost in thoughts of what the weekend holds in store when your bumper is suddenly tapped from behind. Just a tap, but enough to jostle the car and make you check the rearview mirror. You turn around to take a look. It's dark, and all you see are headlights. "Idiot," you think as you shake your head, smirk, and resume your dance between the gas and brake pedals, inching toward home. There's another jolt; a bit more contact with the bumper. You check the mirror and see nothing but the high-beam headlight glare of the car behind, and only the vaguest of shadows of the driver within.

Now you're noticing the anger seething. "He's doing this on purpose! What a &^%$! Can't he see there's nowhere to go! So help me, but if there's even a scratch on my car I'm gonna. . . . " You follow the surge of thoughts, a quickening pulse of peevishness churning deep in your brain.

Another tap of the bumper from behind. You pound the car horn, yelling into the rearview mirror. "What's your problem?!" The swearing and road rage commence.

Of course we, as thoughtful, well-meaning, and highly trained members of society, would never lose control of ourselves in such situations. Of course not. Clearly, however, this person in our hypothetical traffic example is intentionally ramming your car. Your rage is entirely justified. At least until you launch out of your car, storm back toward his, and soon discover that this person heading home to his own family has had a heart attack. He is slumped forward onto the steering wheel.

You've just fallen prey to what social psychologists refer to as "correspondence bias" (it's also called the "fundamental attribution error" because of how pervasive or fundamental it appears to be for people) (Gilbert & Malone, 1995). You assumed the other driver's behavior was his fault; that it was an intentional act resulting from some defect of his character. Simply put, the other driver was a jackass—an unthinking jerk ramming his way through traffic. Your mind jumped to such conclusions and gave no consideration to the possible external or situational causes of this person's behavior. What would you have done if you had really been in this driver's shoes? Would you have jumped to similar conclusions? The data suggests that you would (and that you do on a regular basis, particularly with your more challenging clinical interactions).

Social psychologists argue that when we're watching others do things, we fall into a sort of perceptual tunnel vision; we see them moving and talking, so we assume they are the cause of their own actions, that something internal to them made them act as they did. People act as a result of their traits, personal characteristics, or states of being. Makes sense, right? I picked up the fork and stuffed my face with lasagna, therefore clearly I did so because I was a ravenous glutton. This seems like a valid assumption and indeed it would be until you got more information—until you learned that I hadn't eaten more than dry toast in 3 days due to having the flu (that and the fact that my father happens to be Chef Boyardee).

This is a workbook and not a text on the intersection of neuroscience, evolutionary theory, and cognitive science (nor is it an Italian cookbook). Suffice it to say that our brains appear to be wired for certain mental shortcuts in order to afford us the luxury of tending our television sets and Facebook pages without being completely overloaded with the immensity of sensory input.

Imagine sitting across from a friend at dinner at your favorite local restaurant and having to be consciously aware of every twitch of facial muscle, the tone and timbre of every word, and every possible environmental cause and contributor to your friend's actions. Does this seem daunting? To have complete, consistent, and exhaustive perspective on your every action's causes and implications (and those of your clients) would make you not only the best therapist on the planet, it would make you a good contender for the title of Grand Poobah of the Universe.

Perspective, therefore, is a summit we stand on for a mere fraction of our mental hike. It takes a great deal of effort to get there. Ask any climber of mountains, though, and you will likely hear that the hardship of making it to this hard-to-hang-out-in place is well worth it. Ask yourself: *Is doing your absolute best clinical work worth the climb?*

Think of perspective on your reactions as a muscle of sorts. You would not expect abdominal muscles to pop forth from your midsection from one trip to the gym (unless as a result of an accident on an ab-crunch machine necessitating a trip to the emergency room). A habit of more readily returning to perspective must be built over time. The removal of the obstacles to perspective must be cultivated as a habit. Might this be an important habit for us as clinicians to foster? How might a lack of awareness of the perceptual errors running rampant in one's decision making and discriminations as a therapist block your best work and possibly contribute to negative outcomes?

Here is a partial list of social cognitive biases of relevance to clinicians (adapted from Croskerry, 2003):

- Correspondence bias (discussed above): The tendency to judge and blame clients for their behavior rather than to thoroughly examine the situational factors and circumstances that might have been responsible. "Client X is unmotivated for treatment."
- Anchoring: The tendency to fuse with certain features of a client's presentation early in the assessment or treatment process, to the exclusion of other, perhaps crucial pieces of information (these are the clinical first impressions we find hard to let go of—the judgments about motivation, personality "disturbances," and treatment-interfering tendencies based on gestures, turns of phrase, and anecdotes taken out of context). "Client X's angry interrupting of me during the session showed me his propensity to be the controlling abuser in a domestic violence pattern."
- Availability: Judging things as being more likely simply because they readily come to mind (e.g., "This person is diagnosed with borderline personality disorder and therefore I should be on guard with my personal information because of likelihood that she will violate boundaries with me if I'm not careful").
- Confirmation bias: Looking for evidence in support of a conclusion you've drawn rather than looking for information that might refute it (e.g., "I made sure to take a good look around the client's apartment for any empty bottles—the neglect of these children had to come from somewhere").
- Framing effect: How one's perspective on a client can be heavily influenced by the clinical file, or how others "frame" the person (e.g., former therapist to new therapist: "This kid strikes me as being a potential future sociopath").
- Hindsight bias: How knowing an outcome for the client tends to warp your thoughts as to how things "must" have happened versus a more thorough and realistic assessment of what actually transpired (e.g., "This client has been dissociating and having frequent nightmares—I'm going to need to work hard to help him talk about his repressed memories of sexual abuse").

These errors in thinking are very common and arise for all of us at some point in our work and personal lives. As therapists whose work calls for balanced, insightful, and empathic thinking about clients, it is imperative that we learn to recognize this perceptual hall of mirrors when we walk into it.

LEAN IN

Review the clinician's case conceptualization below. See if you can accurately identify the perceptual biases in any of the statements.

A. "Sam von Trapp is a 35-year-old unemployed man carrying a diagnosis of major depressive disorder who has avoided applying for a job in over 8 months."
B. "Evidence of anhedonia emerged upon interview with the client's girlfriend, who reported that he 'never wants to do anything anymore.'"
C. "Mr. von Trapp's affect in session gave evidence of his well-documented depression in that he rarely initiated topics and was slow to respond to queries."
D. "Based on reports by his former therapist, the client attended therapy regularly and yet failed to generate significant change in depressive symptoms by the time his therapist ended treatment due to a relocation to another city. The client likely experienced secondary gain in his former treatment that went inadequately addressed in session, thereby inadvertently reinforcing the client's depressive and anxious/avoidant symptom pattern."
E. "In our next session, I will probe the client regarding any recent social/interpersonal failures."

Key: A. Correspondence bias—assumption that client "avoided" job applications intentionally without considering situational factors involved. B. Framing effect—clinician is allowing girlfriend's report alone to be the basis for establishing a key criterion of depression. C. Confirmation bias—clinician is "searching" for evidence of depression based on reading the diagnosis of depression in the record. D. Hindsight bias—the clinician has no direct evidence of secondary gain; instead it is a mere guess based on knowledge of a fact regarding the ending of the previous course of treatment. E. Availability bias—just because the client has been diagnosed with depression, the clinician is assuming that social failure has gone hand-in-hand with his mood issues and therefore will probe this area.

LEAN IN

Now that you've practiced catching others' clinical biases, see if you can catch some of your own. Cue up your markers for your own difficult client. Once you have them vividly in mind, write in the space below about the client (in third person—"he/she," "they"). Take no more than 5 minutes and write a case conceptualization without pausing to analyze or censor your responses. Just write whatever comes readily to mind.

Review what you've written. Using the list of perceptual errors above, write the number of the bias or error next to any you identify. If you fail to notice any, congratulations. You get to keep looking until you see one. If we're honest and open with ourselves, we notice that we all fall prey to bias in our thinking about our clients.

(Don't) Go With Your Gut

I think I was a boy when I first experienced what are usually referred to as "finger cuffs." I was at a friend's birthday party when someone popped an interwoven paper tube onto each of my index fingers. "Try to pull them apart," said my friend. "You won't be able to do it." And I couldn't—the more I tried to pull my fingers apart, the more tightly my fingers were ensnared. What was the solution?—moving my fingers toward each other, toward the captive source, and to my amazement, they came free.

As clinicians, we're not supposed to get frustrated by our clients; we're definitely not supposed to loathe them. "I'm a caring, compassionate person," we tell ourselves. "What kind of helper am I if I allow myself to feel these things? There must be something wrong with me." Well, the simple fact is that you have, you are, and you will.

Think for a moment. In just a few simple words, capture what the likely outcome will be if you work to squash these negative thoughts about yourself and your work as soon as they arise.

____

And yet, you'll continue to fight them, won't you? They run contrary not only to your training and professional standards but to your very identity. I find myself reminded of the definition of insanity often attributed to Albert Einstein: Doing the same thing repeatedly and expecting a different result. When we continue thinking we can fight off our extreme thoughts about clients, and the feelings accompanying them, and when these reactions continue, even magnify, what would you call it?

Now ask yourself an important question: What is more important—being right about your thought, or being effective and helpful as a clinician in this particular situation?

According to the ACT approach (Hayes et al., 1999), "defusion" from our tight grip on these negative thoughts can be helpful. The idea is that much of our distress comes from gripping our thoughts too tightly—by assuming we need to view the world *from* them, instead of simply observing them. We are verbal creatures, and though our words allow us to plan, create, and dominate the planet, they also get us stuck in rigid ways of viewing and categorizing ourselves, others, and our world. Suffering and limits on potential for flexible, effective action are the unintended result of fusion in our mental experience.

As clinicians, when we struggle with thoughts of being incompetent or that "Client X is sabotaging all this work I've put into her care," or when the ticker tape of dread and failure shows up in our minds when faced with that next name in your appointment book, it's no surprise that we suffer a great deal of frustration, anxiety, and downright despair. The pain accompanying these fused thoughts is indeed real, and deserves our colleagues' and our own compassion. Just because the suffering is real doesn't mean the thoughts are therefore feasible.

Again, our negative, fused thoughts have served us well across the evolutionary history of our species. Since most clinicians do not practice inside caves and must use techniques other than bludgeoning to leverage change for clients, our evolutionary cognitive baggage seems less than ideal. We need flexibility in our thinking, not hard-and-fast rules. Nuance sparks progress in treatment, not Neanderthal perseveration (I'm betting that grunting as a way to emphasize points to clients doesn't help either).

I've learned to not use clipboards very often in my clinical work. If you could talk to my first psychotherapy client from my training days, you would perhaps learn why—think dutiful, overeager graduate student impatient to prove his therapeutic prowess to colleagues and supervisors; add in a long list of carefully crafted intake interview questions; add a clipboard to hold this list; and add an anxious, angry, and "unmotivated" client who had come to therapy at the insistence of his girlfriend. The formula resulted in me being glued to my clipboard and almost ignoring the human being sitting across from me. I thought it was a great session in that I got answers to every single question I'd painfully written. My client appeared to disagree. He never returned.

LEAN IN

Imagine that I'm sitting with you with my clipboard in hand. Imagine that I've given you a drug, a truth serum of sorts, and you are telling me every thought that passes through your mind. In particular, I want to know the thoughts you have when you're really being hard on yourself as a therapist—the ones when you really are being tough on yourself about your work. List a few of these self-critical thought morsels below. Remember, the truth serum is compelling you. What nastiness does your mind send your way? What does it say about your past work, about your future interventions? What does it say about you as a person? As you write them, I will write them on the big clipboard I'm holding (exercise adapted from R. Harris, 2009).

____

____

____

Now that you're nice and fused with these thoughts, what stories does your always-chattering mind tell you about the challenging client you're using as your focus in this book? Allow your mind to peruse the prickliest, most vexing moments with this person. What pops up in consciousness? What shows up? List those thoughts here, and I'll simultaneously write them on my oversized clipboard—the one I clung to during my grad school days.

____

____

____

Now imagine I'm handing you my gargantuan clipboard to hold. It has all of these thoughts you've listed above written big and bold on it. Imagine holding it up close to your face—as close as the thoughts feel to you when you think them about yourself, and about your client. Now, with the clipboard up close, consider these questions:

- If I were there in the room with you now, how much would you be able to engage me with that big clipboard hugging your nose?
- How much are we going to connect and develop a powerful working relationship?
- How much am I going to feel heard, understood, and willing to work with you if you're magnetized to that thing?
- Is it any wonder that I'm not much into my interaction with you?
- Do you think that your clinging, your fusion, with the thoughts on this clipboard is helping or hindering your desire to do the best work possible?
- Now imagine setting the clipboard down on your lap. How much

> more are you able to get things going with me? How much more connected can we get? Can you notice the difference?

Even as highly trained, competent clinicians, our minds wrap us up in thought-knots on occasion. If we're willing, we can learn to notice this and defuse our thinking. It's our choice to make in every moment of our clinical work.

Defusion is altering the context of the thoughts so we no longer adhere to them, or buy into them, so strongly. Defusion gives us flexibility in which to act. Instead of telling myself (and believing) that I will be eternally damned for my silent profanity as I did when I was a child, I can remind myself that I'm merely *having* the thought that this will happen. This simple reminder creates distance between me and the thought, and I end up feeling less concern, less angst. If only I could have discovered this as a kid. In addition to my inner curse compulsion as a boy, I also let my preoccupation with thought destroy my chances for Major League Baseball stardom. With my placement in the outfield, the time it took for high fly balls to float down toward me out of the sky gave me ample opportunity to chant to myself: "Gonna drop it. . . . Gonna drop it. . . . Gonna drop—" Though humans' capacity for thought allows us to invent games like baseball, thought does not necessarily make for great players (and instead makes you a great benchwarmer).

In order for you to progress in expanding your ability to work with difficult interactions with clients, you need to stop discussing things and give things a try. Practice makes perfect (so long as you don't fuse with such a thought).

LEAN IN

Review your list of fused thoughts about yourself and your client from the exercise above. If you're willing, imagine your client is sitting with you in an empty chair nearby (if there is no chair, imagine one). Try to imagine the client as vividly as possible. What is he or she wearing? Imagine his or her gestures and tone of voice. Now review your list of fused thoughts again. Feel the words as much as possible. Now, please sit upright if possible, with your hands resting comfortably on your lap. Gently allow your eyes to close.

For the next 5 minutes, simply watch your thoughts as they pass through your awareness. Some people like imagining that each thought is a cloud passing by, or leaves blowing across your path, or maybe raindrops streaking a windowpane. Notice any thoughts, sensations, or images that come to mind. Are you willing to merely notice what shows up for the next 5 minutes?

Opening your eyes, note any experiences from this exercise that appear significant to you below.

____

____

____

What happened to your fused thoughts about the client and yourself over the course of the 5 minutes? Did things change or stay the same? How workable, how feasible, is it for you to grip these thoughts so tightly as you sit with this client? Where will all this gripping lead? Are you willing to form a new relationship with these thoughts about the client and about yourself as a clinician?

A metaphor: Our thoughts often drift through the mind as if it was a building with many wildly different sorts of rooms. How odd would it be if you actually walked through a building and found yourself moving from a bedroom to a kitchen to a courtroom to a prison cell to an open meadow back to the bedroom (perhaps hoping to stay there a while—with someone else of your mind's choosing, of course)? As strange as such a stroll through a building would be, that is what our stream of thoughts is often like. We seldom notice the curious and sudden shifting as thoughts drift from one to another, sometimes with a light, pleasant tone about them, and other times taking on a harsher, heavier, more angst-ridden aspect. These darker courtroom and prison cell thoughts often contain a judgmental or evaluative aspect—a sense of "badness" that we attach to others or ourselves. These are the thoughts we'll be working with most directly.

LEAN IN

Cue up your client anchors again for your client. Imagine a particularly challenging interaction or session with this person. For just a moment, try to mentally re-create how you were sitting (or standing) just after this interaction. If you want, you can even assume that posture now in order to add intensity to the recollection. If your mind starts squawking with objections about this exercise, ask yourself: Who's in charge—you or your mind? In the space below, list a few thoughts that show up for you right now.

____

____

Focus in on any negative thoughts that arrived in your awareness, particularly any with an evaluative aspect. If you could somehow magically remove these thoughts from your mind and give them physical properties, what would they look and feel like? The goal here is to play with your thoughts a bit, and the more playful the better. Being playful with these thoughts does not mean that things aren't serious, or that things have not been painful or troubling for you in your work with this person. Playfulness here is meant not as a minimization of your real experience, but is instead an orientation—a vantage point—from which to observe your own experience and perhaps learn from it, loosen from the grip you've felt while thinking such things.

Again, you're aiming for more flexibility in your thinking in the service of more effective action in your work. So with a playful aspect, give your negative thoughts about this very difficult interaction with a very difficult client a size, shape, color, odor, taste, and texture. Pick one and list its characteristics below. If your mind begins squawking, "This is silly—what does this have to do with my effectiveness as a clinician?" simply thank your mind for being so chatty. Let it know you'll be back online with it in just a few more minutes. No mind has ever exploded from lack of attention during such exercises, so relax.

____

____

Letting Go of the Zealot Within

Ask yourself how completely certain you are about these thoughts regarding the session with your client. How true or justifiable are the emotions you experienced? Instead of trying to convince yourself of another way of thinking or feeling, instead of rushing in to tidy up things, ask yourself the following question (that I first came across in the writing of author Robert Pirsig):

How often do I see someone standing in public screaming and warning us all that the sun will rise tomorrow?

Sounds strange, right? You probably don't encounter this very often. That's because we tend to hold things with fanatical certainty only when we're not completely confident in them—when the certainty is actually, at some core level, shaky. Think of holy wars and midlife crises, and you'll have a sense of this. When we're absolutely confident in the truth of something, we tend to assume a calm about us—fanaticism is simply unnecessary.

These thoughts and emotional reactions you're holding on to about your clients—what's fueling your certainty? Why are you giving them your allegiance? Write out your best guess as to what is driving your dedication to these thoughts. What is at the core?

____

____

Think of an interaction in your personal life that led to strong negative feelings. Pick something recent in order to have access to the full flavor of things. In this interaction, what was a thought or emotion you were buying into, or fused with?

____

Imagine that this thought is a large brick that you're holding as you jump into the ocean (R. Harris, 2009). What will be the result if you maintain your grip, your fusion, with this thought? What could you do that would be helpful during your open-water experience if you aren't holding onto this brick? Coming back to your actual life, what actually happened as a result of your clutching of that particular thought? Regardless of what your mind says, what did your experience say? Was it helpful to grip this thought so tightly?

Chances are, particularly if the interaction led to considerable (and likely mutual) upset, there was some degree of tug-of-war—pulling at one another. And just like in the game of tug-of-war, it's hard to yank at the rope without gripping it. When we hold onto our thoughts, feelings, and perspective, experience shows us that things tend to get stuck.

As you may be realizing, your frustration, anger, anxiety, apathy, or upset in reaction to your clients is not really the problem. The true source of the problem is your attempts to force these inner experiences into submission. Ask yourself whether you have ever wished someone ill. I've had many a voodoo doll fantasy moment with some nemesis or another in my life. In the end, I had little actual control over the levels of suffering for these individuals, and I had little ability to make myself not feel guilty for mentally stabbing my mind's stuffed-doll image of them either. The wish, the attempt, to control experience makes sense and comes naturally to all of us. How helpful is it, though? In our work as therapists, how much do our attempts to micromanage our experience of our clients really move the work forward?

Defusion: It's Not Just for the Bomb Squad

How willing are you to consider alternatives to a strong-arming strategy for dealing with your reactions to clients? Have you had enough struggling with your thoughts about these more difficult clients? Again, do you want to be right, or do you want to be effective? All this certainty, buying into, gripping, and fusing with the judgments, labels, interpretations, conclusions, categorizations, and the heart-shaped chocolate box of accompanying angst, may have left you wondering how you might defuse more from the darker, draftier rooms of your mental house.

Before leaping into more strategies, it's important to lay out some caveats lest these techniques become stale and less than ideally helpful.

- Caveat 1: Your pain is real (and you're not alone). As we discussed in the introduction, burnout and compassion fatigue are remarkably common, even among competent therapists. Your upset over work with particular clients (or more generally) is not something to be minimized, and I'm certainly not intending this with any of the exercises (no matter how zany and playful) in this book. It is indeed tough work being a therapist—the role episodically, though inevitably, leads to frustration and distress. The difficulty of a psychotherapist's role requires respect. Think of it like this: How many times have you been to a funeral and witnessed (or found yourself) laughing and joking with others, perhaps while sharing memories of the deceased? This can happen in a very respectful way, and is merely another way to relate to the experience of the pain of death. With defusion, you're looking to create a different relationship with the pain resulting from the challenging aspects of your work.
- Caveat 2: With defusion (and any other strategy in this book) the goal is less to reduce or eliminate your distress than to learn to manage it more effectively. To the degree that you're looking to squash your angst in response to that client who always no-shows but then calls you after hours expecting favors, then you're merely adding another control-focused aspect of tension to the picture. As you work to create a more flexible relationship to your experience as a therapist, often the anxiety, frustration, or whatever else is clogging up your work tends to clear—it does so best when left alone, though.
- Caveat 3: I do not believe you must formally subscribe to ACT or become an ACT clinician, or a Buddhist monk for that matter, to benefit from these strategies. By all means, practice from your orientation of choice. My suggestion is that you consult this approach if you've found yourself daunted by your reactions to clients—if reactivity keeps showing up in your experience despite your best efforts to deal with it. It's here that I believe ACT and Eastern philosophy-consistent strategies can be helpful for the helper.

Below are defusion-focused strategies that aid in creating flexible awareness of one's thought process as a clinician. The goal is to create space for awareness of possibilities for intervention that might otherwise go unnoticed, and for choice in the direction of compassionate engagement and proactive leadership of the interaction. These are not a series of tricks to pull out and try on yourself. These are meant as ongoing experiments for you to conduct in order to shape a new relationship with your thinking as you interact with your clients, and with your mind in the times outside of your office. Approach these as part of an ongoing and essentially neverending journey and see how they might benefit over time. Strategies below were adapted from Hayes and Smith (2005) and R. Harris (2009):

New Perceptual Frames

Defusion in the form of new vantage points or viewing angles on yourself, your clients, and your work.

LEAN IN

Take a step back from the thought or emotion and ask yourself: How old is this? If the reaction seems to go back quite a way, ask yourself whether this is perhaps a piece of your emotional scripting from years ago. Is this script written in words that fit with the direction you would ultimately like to go with your client? What does this suggest?

LEAN IN

Take your thought or emotion and embrace it. Really be grateful for it. Tell yourself this in response: "Thanks, Mind, for sharing this with me about my client!" The more enthusiastic the better. Very importantly, say to yourself that it was your own mind that created this. Your mind is doing what it's built to do—think thoughts and process emotions.

LEAN IN

Think about any feedback you've received when the person starts with a positive comment, inserts *but,* and then tries to give you critical feedback. You, like anyone, reject the positive comment because of the dismissive "but." Simply switching one simple word choice—from *but* to *and*—gives the message that you and your clients have difficult emotions and behaviors that can exist simultaneously. No one is wrong, and flexibility becomes more likely with this simple change. Shift your use of language about yourself and your clients. When you or your client has a negative behavioral response to a strong emotion, instead of thinking "the feeling was X, *but* the action was Y," substitute *and* for *but*.

Similarly, instead of telling yourself that you "are anxious" or "are fed up" or "can't deal with" a particular client, or you "are the worst therapist," shift toward a stance of "having" the thought. "I'm having the thought that I'm the worst therapist" sounds much less rigid and hard-edged, doesn't it? It creates a small space between the thought and you in order for choice to occur.

Small yet consistently applied shifts in your use of language can have a domino effect on how rigid and fused you are with the negative thoughts about yourself, your work, and your clients.

Flexible Experience of Thought Process

Lived versions of defused, flexible perspective.

LEAN IN

Write down the words or phrases that best describe your reaction to your client on an index card. Carry them around with you (but do not throw them out, rip them up dramatically, or do anything else that suggests control or trying to make a change). Just take them out regularly and let them sit in your hands. Maybe you could even try looking at them and reading them aloud just prior to your session with the client. Allow the thought or reaction to sit there, separate and at a distance from you. Also—if you read them aloud, try doing so very slowly—like a tape player that is running out of power. Create emotional distance between you the observer and the thought or emotion. Remember, playfulness, even with intense, "jagged" thoughts, is a great way to create the psychological space for flexible, effective action.

LEAN IN

What is the most startling, dramatic, intense word or phrase your mind uses when you're getting highly fused in reaction to a client, or to some aspect of your work? Sit for a few moments in silence and allow that word or phrase to emerge in your mind's eye. Perhaps it's a word that a client tossed at you in session. Maybe a label that you've conjured for yourself or the client. Whatever it is, list it here: ______________________. Now, take this word or phrase and repeat it over and over as fast as you can for at least 30 seconds. What happens to the words? What do you notice about what they mean after you've repeated them in this way? What has shifted in your experience of their sting? Do you notice the distance you've just created? And ask yourself, who is noticing this distance? Are you those words you repeated?

LEAN IN

Take your fused thought, phrase, or intense word about your work and say it aloud in the voice of your favorite childhood cartoon character (I'm partial to Donald Duck myself and can do a really awesome impression when called upon). Again, this is not meant to make light of how difficult your experience can be. It's meant to shift your stance in relation to it. You don't have to be great at making the voice, just willing to make the effort. What do you immediately notice in your experience of the thought when you do so? What does this suggest about what is possible in terms of your management of the more trying aspects of your work and role as a clinician?

Defusion Metaphors

Catchy images that can go viral and create flexibility in your thought process regarding your work.

LEAN IN

Take your hard-edged thought or emotion (about yourself or your client) and imagine that it is merely a pop-up ad on the desktop of your mind. It is merely an Internet ad, a piece of spam, flashing through your mind. Watch it dart into your awareness, and see what it does if you just let it sit there on your screen.

LEAN IN

With your eyes closed and while sitting in a calm, relaxed position, call up your thoughts about a challenging aspect of your work and watch them as they pass in front of your awareness. Common metaphors are to watch them as leaves floating by as you sit along a riverbank, or to visualize them as clouds in the sky, or maybe as specks of dust floating in the air around you. Breathe into these thoughts as they arise. Try breathing space all around these thoughts.

LEAN IN

Imagine that you're back in your college or graduate school days and you're sitting in class with *that* professor—the one you idolized, whose lectures mesmerized you. Remember how you hung on the professor's words, how you bought into the truth of his or her statements so readily. . . . Well, imagine your thoughts about yourself and your client as coming from that professor in a lecture. See the professor up on the stage or at the front of the classroom pronouncing your reactive thoughts. Your mind *is* that professor—convincing, isn't it? Now, imagine turning away from Dr. Mind and looking around the room—notice chairs, windows, the floor, the ceiling, and notice your own body, your breathing—in short, bear witness to everything else that *is* along with your thought. Imagine the lights brightening in the room and then imagine them dimming until they go out altogether while Dr. Mind is pontificating. What happens? How does your experience shift?

As we've discussed, the only way to learn to effectively manage difficult interactions with clients is to apply strategies in your actual practice. To begin moving in that direction, consider a case vignette.

Imagine you are the clinician working with a client struggling with significant, chronic depressive symptoms. He is in his 30s, living alone with four dogs, and has not worked in over 15 years, relying on public assistance for his livelihood. Your client comes faithfully to sessions each week and is more than willing to discuss and disclose each and every difficult, painful, angst-ridden experience of his daily life to you. He holds nothing back, and typically begins sobbing about halfway through each session. You are planning to begin a course of cognitive-behavioral therapy to help him learn to monitor his thoughts and behavior and make adjustments based on the objective realities of daily life rather than the pull of negative moods. The following are common statements from your client:

- "No one understands me like you do."
- "I can't see why anyone would want to spend more than 5 minutes with me without getting nauseous."
- "Every cell in my body aches. It's all I can do to haul myself in here to see you."
- "I couldn't fill out the thought log you wanted me to do from last week—it won't help me anyway."
- "Please don't make me do these strategies! They just make me look pathetic. Is that what you're trying to do?" (Crying begins in earnest and continues for the remainder of the session.)

You are the clinician. Imagine you are having the following thoughts during your session with your client. You're finding yourself tense and irritable, checking your watch repeatedly and distracted by sounds out in the hallway.

- "This client won't use therapy. He's completely unmotivated for therapy."
- "I should have known better than to take this referral. I'm not good at working with this sort of client."

What strategies of defusion might you apply to either or both of these thoughts arising during your sessions? Consult the strategies listed above, and list those you might apply in this situation, and how you might use them.

____

____

____

What is your rationale for these strategies? What is your goal for implementing these responses?

____

____

____

It will be helpful to return to the actual difficult client from your own clinical work. Remember, practice is far more helpful than mere pondering when it comes to changing behavior.

Take one of your fused thoughts or emotions in reaction to the client you listed earlier in the chapter and apply any defusion strategy. Persist with implementing this, even if your mind tells you it is pointless. Try to hang in with it. What is the result? What do you notice, particularly regarding the intensity of your certainty, your emotional volume? How might consistent application of this strategy change things? What might it create?

Anticipated result:

___

Actual result:

___

As you practice these defusion strategies, you might have ideas of your own for how to do this with your difficult client. A trainee of mine told me that he used to watch the popular show *Sesame Street* as a child. He loved watching the roommate puppets Bert and Ernie banter with one another. He told me that when he berated himself for falling short as a therapist, he was practicing defusion by using a line from the show. When Ernie complained that he was "just ordinary," Bert replied with a friendly rebuttal: "You're no ordinary Ernie." And that did the trick for my trainee. He would tell himself that he was "ordinary Ernie" as a therapist, even mimicking the voice a bit.

It was not any affirmation or personal pep talk that helped my trainee, it was the playful link between his struggles as a young professional and the self-deprecating angst of a television puppet—the silliness of the ordinary self—that gave him space to be the person and clinician he was without gripping himself into a state of effectiveness-choking apprehension.

In the following space, list your own ideas for how to create distance from extreme thoughts and emotions in reaction to your clients. Remember, let go of intentions to squash negatively toned thoughts. Instead of pulling back on the rope, how can you drop it and let things be there in your mind?

____

____

____

____

____

Interior Design for the Thought-Cluttered Clinical Mind

Our work as clinicians requires us to get into bed with language. And just because we have to lie down (and walk around) with words doesn't mean we have to make love to them. This may sound dramatic, but so does our use of language, particularly when we're highly fused and reactive. We talk and think about the toughest pieces of our interactions and roles as clinicians and sound like jilted lovers. We should take a closer look at this relationship we have with the words we use about our clients.

LEAN IN

Imagine that you're sitting in a group supervision meeting. Colleagues are discussing their cases. Consider each of the following statements made about clients.

- "The client finally owned his impulse to drink in our last session."

  ____

  ____

- "The client is an abuser."

  ____

  ____

- "She is a traumatized child."

  ____

  ____

- "My client talks too much at work and therefore others feel squeezed out of conversations."

  ____

  ____

- "Whenever anxiety crops up for him, he shows a compulsive tendency to hoard."

  ____

  ____

- "The client lied to his wife and therefore it's no wonder she won't trust him to manage the finances anymore."

  ____

  ____

- "Her passive-aggressive tendencies are doing permanent damage to her relationships."

  ____

  ____

- "All my client does is complain."

  ____

  ____

Look over each statement and identify any evidence of judgment, evaluation, or opinion. Circle any words that suggest that the speaker was fused with this thought. How might this fusion have impacted work with this client?

In the blank space beneath each statement, rewrite the statement from a perspective of defused observation. You (as the clinician) are merely observing the client's behavior. Think like a sportscaster narrating a game: What are the objective facts of the client's actions? What is happening now? For example, in the first statement, the use of the word "finally" belies the clinician's fusion with how slow and reluctant the client has been to acknowledge the impulse to use. A mere observational statement, free of judgment, might be something like: "My client indicated last session that she has been struggling with the urge to drink. We talked together in session about how important this disclosure is for her treatment."

In addition, on the second line, list a possible defusion exercise you might use in this situation to more flexibly hold any such fused thought that might arise. For the example above, it might be a simple mental notation: "My mind is telling me that the client finally owned her urge" or catching the word *finally* and repeating it over and over while holding the client vividly in mind.

We talked earlier about how our minds create our experience of reality. We've reviewed the role of defusion strategies for fostering space between your observing self and the negative, highly charged thoughts about your difficult clients and yourself as a clinician. Now, before we leave this chapter's discussion of the role of thinking in managing difficult clients, it will be helpful to practice taking up the pen of mental authorship and writing a new perspective on yourself as a therapist.

LEAN IN

In the space below, list the five most self-critical thoughts you occasionally (or often) experience regarding yourself as a clinician. They can be in response to your work with your more challenging clients, or they can be more general.

1. ______________________________
2. ______________________________
3. ______________________________
4. ______________________________
5. ______________________________

Below are a few exercises for you to consider using (in addition to the defusion strategies above) whenever these thoughts plague you. Remember, you are the author of your experience. Do you want to simply act out the script from the past, or do you want to write your way forward in your career? These exercises can help you rise out of your rigid, automatic thinking and create the perspective necessary for more flexible, effective clinical work. They can do so, but only with consistent, concerted effort.

LEAN IN

Take any of the thoughts listed above. Imagine they are *not yours*. They are comments made by a close colleague about herself and her work. What would you say to her about these thoughts and how much she should be buying into them? Notice any experiences that show up in terms of feeling concerned that your colleague is being too harsh and rigid with herself. Notice any inclinations you might experience to want to convince her not to think this way. What leads you to be so critical of yourself? Where is the sense of concern and self-compassion? Why aren't you dismissive of these thoughts when they arise? How attached to them are you?

LEAN IN

Take any of the thoughts above, particularly one that suggests you are lacking in some capacity, skill, or quality (Leahy, 2003). It might begin with "I can't" or "I'm not." Imagine placing yourself on a number line that measures the degree of this particular skill or quality. Press yourself to imagine someone who completely lacks this skill or characteristic. See if you can think of someone that seems to be absolutely devoid of this aspect. What is that person like and how are you different? How do you behave that is a step up in some fashion from that person? Don't feel guilty about making the comparison—we all do it whether we admit it or not.

____

____

____

If you had to talk with this person who completely lacks this skill or ability, how would you describe how you fall short in this area? Can you imagine looking at the person and accounting for your deficiency in this area? Does your connection to this thought shift at all?

____

____

LEAN IN

Imagine a mistake or failure from your work with a challenging client recently. Focus on a time when you tended toward a harsh response to yourself. What is your immediate thought as to why you did what you did? What was it about you that led to this? Don't think—write it below:

____

____

Now, looking at Figure 3.1, press yourself to think less about yourself than about the context of your actions. What aspects of your client, the

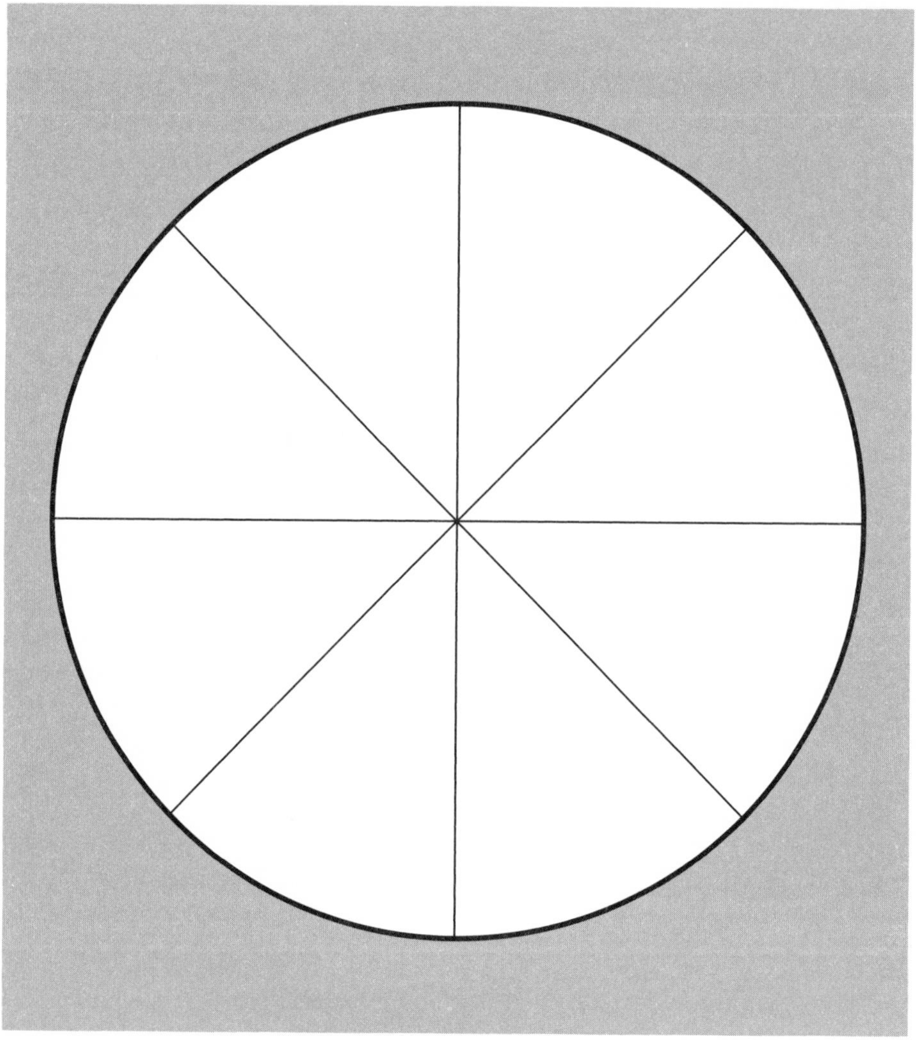

Figure 3.1 Pie Chart Graphic

situation, the environment, other demands, and pressures on you (including time) may have been potential causes of your failure? Without evaluating any, allow yourself to generate as many as possible and write them on Figure 3.1. Draw additional pieces if you need to.

If there were a number of potential causes for this particular clinical outcome, what do you make of the thought you've hooked yourself with? How tightly should it jab itself into you? In the space below, describe any thoughts coming to mind now about this event. Look for a frame on the event that acknowledges your role, your behavior, but takes into account the *full* range of causes, as well as the way in which your actions were inevitable. Finish the following sentence:

"Of *course* I did what I did and things turned out the way they did because in taking everything about myself, my client, and the situation into account . . ."

____

____

____

Sticks and Stones: A New Relationship With Your Experience as a Therapist

In this chapter, you practiced defusion and perspective-taking strategies for creating a flexible mental space and decreasing the likelihood that intense, rigid reactions will fester and block your effectiveness as a clinician. You've perhaps learned to take thoughts a bit less seriously than your highly trained brain has been apt to do. How often have we talked with our clients about how their thoughts are "just thoughts," and yet we enshrine our own? Consider how often your thoughts about your most challenging client don't materialize. On more than one occasion I've found myself fantasizing that a particular client would "do me in," and yet I continue to draw breath. Better yet are the thoughts that these clients might experience a sudden wormhole and be pulled into another universe or dimension, and yet here they sit across from me. Our thoughts deserve less than the crowns we give them.

Now that we've loosened our thinking, we're ready for some serious work on our emotions as therapists. The next chapter suggests a path for managing emotions once they've arrived within and seem as though they're going to take up residence for a while. What can you do if it simply feels impossible to drop the rope with your most difficult clients? And what could be more important for you to work on? Your well-being hinges on this work. And let's not forget our clients—they are always watching us. How we self-manage gives a vivid portrayal of the possible. Their self-acceptance and self-awareness are magnetized by our own.

MAP CHECK

Take a moment and review what we've covered in this chapter. What was one aspect, one piece of content, that resonated with you—sparked your interest, curiosity, or even angst in some way?

Why did this matter to you? What makes this worth writing about? Worth your focus and effort? What is the gravity that this carries for you and your work?

What is one specific action you can take within the next 24 hours related to this issue that feels as though it would be important and has the potential to move you in the direction of what matters?

≺ CHAPTER FOUR ≻

Smelling the Roses (as Well as All That's Rancid)

Mindfulness of Emotion in Clinical Work

IT WAS THE SAME with most games of basketball I played with Teddy at the end of our therapy sessions. He ran ahead of me down the hall and down the stairs of the therapeutic school where I work as a therapist. "Remember," I said. "We can't bounce the ball in the building." I then watched as he slammed the ball into the floor—his dribbling, and my inability to rein him in, echoing down the hallway.

Once we were outside on the court, Teddy reinvented the rules to whatever game we played. For Around the World, he got to have redos if he missed a shot. If I asked him what the score was in a round of Fifty, he would engage in a not-so-slick series of additions for himself and subtractions for me. Sometimes I pointed out the deceptions; usually I let it go. And even if I did point it out, it was in a deferential, "hey there buddy" tone. My hesitance and half-gestures gave the true message: "I just don't want to deal with your meltdown if I press this."

I found it very difficult to tolerate the frustration and, to be honest, the fear involved in working with this particular client. These feelings seemed intolerable to me, and I avoided them whenever I could. I paid the price for blunting and avoiding my emotions in reaction to this boy, and he lost out on possibilities for growth and positive change.

Think back across all your clinical work. Peruse the faces and hear the snippets of dialogue of each client you've encountered. See if you can summarize all of the strong emotions you have experienced in session or out. Please take a few minutes, remove yourself from any distractions or demands on your attention, and think back across all of the many exchanges that together make up the full fabric of your work.

I've always found feelings lists to be a bit too abstract, far removed from the visceral reality of emotion. I work quite a bit with kids, so I'm partial to feelings "faces." Look at the expressions in Figure 4.1. Unless you're just starting out, I challenge you to find a face you have not experienced yourself, even to a significant degree, in the course of your work.

For each of the emotions below, list a client's initials next to those you can remember feeling with a high degree of intensity during a specific clinical interaction. Let yourself spend the time (likely only a few minutes) to conjure clients for each emotion.

Joy/Exuberance: _____
Humor/Silliness: _____
Anger/Rage: _____
Anxiety/Fear: _____
Sadness/Dejection: _____
Boredom: _____
Confusion: _____
Disgust: _____
Shock: _____
Shame/Humiliation: _____
Desire: _____
Hatred: _____

Notice which clients (and the dominant emotion attached to them) come quickly to mind. Notice also which clients and emotions come less readily. Were there any clients you listed multiple times for different emotions? Record any impressions or reactions you have to this in the space below.

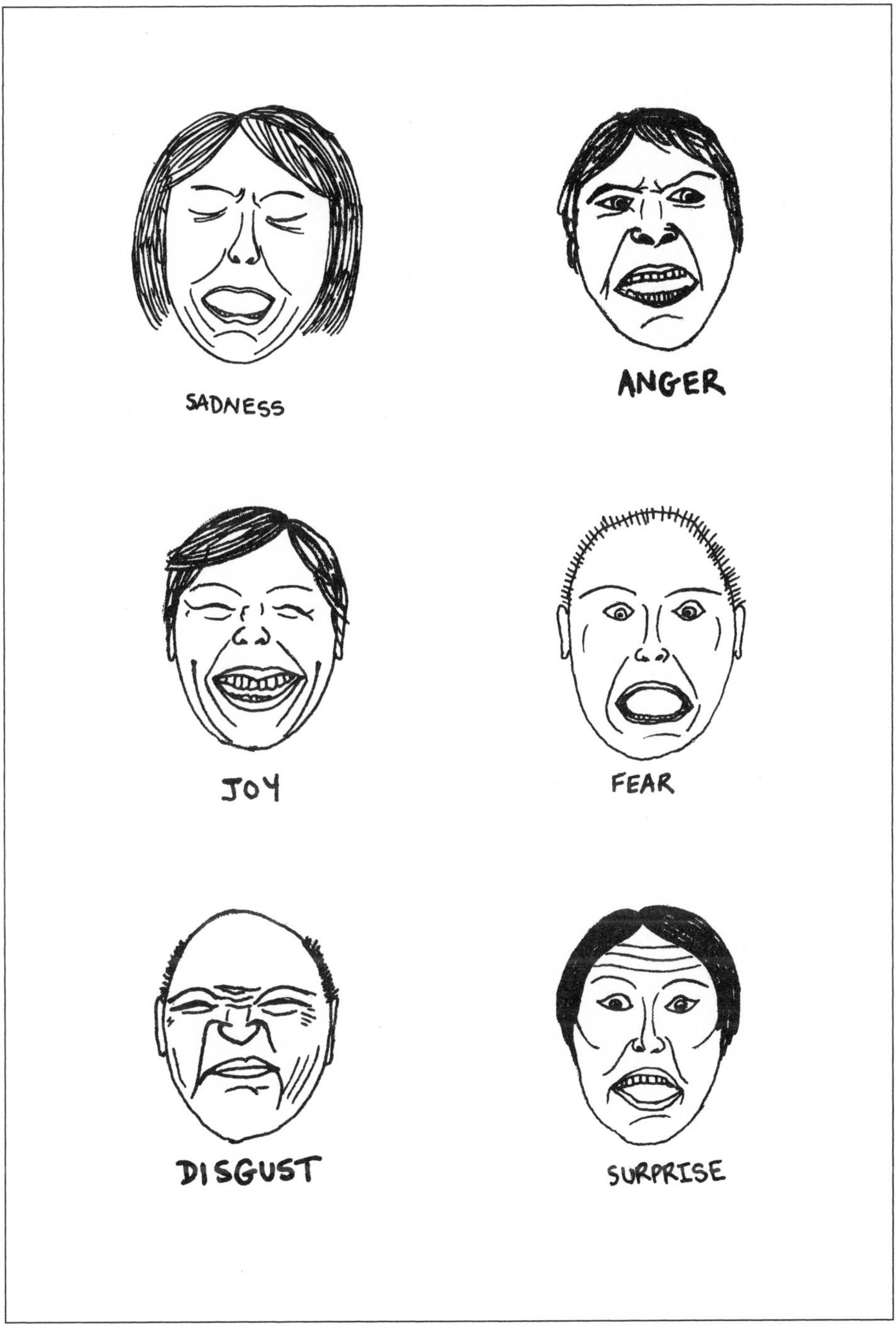

Figure 4.1 The Feeling Faces. Illustration by Diana Elisabeth Dube.

What thoughts come reflexively about you as a clinician and as a person when you consider your emotional reactions to these clients? List any of them below:

____

____

____

____

Can you allow yourself to just notice them for the time being? In upcoming chapters we will actively apply strategies to them, with the goal of increasing your capacity for managing your experience and maintaining a therapeutic stance in your work with clients.

Let's shift gears a bit. If strong emotions are inevitable in clinical work, it is imperative that we develop our capacity to allow them to move through us. Mindfulness strategies can be extremely helpful in this regard. Much has been written in recent years, especially in professional journals, about the benefits and efficacy of mindfulness practices. Numerous studies (in the thousands) document that developing the skills for centering one's mind on the present moment can change physical structures in the brain involved in attention, monitoring action, and regulating emotion (Luders et al., 2012) and can lead to benefits such as increased tolerance of stress and physical illness, as well as reductions in conditions such as anxiety, pain, and depression (Baer, 2003; Shapiro & Carlson, 2009). It has also been linked to decreased health care costs (Herron, 2011). Mindfulness is no mere fad or neat psychological parlor trick.

What is mindfulness? Maybe the best answer to this question begins with what mindfulness is not. It is not . . .

- An activity that requires chanting, the striking of gongs, and the wearing of robes
- Something that requires a dabbling in things supernatural and surreal
- A simple caving in and resigning yourself to negative, inappropriate behavior from your most difficult clients
- A weak, passive approach, inviting trampling of your personal boundaries

Very important, mindfulness is not something you do in order to achieve deep relaxation, especially in the midst of clinical chaos or intensity with a difficult client. While mindfulness practice, done consistently, may help generate feelings of relaxation more regularly, it's not realistic to aim for flower-filled meadows of bliss.

So what is it? As the Zen saying goes, using words to describe mindfulness is like fingers pointing at the moon. Ask an astronaut and you'll learn that the moon is more something to be experienced than concretely depicted. Mindfulness is similarly difficult to describe and requires doing. As pale as the words might be, descriptions of mindfulness point to it as "mirror thought . . . nonjudgmental observation . . . impartial watchfulness . . . bare attention . . . nonegoistic alertness" (Gunaratana, 2002). In his poetic (and "moon-like" description) Gunaratana goes on to write that with mindfulness "one is an unbiased observer whose sole job is to keep track of the constantly passing show of the universe within" (p. 141).

Mindfulness, in the context of working with challenging clients, is allowing yourself to fully feel, to contact, the understandable and inevitable reactions in yourself that arise in the moment during interactions with these people. It is the *you* inside Robert Pirsig's engine car. It is . . .

- A willingness to compassionately and gently allow yourself to feel your emotional reactions to provocation, rants, disrespect, and disavowal of your therapeutic efforts without harsh holding of yourself.
- Leaning toward, or into, tough, unsettling experiences.
- Entirely focused on what is here now in the present, and on learning to foster connection with yourself and your clients there.
- Something you choose to open yourself to. It is a cultivation of flexible awareness of what is.
- A commitment to courageous openness. It is a willingness to feel the intensity of whatever is here now, no matter how bitter, biting, or aversive. It requires the fuel of effort, consistency, and compassionate bravery.
- Essential for self-awareness and effective self-management. You can't handle yourself well in moments of complex and perhaps intense interpersonal exchange without it.

To me, what we're talking about here is the gentle holding of moments such as watching my daughter's birth, or even standing amid a wave of pain and regret at a family member's funeral. It is the deep knowing, the penetrating surge of these moments that suggests mindfulness of emotion. Instead of waiting for these big experiences, we can choose to open ourselves to such fine-grained contact in daily life. Here in this book, we're talking about opening to the raw moments of clinical work, allowing the full range of our emotional experience.

Mindfulness is open awareness, good or bad, of what your clients bring to you, and what your mind and emotions shoot around inside your brain like a machine gun's barrage. For the clinician, mindfulness is the ring holding all the keys to effective management of reactivity within and toward the client. The behavior and intensity of your most difficult clients passes through your awareness, and mindfulness lets these experiences be, without attempting to make them be other than what they are—hard or soft, pained or pleasurable. You notice, observe, and allow, and in the process of doing so, you create space for movement. You carve out the space for taking nonreactive, centered action to move the clinical work forward.

Again, consult the references for a more exhaustive treatment of what exactly you might make of mindfulness. Just know that science has told us much in recent years about how mindfulness awakens and focuses the mind, allows more capacity for holding intensity of negative emotions and pain, and even shapes the structure of the brain in a measurable fashion. Research has shown that mindfulness develops new wiring for approaching, rather than avoiding, difficult experience (Siegel, 2010). Mindfulness is not reserved for the spiritual seeker. It is a tool for universal connection to life, positive adjustment, and change. For our purposes in this book, mindfulness allows you to develop the skill of increasingly noticing and monitoring your physical cues of emotional arousal to clients' behavior. Though mindfulness promises no foundation, no bedrock of certainty, it does help you learn to ride the current of experience.

Guts, Not According to John Wayne

I grew up watching John Wayne war and Western movies. I loved to see him saunter into the rowdiest of bars and storm up the deadliest of machine-gun infested beachheads without an ounce of fear evident on his face. John Wayne symbolized my early definition of courage: unflagging power and strength without fear. When courageous, you run forward without flinching.

And then I grew up and became a therapist. Fear, doubt, and frustration poked at me with frequency (and my colleagues as well, as best I could tell—though often I felt myself to be in solitary, weak company). I also, as a young therapist, worked with actual war veterans. I listened to their tales of fingers unable to pull triggers due to waves of terror, of intense despair after the deaths of friends. From them, and many other clients, I've borne witness to a more accurate definition of courage: doing *despite* pain. John Wayne movies are engaging to watch, but they fall short when it comes to what courage is really about. And courage is what we seek to build in our clients—courage to accept the emotional pain that arises in their experience, and to do what needs to be done to live lives of meaning despite this.

In Chapter 3 we learned skills for defusing and creating flexibility and distance from unhelpful thoughts. In this chapter, we learn about the power of mindfulness of emotions themselves. Here, we're exploring how, through acceptance of our emotions as clinicians, we can more fully wade up onto the beachhead of our difficult interactions with clients. There is no passivity here, no sitting around on cushions resigning ourselves to what's hard about our situations. We're leaning into our boredom during sessions, our fear of that loud, volatile client, our dejection over things not getting any better for our clients, for the financial and personal woes that press at us in session. Acceptance is a willing choice to open up fully to our current emotions, no matter how distasteful they may be. Gandhi said that we should "let good news as well as bad pass over you like water over a duck's back" (1962, p. 271) and that it is important to "forget the past and think of the task before us" (p. 50). Doing so—opening up to what is—allows you to invest energy into moving the work forward rather than squandering it on struggling against yourself. Doing so opens you to range and depth as a clinician. John Wayne would be envious.

Setting aside definitions and descriptions for a moment, are you interested in learning to encounter mindfulness and its potential for helping you in your work with the most vexing clients in your caseload? If you're sufficiently open and willing, take a step forward with the following activities.

LEAN IN: BASIC MINDFULNESS EXERCISES

1. Sit with a straight (not rigid) spine either on a cushion or a chair. Gently close your eyes and for at least 5 minutes focus on the sensations of your breathing. Focus your attention on where you feel it most notably (nose, belly, or chest). If there's any thinking, any mental meandering, come back gently to the awareness of the sensation. This gentle return, no matter how many times you do it, is by itself an extremely useful practice in developing the capacity for nonreactivity. Simply (though not always easily) notice the thoughts as they come and regard them as bubbles. You are not swatting at them or poking them away. Instead, you are reaching out with gentle intention and lightly touching them as if with a feather. Allow yourself to rest in the sensations of your breathing. Be as curious as possible about each breath as it comes and goes. Notice the gap between inhalation and exhalation. Collect details of every sensation. Learn as much as you can about each moment: Are your inhalations longer or shorter than your exhalations? Does the breath flow smoothly or does it swirl a bit in your body? If your breath had shape and form, what would it be? Allow your awareness to expand, to go in all directions, to create vast space, with each breath.

2. Again, sit with a straight spine (this facilitates alertness in your system). This time, keep your eyes open (but softly so—without forcing your eyes wide open), and for at least 5 minutes allow your mind to notice *any* sensation that arises. Whatever arises in any of your senses, observe and collect the detail of the sensation. Notice the sounds near and far. Collect the subtleties of movement—digestion, twitching, churning—within your body. Notice any soreness or tension and simply let it be as it is. If your mind is drawn into thoughts or some storyline, gently direct your awareness back to whatever is now in your awareness. Observe each sensation closely. Inspect it without analysis or judgment. Watch it as if you were feeling it for the very first time in your life. Can you notice the contours and edges of each sensation? The subtle beginnings and endings? What is strong and what is weak? Breathe into every sensation and gently return from any thinking, judging, or analyzing. If you stray into the past or the future, simply note "past" or "future" to yourself and come back to the sensations in the present. How are things changing with the passing seconds?

Open and expand into your experience as it shifts (or not) within and around you.

The goal with these exercises is to learn to hold the sensory aspect of your emotional experience without the usual reflexive attempts we all make to change them. This is acceptance of emotion and, again, it is anything but passive and weak. It requires effort, focus, and a cognitive and emotional resilience shaped by frequent practice. Noted meditation instructor Joseph Goldstein points to two basic forms of mindful awareness highlighted in the previous exercises, the first entailing single-pointed focus on a primary object of mindful attention (here the breath), and the second resting in "open, natural awareness" (1993, p. 35).

The focused, single-pointed form of mindful attention can be quite useful for narrowing one's focus, particularly when emotion and thought are flooding the mind, such as during periods of worry and apprehension. The second, expansive form of mindfulness can be indicated when broadening awareness would be of benefit. This might be the case when the mind is tending toward restrictive, fused focus on a specific negative or painful emotion. Basically, this open form of mindful awareness facilitates acceptance by asking "what else?" of present-moment experience.

In building your basic repertoire of mindfulness skills in order to manage your emotional reactions in the midst of client work, it is important to experiment with how limited and constricted our experience often is. Particularly when the work is difficult over a long period of time, we find ourselves sensing and feeling with one lobe of our limbic system tied behind our backs. The exercises here are meant to be the start of a new path—one in which you learn to open into your emotional experience as a clinician. Your best work emerges from this spaciousness. Take these exercises as mere appetizers whetting your appetite for the ongoing mindful consumption that will expand you as a clinician. Speaking of appetizers . . .

LEAN IN

You've been doing such a nice job walking through the explorations and persistent self-questioning of this book. You deserve a small snack. Seriously, please take a moment, go to your kitchen (or the vending machine down the hall) and get yourself something—anything—to eat. Don't eat it outright. We'll need this snack item for our next exercise. Follow the steps below:

1. Remove a small piece of the food item (raisins, grapes, even chocolate are great for an exercise such as this) and let it rest on the palm of your hand. Just look at it for at least 30 seconds. See how many things you can notice about it—size, texture, weight, what it reminds you of, anything. Just let these observations pass through your awareness. Allow yourself to merely notice each sensation or thought as it comes along.
2. Place it in your mouth, but do not chew it. Notice what shows up in your experience—the feel of it on your tongue, perhaps bumping up against the roof of your mouth. Take an inventory of every sensation that passes by.
3. Slowly—very slowly—begin chewing it (counting to 30 as you do so). Let yourself take in each moment of what it tastes and feels like. What comes to mind as you do so? Just allow these thoughts to come and go as you continue chewing slowly.
4. Slowly swallow what's in your mouth. What remains? How would you describe the taste lingering there?

Take a moment and write in the space below any reactions or experiences you had during this exercise. How was this experience different than the last time you ate this type of snack? How much might you take simple things like eating for granted without mindful attention? What might happen in your clinical work if you attended this way consistently to your inner experience, particularly when things are hard?

I'm sure you are extremely busy and you're not sitting around your office eating bonbons all day. Your schedule is probably as much an exercise in wishful thinking as mine is. How could you possibly have the luxury of time for mindfulness? In order to begin realizing what you might do with increased mindfulness, I'm recommending the following experiment.

LEAN IN

For one full work week, commit to a practice of pausing whenever you hang up the phone, whenever you log on or off of your computer, or before or after some other regular, frequent activity, and merely pause to "collect" the moment you are in. Be a "momentologist" and take three deep, fully felt breaths and ask these questions: What is happening? What's here? Become as deeply aware of what is going on inside and around you as possible for just those few seconds before resuming your regularly overscheduled daily programming. What arises in terms of bodily sensations? Where does your mind go? What comes and goes in your environment?

Before you've become more familiar with it, it's easy to wonder why you should bother with mindfulness. It can seem overly abstract and mystical—not fit for a serious clinician. What you'll find, however, is that with consistent practice in collecting moments, you begin to notice previously neglected or overlooked aspects of your experience. You also notice all the emotional burden from your clinical work you are carrying about. It can be striking how much we carry without awareness. How might this weight be bogging down your efforts with the clients who press at you the most?

LEAN IN: TAKING A STAB AT YOUR MOST DIFFICULT CLIENT

Cue up your anchors for your sample, most difficult-to-work-with client. With eyes gently closed and while sitting erect, visualize your client as vividly as possible—how he or she sits, talks, gestures, word choice, intonation, anything. Conjure up a moment of particular challenge and difficulty with this person. See the scene moment by moment, allowing it to unfold in an unedited fashion. Keep playing the scene and watching your client until you notice tension or difficulty arising, even if only slightly so, in your experience.

Allow your awareness to gently touch all sensations that arise as in the "expansive, open awareness" form of mindfulness we practiced earlier in this chapter. Notice any bodily experiences in particular. If your mind gets caught up in thinking (particularly judgments, analysis, diagnostic considerations, theoretical conjectures, treatment planning), simply note the word *thinking* to yourself and come back to your emotional experience.

Get as curious as possible about the harder edges of your emotional experience. Watch the ebb and flow of any negative sensations of tension or aversion. Breathe into them and make space around them as they arise. Give them motion, sound, shape, and texture. What would this emotional experience look and sound like if you were to set it out in front of you right now? What else is there within and around you in addition to this emotional thing? Watch this emotion as if it were the most interesting thing you've ever encountered. You're Columbus and you've just set foot for the first time onto this emotional new world.

With the exercises we've covered thus far, you're well on your way to fostering a new relationship to your emotional experience as a clinician. Instead of stifling your emotional reactions with the heavy weight of any texts in your clinical library suggesting you do so, you are learning to get acquainted with these reactions. You're leaning in toward their cold, their warmth, and you're giving their rough, sharp, gritty aspects a gentle squeeze. In closing the distance with these reactions, you're working to go the distance with the most challenging aspects of your work, with the most difficult of your clients.

A quick analogy: Have you ever been trying to get some paperwork done when a huge housefly bursts onto the scene and buzzes around, strafing your head from time to time? Have you ever gotten so annoyed by this nuisance that you've had the strong urge to stand up and ferociously swing away at it with any available item (I've been known to throw cushions and magazines at the hapless creatures)? How much work do you get done if you're obsessed with making the fly leave you alone? Is it possible for you to simply let the fly be and get work done anyway? The latter option is what we're about: letting what buzzes at you from your clients simply share the space with you as you do what's important, with mindfulness of your emotional reactions as a core skill in doing so.

LEAN IN

Remember the staring contest exercise from the Introduction? Just when you thought I was done with it, I've decided to bring it back. I call it Stare-Down, the Sequel. As before, find a willing colleague or partner.

Once again, sit facing each other, within 4 or 5 feet. Make eye contact and hold each other's gaze. The instruction last time was for the two of you to not communicate anything to one another. It's different this time. Taking turns, and for approximately 1 minute apiece, maintain eye contact and keep to the only instruction in this activity: The person whose turn it is must communicate *every* thought, bodily sensation, or emotional reaction that comes to consciousness. Do not censor anything—let your judging, socially proper mind go limp. The task for the listener is to absorb everything expressed by the other person. Take in the energy of the words, gestures, and expressions without responding. Simply observe, and in turn observe the thoughts, sensations, and reactions in yourself. Ready, set, communicate *everything*. . . .

Note your brief reactions to this activity in the space below. What did you experience while openly expressing everything that emerged? What reactions showed up in you as you attempted to do so, and how did you relate to them? How distinct is this communication stance from how you typically communicate in your clinical role?

____

____

In the space below, relay your experience of being the listener. What emerged in your thoughts, sensations, and emotions as you faced your partner unleashing his experience in your direction? Did you notice any fluctuation in your willingness to fully and openly receive his communications? What did you learn about yourself and your possible left-sided tendencies? Were there any specific aspects of your partner's communication that sparked reactions for you and, if so, what do you make of this? How much were you truly accepting of what your partner shared, as well as whatever arose in your own inner landscape?

____

____

Surfing the Air Waves

Now that you're well on your way forward with experimenting with mindfulness of your work experience, consider this next activity. Now, we're wading in closer to what we might typically look to avoid. All of us get annoyed at times when we're flipping through TV channels and end up watching a news magazine show in which political pundits argue, debate, and interrupt each other. It's repetitive, pointless, and always seems to play out a familiar script. Yes, these shows can be aggravating, but guess what: For our purposes in learning to cultivate space within us for working with difficult clients, these shows can be downright juicy.

LEAN IN

Select one of these sorts of political pundit shows (unfortunately, there are many to pick from), and prepare to watch it. Turn on the television, sit comfortably and yet upright in a chair or on the floor (a straight back is best), and turn the volume all the way down. Now, do the following:

1. With your eyes closed, focus your attention on the flow of your breath in and out of your nostrils. Do so for a few minutes, focusing on the sensation of breathing wherever you feel it most noticeably (e.g., tingling in the nostrils, rise and fall of chest). Try to focus less on thoughts of breathing and instead focus on noticing the sensations. If your mind wanders, that's fine—just gently come back to the sensation of the breath. As we've done before, see how much, how many details, you can notice about each breath.
2. Now, for the next few minutes, shift your focus from your breath and instead focus on any sounds you can notice in your immediate surroundings. What's here? Perhaps the ticking of a clock, air coming through vents, the hum of a refrigerator—whatever is nearby. Try to collect the sounds around you, noticing how they come to awareness and then pass away. Let the sounds come and go, passing through your awareness like clouds. Allow yourself to open up and lean in toward any sound that arises.
3. Once you are centered in this noticing and observing space, gently turn up the volume on your set to a moderately loud setting (a bit

louder than you would typically set it is fine). Close your eyes again and continue noticing the sounds as they come. Notice the words and tone of the pundits in the program. Focus on the sensations in your body that are prompted by the bickering, the arguing, the loud talk from these people. If you find yourself getting caught up in the content of what they are debating, that is fine—gently come back in your awareness to noticing the sensation of experience in your body. Watch as the words and their impact on your body come and go like passing clouds, or like pounding rain that runs down your window, soon to disappear. Notice any thoughts too as they arise, and gently observe them, letting them come and go without grabbing onto them. How do you get tangled up in your thoughts? Don't wrestle with them—just see that you've gotten hooked by them and continue to watch them.

4. Continue listening and noticing for at least 5 to 10 minutes. Let the sensations of sound, and the ebb and flow of reactions within your body and mind, pass through your awareness with as little ownership by you as possible.

In the space below, note any observations you have of this activity. In particular, what do you notice about your ability to move toward angst-ridden, pressured, ego-filled exchange? What was difficult? What did you learn about your own tendencies in such situations? What pattern might exist here?

____

____

____

____

____

LEAN IN

While this experience is still fresh and present for you, quickly cue up the anchors for your difficult client. If you're willing, close your eyes and allow yourself to imagine this person sitting with you. Allow yourself to hold onto the images and sensations that arise as you do so just as you've done for the activities in this chapter so far. Give your thoughts and sensations about this client the same degree of mindful attention. Try not to worry about what to do with what arrives in your experience. See if you can just let whatever comes be just as it is. Write a sentence or two to describe anything that shows up as you make contact in your imagination with this client.

____

____

____

Conjure your client's anchors once again and visualize your client as deeply as possible. Do so until you notice yourself reacting with negative emotion. Notice any accompanying thoughts and allow yourself to grab them as tightly as possible.

Once you're good and fused with the thoughts and emotions, take a moment to stand up and swing your arms in wide circles as quickly as you can. In addition, bring your index fingers to the tip of your nose as rapidly as possible, one after the other. Why is this suddenly seeming more like a book about Pilates than a primer on clinical work? Thankfully for us both, it's not, but now ask yourself: Can you successfully control away your feelings in reaction to this client? Can you make yourself not have this experience? You were just having a negative emotion about your client. Could you manage your actions even though you were feeling this? In a simple sentence, write below where your control efforts make the most sense. No matter what your emotions shout from within, what might you be willing to do in actual moments with your client?

____

____

____

____

If you continued to allow the feelings, the physical sensations, to arise without trying to mold or change them in any way, what is your mind telling you will happen? If your mind is like most (if not all), you might entertain thoughts such as how your client is stepping on you or that you're not cutting it as a clinician, and that sitting here just noticing is the same thing as giving the client permission to act out. "This work is a complete failure," you might say. The feelings arising in reaction to such thoughts would be a malicious marinade of negativity for your body and mind.

Mindful detachment and observation of these emotions does not, however, mean you are fostering an uncaring or apathetic attitude toward your work or the client (or yourself for that matter). Quite the opposite—you're actively developing an open, receptive quality in yourself. You're flexing a mindfulness muscle that will only help you craft a more therapeutic connection to your most trying clients.

In order to build this muscle, you have to show up regularly and exert the effort mindfulness requires. What you'll find is that mindfulness does take effort, and does not always equal blissful relaxation. It is allowing whatever is present to fill your awareness, and the whatever can be extremely distasteful or painful. In that regard, mindfulness is not the weak, passive approach some people might assume. It is a path requiring courage and conviction. To apply it to your clinical work requires that you make a commitment to cultivating the deepest reaches of your healing presence.

Perking Up for Positive Impact

LEAN IN

After reading through the instructions for this activity, please close the book and sit where you won't be disturbed for at least 10 minutes. Turn off any media and sit so that you're not facing anything interesting—no picturesque landscapes out your window, no lovely framed photos of loved ones, nothing but (ideally) a blank, empty wall or swath of carpet. Sit comfortably and simply do nothing for 10 minutes. You're not even allowed to daydream or fantasize. The only thing you're allowed to do is track the flow of your breathing. If your attention wanders, bring it directly back to the breath. Do this now before reading further. . . .

Hopefully you're not one of those people who skip ahead and ignore instructions. If you are indeed such a rebel, please stop reading now, and settle into a short span of do-nothingness.

How "fun" was that? It's a safe bet that at some point during the past 10 minutes you were notably, and perhaps deeply, bored. Imagine yourself in a room packed with other clinicians. All of you must now raise your hand if you have ever been extremely bored while working with a client. How many hands would go up? (All of them, of course.)

I once had a trainee who (sheepishly) admitted to falling asleep in session with a client. While this is a definite no-no, and an extreme boredom-related behavior, it is not the norm. Moments of lackadaisical engagement are indeed typical. We all get bored from time to time in our interactions with clients. What does this mean? What is boredom in the context of clinical work?

In my opinion, here's what boredom for a clinician is not—it is not an insufficiently "goal-congruent" or "clinically relevant" client presentation. It's not about the client being a dud and failing to sufficiently stimulate us. Clinician boredom is not due to a client's inability to give us a Broadway production. It says much more about us, the clinicians, than it does about our clients (though we all tend to assume that boredom is the result of a less-than-interesting environmental context).

LEAN IN

Go back to the exercise above where you got bored with your breathing. Try holding your breath right now. Do so for at least a full minute, maybe even two if you're so bold. How boring is it now?

Boredom has to do more with our difficulty giving our full, open awareness to the moment than it is about any inherent quality of our context itself. As clinicians, it's important for us to catch ourselves in moments of mindless haze, and realize that it's not our clients' faults; it's a flagging of our mindful focus. Even the breath can get exciting if we really allow it. As meditation teacher Joseph Goldstein has observed, "boredom becomes a tremendously useful feedback for us . . . that our attention at that time is half-hearted" (1993, p. 80).

Finding Your Mindful Groove

I'm suggesting that you consider adopting a habit of regular, at least weekly (but ideally daily) mindful contact like this with each client, or at least the clients toward whom you've experienced intense emotion. Are you willing to commit now to at least 15 minutes at the beginning or end of each week to mindfully review your experience of your clients? If so, consider the following sequence of focus during your mindful review of your work.

LEAN IN: MINDFULNESS ROUNDS ROUTINE

1. Five minutes of mindful focus on the breath. Again, focus your attention on the sensation of breathing, wherever you feel it most notably. For me, it's the inner rim of my nostrils. Count your out breaths if it's helpful to get started. If there's any mental meandering, come back gently to the awareness of the sensation. This gentle return, no matter how many times you do it, is by itself an extremely useful practice in developing the capacity for nonreactivity. Simply (though not always easily) notice the thoughts as they come and regard them as bubbles.
2. Five minutes of mindful noticing of sounds, sensations, and the flow of thought. It may help to do this with eyes closed in order to minimize distraction, but if you want to keep eyes open, it can convey an openness to whatever might arise. Allow yourself to realize that there is space for whatever might arise, be it sound, sensation, thoughts, or feelings. Let them rise and fall like waves, or pass by like leaves on the breeze.
3. Ten minutes (or more) of cueing up specific difficult client exchanges from recent work. It may help to have prepared brief notes in advance—perhaps phrases on note cards of what was most taxing, upsetting, frustrating, confusing (insert difficult experience here) regarding your work. Sitting in this centered experience of your body, mind, and surroundings, bring each statement to awareness by glancing at it briefly. And here's the crucial task—notice, observe, and allow whatever arises. That is your task—there's nothing to do in this moment other than hold your experience. Remember, there is space for whatever arises. No matter how displaced you become from a particular reaction about your client, allow yourself to come back to your center through gentle observation of the thoughts, feelings, and sensations.

4. Open your eyes, take a full, deep breath, and immediately take an action with regard to your clinical work with these individuals from this centered place. The point here is to experience what it's like to place a call, write a session note, or plan the next phase of the work from a place of mindfulness. What do you notice about any changes in the quality of your actions immediately following mindful presence with your experience of recent work?

   ____

   ____

What might happen if you were willing to consistently implement this new habit?

____

____

What obstacles do you anticipate will make implementing this mindfulness habit difficult? How might you address them?

____

____

____

Catching Ourselves

A couple of months ago, I was driving home from work and realized I was driving very fast, and I was much edgier than usual. Slipping into my old script, I was seething with irritation at the abundant and annoying Boston drivers around me (I still, after 12 years, can't fathom why people here think red stoplights are "stoptional"). Thankfully, I caught myself and used the opportunity to conduct a mindfulness check-in.

With attention to my breath and observation of the flow of sensation and thought, I encountered rapid-fire images of the day's work. Among many other tasks, I had conducted two family therapy sessions. In each, there was a father who regarded his son with distance and withdrawal. I knew these boys well and I was certain they felt their fathers' disengagement. The insight, born of this mindful awareness, was that I had just had a day of "distant fathers," and that it had hit an old button within me regarding my own experience of distance with my dad from many years before. I had struggled to engage these fathers in the sessions, but as I drove home and allowed the thoughts, sensations, and old mixture of resentment and longing to rise and fall, I found myself in a different place. Suffice it to say, my subsequent work with these dads (though I'm sure far from perfect) was charged with more engagement. I was less pulled away by my old resentment-based script of reactive withdrawal. Mindfulness had helped me to lean in toward these clients. Mindfulness cannot do everything in our clinical work, but it can help us with such shifts in our emotional posture. It transforms our presence and opens up possibilities that would otherwise be missed. With mindfulness, more is available to our therapeutic intention.

As you may have deduced, I indeed love metaphors. As we're working to use mindfulness to build acceptance of our emotional experience as clinicians, it can be helpful to remember metaphors such as the clipboard from our discussion of defusion in Chapter 3—that our emotions that show up in reaction to clients are simply there on the clipboard. We can benefit from observing as our negative emotional experience "writes itself" across the clipboard and then asking ourselves how useful it will be to try pushing the clipboard away. You can also envision your emotional reaction to your work as a pit of quicksand you've just stepped into. Where will your struggling against the quicksand lead?

Here's another metaphor—mindfulness in clinical work is like the time recently when I was absentmindedly slicing a tomato. Anyone who has done any serious slicing of large tomatoes knows that it's best to slice it from either the bottom to stem or vice versa. I was distracted, and began lopping off slices from the sides. If you've made this mistake you know that the tomato usually won't hold together well when you come at it from the sides—all the guts of it start sliding about and the slices fall apart. The same tomato, the same "reality," cut from top to bottom holds together.

It's the same with our experience of our work with clients. If we allow ourselves to notice and observe from top (thoughts) to bottom (emotions and physical or bodily sensations) or vice versa, then our experience holds together. We can contain it, allow it to come and go. If we approach our work from the sides—a complete focus on the content of what the client is pushing toward us—we get distracted, are overwhelmed, and lose our therapeutic stance. We become unbalanced and less effective. I'm not saying that you can never attend to the content of your clients' problems. Of course you will need to. If you get lost in the words, the twisted logic, the theoretical jargon and technique, and you neglect your own inner experience, things will go awry. What I'm saying is that, particularly when things are difficult, it is crucial to slice the moments "top-down" (brain to body) and give yourself a handful of seconds to notice, observe, and allow. From this mindful space, you will be much better able to take effective action.

LEAN IN: NEWS FLASH!

You are indeed a human being. And as a human being you are supposed to experience emotions in response to your work. You are allowed to have these reactions (despite any training you may have had to the contrary). Since you're here existing with all these emotions that show up in response to difficult clients, it's helpful to develop your own mental hooks to hang your emotional experience on—your own metaphors for mindful acceptance of what shows up for you. For this exercise, take some of the more common acceptance-related terms we've used in this chapter, such as "opening up," "leaning in," or "noticing and allowing," and spend a few moments brainstorming and creating your own metaphor that captures this stance toward your emotional experience as a therapist. Make it visual and allow it to tap into multiple senses if possible. What is your metaphor for what mindful acceptance of your difficult emotions looks like?

____

____

____

Mindfulness of Difficulty: The Advanced Course

LEAN IN

Let's assume you've tried all the mindfulness exercises described in this chapter. You've even created a daily mindfulness rounds routine. Let's assume that despite all this great effort, you're still reacting to strong negative emotions in the midst of your work—you're withdrawing from that irritating client, lecturing that client who has failed to follow through on your solid recommendations yet again—now what? Things are really heating up (or freezing over) internally and you need a procedure that has a decent chance of getting things better regulated. It's time for an emergency mindfulness practice that follows the following steps:

1. Identify the key markers or cues within yourself (cognitive/thought, emotional/physiological, contextual/environmental) signaling that being overwhelmed or zoning out are in the offing for you. Cue up the anchors for your sample client and imagine a situation that involved significant reactive emotion on your part. List the inner and outer markers predicting that your emotion was on its way.

- Cognitive/thought markers:

  ____

  ____

  ____

- Emotional/physiological markers:

  ____

  ____

  ____

- Contextual/environmental markers:

  ____

  ____

  ____

2. Wherever you are when these markers emerge, regardless of the moment swirling about you, begin a brief (perhaps only a few seconds long) interval of delving into the sensations of your breathing. You do not need to breathe in any special way—just attend to it, watch, and note how it feels as it comes in and out. Get extremely curious about how it feels for just this moment. Where do you feel it most notably (chest, abdomen, nostrils, or throat)?

3. All of us have special things we've accumulated in our lives. There are objects that have little monetary value yet we would trade a great deal to keep them—photographs, a note written on a napkin, an heirloom. Mentally peruse your life's collection of objects and select one that to you symbolizes deep meaning—that when you even think of it, you find yourself a bit more centered, more stable in what truly matters beyond the turbulence of the moment you find yourself in. For me, a core object is a small, flat black stone I picked up off the driveway at home in the moments after my toddler greeted me at the kitchen window. She was laughing and was clearly glad to see me after my long day at work. I can register and readily conjure that moment and the gravity of it with the actual or merely imagined feel of that small, smooth, "worthless" piece of rock.

As you continue mindfully breathing, center your mind firmly on this visualized object you've selected. Fix the form, feel, shape, color, and certainly the meaning of it as you breathe in. Mentally see and feel this object as you bring in each new breath during this brief break from engaging the difficult moment in front of you.

4. Last, I want you to think of just one word. What single word shouts out why you are a clinician? In Chapter 2 we surveyed the basic values that inform and direct your work as a therapist. Don't think much about it. Feel the word. Whatever it is, let it emerge in your mind and breathe it out. With each exhale, give that word out to the moment you are in, no matter how charged, tense, or tedious.

These steps can be accomplished very rapidly. In the span of a few seconds, you can connect yourself with the markers of difficulty, your breathing, and begin breathing in a centered foundation and breathing out the direction you most want to move in your work as a therapist. How much less reactive might any intervention of yours be that follows such a procedure? How much more on target with the needs of the moment?

* * *

Before leaving this exploration of creating space in the present for mindful contact with your emotions, it's important to give yourself credit for working to manage these experiences. Occasionally, despite your best efforts, you may experience flooding of emotion—you may feel yourself overwhelmed with reactivity. At these times it's crucial to seek out support from colleagues and supervisors.

Particularly if you're experiencing flooding, it will be important to develop a specific plan for managing your reactions. This plan may include self-care activities, breathing and visualization exercises such as those above (or others you create), planned breaks and time away, and possibly a plan for setting new limits and boundaries on the work with particular clients (see Chapter 10). The more specific your plan, and the more you commit to its implementation, the better you will manage your emotional reactions to clients, and the more your alliance with them will develop in the service of treatment goals.

Remember, mindfulness need not be viewed "narrowly" as a spiritual commitment. It is a tool for expanding your awareness of what is—emotional and mental moments with each of your clients. Regardless of your theoretical leanings, and no matter the pressures of your busy schedule, there is always time for consideration of the moments of your work. Your brain and your work can only expand with the effort of such increased awareness.

MAP CHECK

Take a moment and review what we've covered in this chapter. What was one aspect, one piece of content, that resonated with you—sparked your interest, curiosity, or even angst in some way?

____

Why did this matter to you? What makes this worth writing about? Worth your focus and effort? What is the gravity that this carries for you and your work?

____

What is one specific action you can take within the next 24 hours related to this issue that feels as though it would be important and has the potential to move you in the direction of what matters?

____

≺ CHAPTER FIVE ≻

Crossroads

The Juncture of Past and Present in Your Clinical Work

ONE OF MY absolute favorite film characters is Al Pacino's Michael Corleone in the *Godfather* trilogy. In the 1990 final installment of the series, the aging mobster godfather, played by Pacino, is hoping to step down once and for all as the head of the crime family initiated by his father. But, after the threat posed by a rival mob faction, Pacino famously, and with existential anguish, declares, "Just when I thought I was out, they pull me back in!" Michael Corleone had been his father's hope for a legitimate path for the family—free of the stain of violence and malice. And yet, as the trilogy brilliantly displays, family patterns (and the scripts we overlearn from a young age) die hard.

We do not need Hollywood to teach us about the fundamental role of our scripting—our collective conscious and subconscious patterns of expectation and emotion—in shaping our social responses (or more impulsive reactions) to others. A lavish cruise, or an exotic beach, can be equally hell or heaven depending on what the script dictates.

A study by John Ruiz et al. (2006) of Washington State University brings this ancient wisdom into the modern world of psychological science. Ruiz and colleagues analyzed the health outcomes of 111 artery bypass patients to see if psychological characteristics could predict how well these individuals did postsurgically. This sort of study is not new in the literature. It is well established that the more psychologically stable (less anxious, less depressed) patients are, the better they fare after the ordeal of surgery. Ruiz didn't stop there, however. He looked to see if the psychological characteristics of the patients' spouses also predicted how well the healing went. The more neurotic the spouses, the more the patients reported postsurgical depressive symptoms, lower marital satisfaction, and greater caregiving burden and strain—unless (and here's where it gets interesting) the patients were satisfied in their marriages. Those patients who were more dissatisfied in their marriages experienced their spouse's neuroticism as more damaging. What this may suggest is the protective role played by a spouse's acceptance of the partner's neurotic tendencies. The mindset of the patient may serve as a buffer against the emotional contagion from the spouse's negativity. This study points to the crucial importance of perception, of the interpretative filter we use in our interactions with others from whom we seek care and support.

Shoulding All Over Your Clients

In the space below, take a moment and list some of the thoughts or beliefs about your clients that seem most important to explore. In particular, list thoughts that include a sense of certainty in some way (e.g., "must," "should," "always"). Write down the firm beliefs about your clients that would pass the "nod test"—if you heard a colleague come to the same conclusion about your client, you would nod in agreement without a moment's hesitation.

____

____

____

____

____

____

Ask yourself: Where do these firm beliefs—especially the "shoulds," "musts," and "cannots"—come from? Remember, all human interaction is mutually and reciprocally causal. Elements of you are shaping these perceptions of the client. (Remember the eye contact exercise from the Introduction?) Your own lens for emotion and expectations for how people should manage the meeting of their own (and others') needs are directly filtering what your clients present to you. The meaning you make of your client's emotional and social behavior is a direct result of what psychologist John Gottman (1999) refers to as "meta-emotional philosophy." This philosophy shapes how you think, feel, and respond to others' emotions and behavior. It is your script, your pattern, for how to channel and express the emotions spawned during your interactions.

All the World's a Stage

We each have scripts telling us about what emotions mean and what we're supposed to do with them. The raw ingredients, let's call it the ink of this scripting, is laid down genetically in terms of biological predispositions toward certain ranges of emotionality (e.g., I might be more tolerant of risky situations than you, but you might be more comfortable with being separated from loved ones) (Kagan & Snidman, 2004). But it's not all genetic—our brains have laid down a lot of neuronal cable over the years in response to things we've learned during interactions with others. Specifically, our early interactions with caregivers and attachment figures provide relative degrees of match or mismatch with our genetic emotional and temperamental predispositions and our core emotional development needs for security, love (or connection), and comfort or valuation (Brazelton & Greenspan, 2000; Daniels & Price, 2009).

For all of us, during our early lives, our brains developed tendencies (based on interactions with significant others) that dug biological grooves into one of three systems of emotion—fear/anxiety, sadness/separation, and anger/rage (Siegel, 2010). Our brains have registered various emotional scripts telling us which way we should go (i.e., which of these emotional systems will dominate) when challenging experiences crop up. Our behavioral reactions in response to situations that trigger these emotional systems are therefore a complex interplay of biology, environmental context, and repetition across time. If you think for a moment (and we'll think much more intensively along these lines shortly), you have probably noticed certain tendencies involving fear, sadness, and anger within you, perhaps across multiple members of your family, and perhaps even across generations. When tempers are flaring, or pained looks are projected in your direction, where does your emotional mind fly? What is your default across situations and people, and across time? As dutiful clinicians looking to broaden our therapeutic reach, it is to these patterns that we now turn.

We are all lovers of patterns. We spend much of our daily lives acting and reenacting well-rehearsed patterns of action and reaction, from showering sequences (do you wash your hair first, and if so I bet you always do so, right?) to social dances with others. We tend to move through our lives in a series of repeating patterns, which are largely learned. You do not have specific genes telling you to wash your hair before picking up the bar of soap, and you don't have genes telling you to assert your absolute correctness when clients are dismissing your logic in session. Remember, genes give you the emotional ink, but the script itself is written through experience.

Multiple lines of research have begun to link the patterns of managing and expressing emotion we learn from caregivers growing up with outcomes later, sometimes much later, in adulthood. For example, John Gottman's research has associated parents who exhibit an ideal "emotion coaching" philosophy with their children (a combination of structure/guidance and support for expressing emotion) with positive parenting (and less harsh) behaviors, as well as increased self-soothing in children (Gottman, 1999; Gottman, Katz, & Hooven, 1996). Research on styles of attachment (e.g., secure, avoidant, ambivalent, or disorganized) has suggested that people learn emotion regulation strategies through interactions with caregivers in childhood, which impact their management of emotional interactions later in life (Mikulincer, Shaver, & Pereg, 2003). Longitudinal research (Simpson, Collins, Tran, & Haydon, 2007) has indicated that more secure attachment in infancy predicted successful friendships later in childhood, and that, for this same sample, social competence in childhood predicted secure, connected romantic relationships in adulthood. Social scientists such as Ann Duffy and Julianne Momirov (2000) have labeled "intergenerational transmission" as a process by which children who grow up in violent families develop emotional and behavioral patterns that lead to repetition of roles in adulthood.

Patterns of managing emotion in the context of relationships with others come from repeated observation and enactment with others over time. Actors can't perform without a script to guide them. We can't perform in our interactions (particularly difficult ones) without scripts of our own.

It's not an insight into authorship of these scripts that we're after. It doesn't matter as much whether Mommy or Daddy did or didn't do such-and-such and what that might say about your tendencies toward lollipops or messy desktops. It's a sense of the here-and-now impact of the learning; of what our minds are doing to mold the emotions we experience right here in session with clients. In the theatre of our minds, we can improvise if we so choose. Though our emotional philosophies or scripts were etched into our brains many years ago, they are by no means permanent. Modern neuroscience (as we discussed in Chapter 1) has repeatedly documented the plasticity of the (even adult) human brain. We can write a new script for how we want to manage the reactions cropping up when our clients do whatever it is they're doing. We can become increasingly mindful of our patterns of emotional reaction and learn to respond in a more flexible fashion.

While intensive psychotherapy and/or ongoing supervision can be necessary tools for developing greater understanding of one's own emotional scripting, in this book let's take a glimpse at what some of your own patterns might be. This will only be a sampling, and it will be important to take your time and put serious effort into understanding your patterns of emotional enactment with others in order to maximize your ability to manage difficult clients (as well as your clinical work generally). While some of this exploration may not necessarily be fun, I would argue that it's at least more enjoyable than your last trip to the dentist (although my dentist happens to be an amateur comedian, making it a great experience—hard as it is to laugh with someone else's fingers in your mouth). But I digress.

Learning Your Lines

In this section, we'll do some exploration of your current understanding of some of your past experiences of emotion in order to distill a sense of some of the scripts that guide your reactions to clients. Similar to our perusal of mindfulness strategies in Chapter 3, we are now approaching each of the exploratory questions below with focused attention. Though you don't need to be formally meditating, striking a full lotus pose while pondering each question, it will be helpful to clear your schedule of other demands, and your mind of any significant distractions.

LEAN IN

Spend a few minutes now before you begin, using the following prompts to create a more open, receptive space for yourself.

1. For a few minutes, simply sit with your eyes closed, noticing the play of sound around you—air in the vent, your computer's hum, birds outside perhaps. Gently nudge yourself to expand your awareness of more and more sounds around you.
2. For another minute or two, focus your awareness on sensations in your body. Scan your body from head to toe, not trying to think about your body but instead noticing what shows up in terms of actual physical sensation. Notice each sensation (the press of your back into the chair, your feet on the floor, the itch on your scalp) until you have fully scanned your body.
3. And last, notice the flow of thoughts through your awareness. Just notice your thoughts as they come, one at a time. Imagine them as flakes in a snow globe, settling slowly to the bottom until the water (your mind) is relatively clear. No matter what thoughts arise, see if you can let them be there in the open space of your mind. Assume a stance that welcomes whatever emerges. You are a spectator to a passing scene. Your mind is an open sky and the thoughts are merely the clouds, the weather, moving through. Just as you can't clutch a cloud, there's no need to grab at the thoughts.

After you have attained this more settled awareness, turn to the questions below by following these steps:

1. Fix your attention on each question after getting yourself centered and in a mindful state of focused awareness.
2. Sit and observe what emerges in your experience in response to the question. Try not to analyze, judge, or pursue the storyline of any thought or image that arises. Again, the goal is not an insight into what happened in the past. Instead you're looking to make experiential contact with what emerges *now* in response to questions that may reflect ongoing patterning regarding emotional or interpersonal demands. Simply (though not easily) allow sensations, thoughts, and

images to come into awareness. Note them and then watch (with earnest curiosity) what emerges in the next moment.

3. Pause to write your immediate reactions and reflections.
4. Repeat the steps for centering with each question. If you find that you are stirred up while working through the remainder of this chapter, try noticing or watching this stirred-up aspect—the rush of thoughts, the memories of episodes in the past, the surge of old feelings, or whatever else. Remember to take time with these questions, and approach them with an atmosphere of kindness toward yourself. You are not wrong or insufficient because of any experiences in the past that have scripted you. We all have these twists and turns that bring us to where we are today. Again, it is what you will choose to do with these scripts in the here and now that is of utmost importance.

One last question to consider before centering yourself with the steps above and embarking on your exploration of the questions below: *Who* is doing the noticing as thoughts, images, and sensations arise in awareness? Okay, I lied. Here's the last question: If you are the one noticing these experiences, can you *be* them? Are "you" one and the same with these experiences if "you" are watching them come and go?

If your mind is not completely blown and twisted from this cognitive contortion, then *mindfully* proceed with the questions that follow in order to refine your understanding of your emotional scripting.

An Oscar-Caliber Performance of . . . You

1. How would you describe the overall emotional volume level in your home when you were young? What number on a scale from 1 to 10 would you give it, and what words or images come to mind?

____

____

____

____

2. If others were upset with you when you were young, what would you tend to do? What was it like to be with others when they were upset with you? How would it feel after the interaction? Describe anything coming to mind.

3. If you were upset with others while you were growing up, what would you typically do with your upset? How was your experience of vulnerability responded to by others when you were young? What did you learn to do with that experience?

4. Who was the person you felt closest to growing up? What five adjectives come to mind to describe him or her? What arises for you as you list these characteristics for this person?

5. Who among your family did you feel most distant from while growing up? What adjectives come to mind to describe this person?

____

____

____

____

____

6. List the most challenging emotion (or emotions) for you to experience and openly express when you were growing up. What did you learn about this emotion that made you less than completely comfortable with it? What was the unwritten rule about it? To be ______ (strong negative emotion) means that ______. How would you fill in the blanks?

____

____

____

____

____

____

7. What lessons do you think you learned from each of these individuals about managing strong, negative emotions that have affected how you experience and express emotions now? Also, where do you think they learned this?

____

____

____

____

____

____

Now comes the more challenging part. Here is where we wonder how these emotional lessons from your early years might be echoing into the present.

Look back over your responses to these questions. What patterns, what scripts, do you notice? What emerged in your thoughts, feelings, and perceptions with your mindful reflection of each question? What showed up *now* about your life *then*? In particular, look for patterns that appear to have repeated with people in your personal and professional life. To use Gottman's terminology, what aspects of turning toward, away from, or against others during negative or upsetting exchanges do you notice in your patterns of reaction? Look for at least one or two thematic scripts that you seem to enact with some consistency in certain emotional situations. Be able to complete the following: "When faced with strong _____ [emotion], my tendency is to _______ [pattern of thought, feeling and action]."

Pattern 1: ____
____
____

Pattern 2: ____
____
____

It can often be difficult to readily cue up a core emotional script for yourself. Here, it can be helpful to conduct what cognitive therapists (Leahy, 2003) refer to as a "vertical descent"—answering a series of questions that deepen the understanding of what might be at the center of certain emotional or social interactions for you.

LEAN IN

Take one of the more challenging emotions you listed above. What specific situation happened for you recently where this challenge in experiencing and/or expressing this emotion presented itself? Summarize this situation below.

____
____
____
____

Holding it vividly in mind, imagine you are in this situation again. What might you have thought would happen? What were you concerned might occur?

____

____

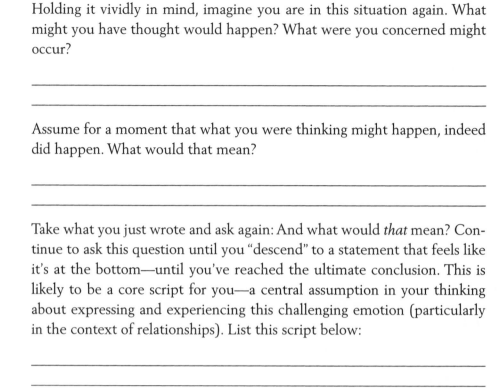

Assume for a moment that what you were thinking might happen, indeed did happen. What would that mean?

____

____

Take what you just wrote and ask again: And what would *that* mean? Continue to ask this question until you "descend" to a statement that feels like it's at the bottom—until you've reached the ultimate conclusion. This is likely to be a core script for you—a central assumption in your thinking about expressing and experiencing this challenging emotion (particularly in the context of relationships). List this script below:

____

____

If you wish, use vertical descent to flesh out your scripting for other challenging emotions or social exchange situations in order to develop an inventory of scripts or patterns for yourself. The more effort and attention you put into this process, the more aware you will be of the influence of patterning in the moment during your interactions with clients. You will have more room for choice and change as a result.

In order to better understand whether your emotional behavior in social situations is likely being influenced by old scripts from your relational past, it may be helpful to conduct another simple thought experiment. At present, only in the outer orbits of science fiction do we have MRI-style scanners that can pinpoint (and erase) our very thoughts. For now, we'll have to be content with scans that we can produce through conversation, meditation, or mere reflection. Consider the following.

Take any emotional pattern you suspect may be relevant for you and boil it down to a single phrase or sentence (e.g., "When I think others are disappointed or frustrated with me, I go to extreme lengths to convince them not to be upset with me" or "When I get angry at someone close to me, I tend to stifle my anger and get very distant").

If you were to let close, trusted friends or loved ones in on the secret of your scripting, how would they respond? What would they say if they read your distilled sentence about yourself? Would they think it a helpful or unhelpful approach? Effective or ineffective? Would they say "Sure! That's how you should handle things"? Or would they scrunch their faces into something other than agreement? Imagine their responses and describe them below:

____

____

____

If in this quick thought experiment you found yourself realizing that those who know you best would tend to view this script (if stated clearly and directly) as less than ideal—not the best route to take—then you can be more confident that this is indeed an unhelpful script you are enacting. Can you imagine yourself actually asking people close to you for this sort of input about your reactive patterns? If you have any hesitance, what do you make of that? What does it suggest?

These maladaptive patterns are highly resistant to the light of reason. Instead, they are muddy and logic can't penetrate, but logic has little to do with what we do in emotional moments. Our limbic, emotional brain relies heavily on easily accessed memory circuits to guide our reaction—the scripts floating about like silt in stirred-up riverbeds. It takes more than the bright logic of one thought experiment to clear things up and produce a more adaptive, nonreactive (and therapeutic) response—it takes concerted effort to hone new skills of emotional observation.

Now, look back over the list of thoughts you generated about your work with clients at the outset of this chapter—all of the shouldas, wouldas, and all the mustiness your mind produces when clients are doing whatever they do that breaks the back of their daily lives and brings them into your office. In the space below, wonder a bit about how these thoughts may be influenced by what you've gleaned about the social scripting you've carried all these years. How might your own patterns be influencing your more certain or extreme thoughts about them?

____
____
____
____
____
____

Take a moment to review the Interpersonal Process Grid (Figure 5.1). As you consider the potential emotional themes or scripts that you bring into your therapeutic work, where on the grid do you see these tendencies depicted? For example, if a client presents with hostile behavior in Quadrant C, what has your exploration of emotional history in this chapter re-

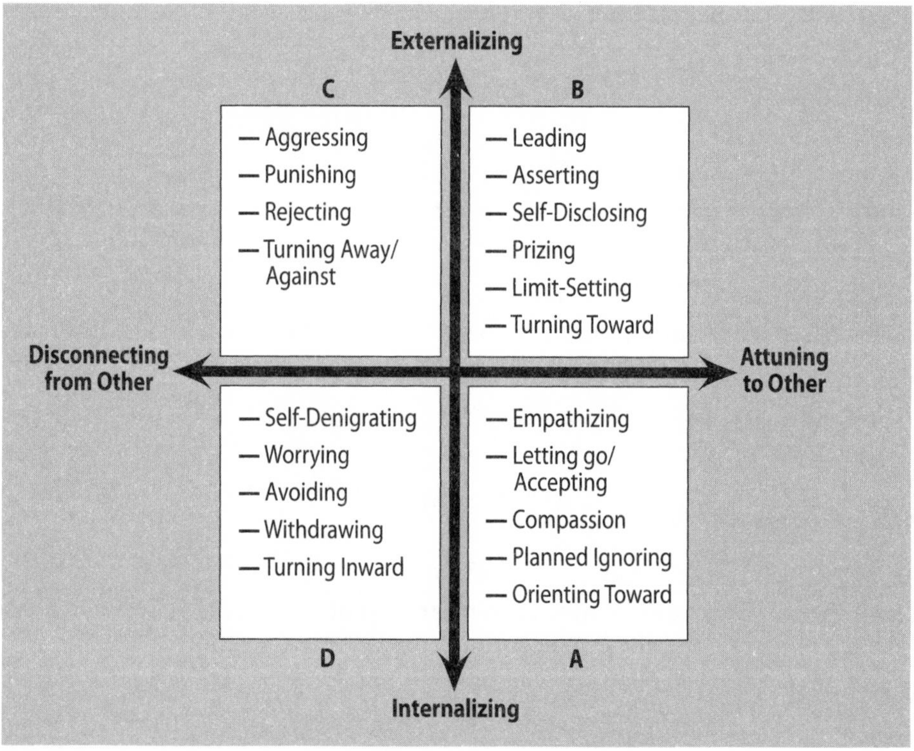

Figure 5.1 Interpersonal Process Grid

vealed as to what your reactive pattern is likely to be? What reactive patterns are possible for you when you are fused with the *must, always*, and *never* that show up in your thinking about specific (perhaps challenging) clients in your caseload? Which patterns do you find acceptable? Which are you willing to work on altering?

As the clinical director of a therapeutic day school for children with emotional and behavioral issues, a sizeable portion of my job has been to witness kids in the midst of tantrums and high states of agitation. I've watched kids swear, kick, spit, punch, and break things, and I've watched those trying to care for them struggling with the emotional impact of proximity to all this intensity. And here I am—a guy who grew up under a mix of Gottman's (1999) emotion-coaching and laissez-faire meta-emotional philosophies. It depended on the situation, but there was definitely a theme, a pattern, of anger and conflict being taboo, things to be avoided at all cost. Particularly when I sensed others were angry or frustrated with me, I tended to find significant anxious reactions cropping up—thoughts of having to do something, anything, to prove that such displeasure with me was unwarranted. Others' anger, instead of being a notice, a nudge toward action, was—based on the years of experience within my family—a noose of passivity, a declaration of defeat. I learned to have keen radar for conflict and how to sidestep it because my mind had me convinced I would not fare well on the other side of others' anger.

You can imagine the challenge I experienced when first beginning my job at the school where anger and conflict—the emotional buffeting of volatile child agendas against those of staff members and peers—was a regular, unwelcome guest in my routine. My philosophy was woefully unworkable. My thoughts about my work (my emotional patterning) screamed for avoidance, and I had a choice. I could either cut and run, or learn to hang in and see what might happen. Enough about me—let's (thankfully) get back to you.

The View From the Balcony

As you have probably realized, either personally or in your clinical work, perspective on one's negative emotional experience is very difficult to maintain. You may come to a strikingly high vantage point—an Everest summit of sorts—on your anger, sadness, or malaise, and you may indeed see the hot, red thread of scripting weaving all the way back into an early emotional philosophy, a style of attachment with your caregivers. And yet you will almost certainly lose that thread and find yourself left-side reacting to a particular person as if you had never stood on the top of the world. Why is this? What happened to your hard-won perspective?

I train others in the pitfalls of perspective in daily life on a regular basis and yet I still yell at people in traffic (although, to my wife's relief, much less often these days). If I were able to maintain comprehensive and unfailing perspective on others' actions, I would never allow myself to spout off while white-knuckling my steering wheel and pounding my car's horn as if it were the firing button on a missile launcher. I follow my mind down the rabbit hole of distortion—this jerk cut me off "on purpose." I forget my preaching about social cognitive errors such as correspondence bias (see Chapter 3) and how it leads us to neglect the influence of situational context on people's actions. I am better about catching myself, but, as I'm saying, it's a muscle—a habit that requires constant tending. If you don't use perspective (and act from it), you indeed lose it (emotionally). Perspective on our scripting, particularly that which is limiting our work as clinicians, is a muscle we are capable of building.

Dress Rehearsal: The Curtain Is Calling

Take a moment and review the list of clinician comments below. These are common thought patterns that may cloud one's perspective on work with clients. Mark in the spaces whether you have had, if not tightly fused, any of these in the past, as well as any you are currently experiencing with a client.

Past? Present?
"This client is unmotivated for change."__________
"This client won't accept help/won't help herself."__________
"This client is broken."__________
"I have to save him or her."__________

"This is too much for me to handle."__________
"This client is trying to take advantage of me."__________
"This client is so Axis II."__________
"I'm wasting my time with this client."__________
"This person is a manipulator."__________
Other? ____

For any of the thoughts you endorsed, look back to your exploration of emotional scripting. Circle or underline the thought patterns that may have been influenced by this scripting. You need not have definitive proof of the influence of scripting (and you never really will). A hunch is the best you can do at this point.

Take any of the thoughts above and rate them with the following scale. How intense is any negative emotion you experience after gripping this thought in your awareness?

1	2	3	4	5
Not at all		Moderate		Very Intense

Now, ask yourself: How much has this reaction cost me when I struggle against it? How does it get in the way of what I want to be about as a clinician?

How workable are these reactions? How much do they take you in the direction you really want to be going in your work? How much do they give you the satisfaction you desire in your role as a helper?

1	2	3	4	5
Not Workable		Somewhat Workable		Very Workable

Now take this thought and feeling (or any other about your client you experience with significant intensity) and ask yourself this final question: How willing am I to simply notice this thought, and the feelings accompanying it, without attempting to change, alter, or make them be otherwise? You are not rating how much you agree or disagree with the thoughts. Instead, you're considering how much you can allow them to be what they are—the chatter of your mind and the fluctuations of your physiology—without any reactive attempt to change them. What is your degree of willingness to notice them?

1	2	3	4	5
Not Willing		Somewhat Willing		Very Willing

You are reading and writing your way through this book because you sit across from angry clients, intrusive individuals, people who rant, some who poke at you, others who avoid any emotional strain in the direction of growth, people who grate and ingratiate. You're hoping to create stronger alliances and feel effective in treating such clients. And now, you've considered the nature and intensity of the thoughts and feelings you experience in response to these people. We've walked across an Interpersonal Process Grid in order to see how we inadvertently play tug-of-war with people when they prod us in a provocative left-sided fashion. You've wondered about how you've learned meta-emotional patterning in the past that ripples out into your work with clients in the present. You may have noticed a tendency toward gripping certain thoughts and feelings about these difficult people that—after you've stepped back far enough to really see—are unworkable.

As understandable as your experiences certainly are (remember, this is difficult work, you're doing the best you can, and these clients are quite adept at button pushing), you're realizing that your thoughts and emotions are blocking things to some degree. Perhaps you've become aware of certain patterns that keep replaying with specific clients. Whatever the thoughts, and however intense the corresponding emotions, you may be noticing this rock-bottom sense of things not being as you would like them to be. You may be wondering whether there is a new path for your work with such clients. Well, my fellow emotional Magellan, it will be a process for you to rewrite your scripts and begin walking with these individuals in a way that moves them, and you, forward.

The process will involve three primary steps or phases: assessment of the scripts from the past, collecting data and tracking patterns in the present, and then practice in interrupting patterns, evaluating progress, and writing new scripts for the future. This chapter has been a mere introduction to the first step of assessment of your unique emotional patterns as they may manifest in your clinical work. After writing your way through this chapter, I encourage you to keep a journal open for ongoing documentation of how emotional patterns emerge with reactive thought, emotion, and behavior in your challenging interactions with clients (and perhaps in your personal life as well). Using the mindfulness strategies in conjunction with reflective writing will integrate your exploration and provide the most comprehensive understanding possible of the unique contours of emotional and interpersonal scripting that your early life wrought in your brain.

After you've spent a period of time (months perhaps) tracking and monitoring yourself, you will have a fairly comprehensive account of the primary scripts that enhance and inhibit you in the harder moments of exchange with clients. You are now ready for the second phase of interrupting the old, unworkable patterns, and will here find the strategies of mindful management of thought and emotion from Chapters 3 and 4 helpful in creating defused perspective and an increased stance of acceptance toward whatever arises. Then, in the third phase, I recommend a return to Chapter 2's exploration of the core values giving direction to your role as a clinician. Use these compass headings to get your bearings and guide you in writing the new scripts for managing what's hard—the gentle ripples (or giant tsunamis) of attraction and aversion, rage and resignation that buffet you from inside as you sit facing these people you intend to help. You will need a deep connection to what matters to you at the center of your professional life in order to write new ways of relating. You will need to want this change in a massive way in order to turn around the momentum of the years of rehearsal we've all put into the patterns we enact.

When I was 13, my family moved from Ohio to Florida. After the initial belief that life in Florida would be a perpetual vacation faded, I was left with the residual reality that I was lonely and needed to make friends. In class one day, I overheard some kids talking about a get-together they were planning at a local roller skating rink for that coming Saturday. I went home that afternoon and announced to my parents that I needed new skates. "I've been invited to come," I said. My parents, eager to help me ease the angst of our relocation, were more than willing to take me shopping and buy me a flashy new pair.

That Saturday, I sat with my dad in the parking lot of the skating rink. I looked at the front door of the building and gripped my new skates. "Okay," said my dad. "I'll be back in a few hours to pick you up. Have fun."

I sat in silence. "Something wrong?" he asked.

"Take me home," I said.

It took a few more minutes of me repeating myself (and adding more angst and intensity with each repetition) before my poor, confused father drove me home.

There had been no invitation from peers to join them at the rink that Saturday. There had only been my understandable wish to connect with other kids, and there had only been my long-standing pattern of social anxiety and avoidant escape tactics. What I wanted was more than reasonable. My brain groove for anxiety in such situations was quite strong, and remained so well into adulthood.

Flash forward until only a handful of weeks ago. I'll spare you the details of my experiences within my own psychotherapy, as well as numerous formative encounters with supervisors, colleagues, and clients. There I was just a short time ago sitting again in a car facing the front door of a building where a professional social mixer of sorts was to transpire. This time, I had been invited but, like the skating rink many years prior, I did not know a soul inside. Also, like my teenage days, I very much wanted to connect, to be included. As I sat gripping my umbrella, I felt the familiar pulse of fear, the urge to cut and run and feed my escapist script.

But thankfully, there was no parent in the driver's seat to take me home. I was alone with my thoughts, and had (through considerable effort and support from others) learned a thing or two about abiding my anxious thoughts and bodily sensations. I mindfully surfed what showed up in me and sidestepped what the decades have dictated. Believe me, I haven't been able to do so in every such situation, but on this occasion, I acted from a new script. And I indeed connected and broadened my professional prospects as a result.

It is my experience; it is likely our shared experience as clinicians from our work with many clients; and it is likely our shared hope that the effort we put into understanding, interrupting, and reshaping these patterns will ripple out for the betterment of many. And now that we've worked on these patterns within ourselves and begun harnessing skills for managing our own inner experience, we can now turn once again toward our clients—we can explore how to orient toward them in profound ways in order to deepen the alliance and the scope of the therapeutic work itself. We are now ready for the role mindfulness and perspective can play in a full consideration of the pained human being facing us.

MAP CHECK

Take a moment and review what we've covered in this chapter. What was one aspect, one piece of content, that resonated with you—sparked your interest, curiosity, or even angst in some way?

Why did this matter to you? What makes this worth writing about? Worth your focus and effort? What is the gravity that this carries for you and your work?

What is one specific action you can take within the next 24 hours related to this issue that feels as though it would be important and has the potential to move you in the direction of what matters?

≺ CHAPTER SIX ≻

Really Knowing Your Travel Companion

Skills for Orienting to Difficult Clients

REMEMBER THE freight train metaphor? Until this point, we've been focusing on the past (the freight cars—your and your clients' histories and emotional patterning) and the present (the engine car—the here and now of difficult exchanges with clients). You've developed a greater understanding of the past and present factors (in the brain and social context) pulling you toward tug-of-war interactions with clients. You have greater clarity as to how your emotional patterns from the past may be influencing your work, and you are applying defusion and perspective-taking strategies to manage the less-than-helpful thoughts emerging during your work. You're delving more deeply into the moments of your work with the practice of mindfulness strategies. Emotions are less likely to knock you off balance because of consistent practice of mindfulness strategies that call for noticing, observing, and allowing your experience.

But so what? When are you actually going to *do* something about your difficult client? These people call at three in the morning because they have no boundaries. They yell at us. They refuse to do the obvious things to make their lives better. They blame everyone but themselves. They get worse. All this work on us—our thoughts and feelings—is great, but when will this book get on with it and give the strategies for really managing these immoveable clients?

Yes, you'd be within your rights to ask such questions. And yes, we will delve deeply into what you can do to be a "relational leader" (Chapters 9 and 10), how to intervene with good timing (Chapter 8) and with authenticity (Chapter 10), and also how to respond to the most challenging and precarious client behaviors (Chapter 11), but we're not there yet. Don't do it! Don't skip ahead. Apply some defusion and mindfulness to yourself if you need to, but don't jump toward taking action until you've fully learned how to do so from the right place—from a deep reservoir of compassion within yourself. You can't lead until you know where you're going (the tracks in our train metaphor). You can't lead until you care enough about those you're helping (and yourself) to truly hang in with them when the road seems impassable.

Take Your Compassion Temperature

One of the most difficult clients I've ever had was the mother of one of the children I saw for therapy. I'll call her Melinda. Her daughter was difficult enough with her acting-out behavior, instigation of other kids, and her emotionally slippery quality in sessions, making her hard to connect with. All of that I could deal with. It was her mother that sent me over the edge. It got to the point that when I came into my office in the morning and saw the red light on my phone indicating a voice mail awaited me, I knew it was her, and my gut tightened with anxiety and anger.

For much of my time working with this mother and her daughter, it's safe to say that my compassion reservoir had drained dry. The mother questioned my expertise on occasion. "Well, maybe I should hire a consultant to come teach you and your staff to work with my daughter," she said during one interaction. She insisted, second-guessed, and inserted herself into every aspect of her daughter's school life. And heaven forbid that her child have a serious acting-out episode within the program. "What did your staff do to prevent this?" she would ask. "They aren't doing enough" or "They're doing it wrong" was always the implied message. And the message to me seemed clear: "You're incompetent." Or at least that's how I (and my patterning) saw it.

No sooner would the door to my supervisor's office close behind me than I would launch into my latest rant about this mother. "She's impossible! I'm done with this," I'd say. I used a metaphor (yes, I know you're surprised) with my supervisor to capture my intensity of upset with this particular mom. No other client required such measurement—she was special. I'll call it my Melinda Meter. I would show my supervisor my off-the-charts angst reading with a dramatic lateral swing of my arm as if it were the needle on a gauge gone wild. Compassion? I had none for this client.

Before launching into our exploration to increase your skills for orienting toward the most difficult clients, let me tell you how things ended up with my situation. She and I wrangled, disagreed, and ultimately agreed to continue disagreeing. She pulled her daughter out of our program. I contented myself with my Melinda Meter descriptions of her to my supervisor. It was her fault, after all, that her daughter would fail at her next placement. But her daughter ended up doing quite well, from all that I later gleaned. With the distance of some time, I began realizing that, as inappropriate as some of her ways of communicating were, this mom was correct about much of what we argued about. And only now, looking back years later, can I find the space to remember that this mother who poked at me had survived a serious heart attack, was a staunch advocate for her special-needs child, and gave up much in her personal life in order for her daughter to have what she needed. I learned to put my Melinda Meter in my desk drawer and leave it there.

LEAN IN

Close your eyes for a moment and let your mind flash to the most distasteful, despicable, angering, ruthless (insert your extreme negative adjective here) person (alive or dead, client or not) that you can imagine. Write the initials below:

____

As you look at these initials, think about the person and everything you're aware of that the person has done to impact others, and ask yourself how much you feel genuine concern—compassion—for this person. If he or she were sick and suffering, how much would you feel moved to care? Go ahead, be honest. . . .

1	2	3	4	5
Not at all		Moderate		Very Much So

Are you surprised by your rating? Does this make sense based on this person's actions? Isn't this what he or she deserves? But now ask yourself, what is the impact of your low sense of compassion on this "empathy-hard" individual?

Consider this difficult person again, but now think of him or her as an infant, swaddled in blankets and in your arms. Or maybe the child is 5 years old and walks up to you on the street, bloodied at the hands of an afterschool bully. Or perhaps the person is lying on the bed at home as a 10-year-old, covering his or her ears as violence erupts again between parents with only a too-thin wall to lightly muffle their screaming. If you were bearing witness to such circumstances for this person, what would your compassion rating be then?

1	2	3	4	5
Not at all		Moderate		Very Much So

Of course we have strong reactions to people who do despicable things, and of course they should be prevented from harming others, and of course they should be accountable for their actions. But we're not working here to address others; we're still working on your orienting skills, your inner stance. The key question here is this: When others are extremely difficult, can we hold them with compassion anyway because of the potential that compassion (versus antipathy or apathy) has to shift interactions in a more useful direction? How much do things improve when we meet hate with hate? What might happen if hate is mingled with compassion?

Why Compassion?

In one of his books, the Dalai Lama (1999) wrote about the Buddha's definition of compassion. He said that true compassion is what a mother feels for her sick or suffering child. While this definition makes sense in the abstract, it was only after my wife and I had our daughter that I fully experienced this definition of compassion. I felt it while watching my wife's tears at the mere telling of the story of a medical procedure our daughter had undergone. Everything was fine with our daughter, but the mere description of my daughter's pain was enough to spark it in actuality for my wife. This was compassion, without a doubt. My question for you is whether it makes sense to define compassion for your most difficult clients in the same terms. Is it even possible? But, your mind screams, they don't deserve it the way one's suffering child does. It's just different. Thanks, mind, for sharing. . . . (Remember defusion?)

The Dalai Lama has also suggested that "compassion can be roughly defined in terms of a state of mind that is nonviolent, non-harming, and nonaggressive—it is a mental attitude based on the wish for others to be free of their suffering" (Dalai Lama & Cutler, 1998, p. 114). Notice that nowhere in this definition of compassion does it require that you condone or endorse the difficult or downright destructive behavior of others. It does require that you hold an attitude of intending that this person no longer suffer. If the person is no longer suffering (e.g., from hate), then what might flow from his or her actions instead? Such a mental attitude is crucial for all helpers. One could even argue that it might be our responsibility as clinicians to develop our compassion, even for those least deserving.

In preparation for doing some work together to build up your compassion muscle, it's important to take a step back for a moment and begin with a proper perspective. As we've discussed, you as a clinician are tethered emotionally (and therefore biologically) to your clients during every interaction. Contemporary psychodynamic writers such as Paul Wachtel (2008), Jeremy Safran, and Christopher Muran refer to this tethering as intersubjectivity, wherein the therapy relationship is "an ongoing interplay of separate subjectivities . . . particularly salient during the negotiation of alliance ruptures" (Safran & Muran, 2000, p. 52). The idea here is that therapist and client coexist in a cycle of interaction where each person influences and shapes the other's perceptions and behavior and that this cycle results from the "mutual, bidirectional interplay" of subjective experiences and actions on the part of both parties (Wachtel, 2008, p. 157). This mix of therapist and client subjective experiences is most notable at times of difficulty in their relationship—a time when compassion is most needed.

Compassion can be thought of as a sense of openness, a willingness to be penetrated by others' suffering. Whether you intend to be affected by your clients' suffering or not, you indeed are. If we cultivate compassion, healing is more likely to result from the interaction.

Poet, monk, activist, and Zen master Thich Nhat Hanh (2001) has said that "without a cloud, there will be no rain; without rain, the trees cannot grow; and without trees, we cannot make paper. . . . So we can say that the cloud and the paper *inter-are*" (p. 55, italics in original). There's an ecological point of view to our work as clinicians—every breath taken in session is shared air, and the brain-to-brain dance leads to inevitable mutual influence. We, as Thich Nhat Hanh suggests, "inter-are" with our clients. And when our exchanges with them are most challenging, when they toss emotional and behavioral garbage in our direction, we need the openness of a compassionate perspective. If all interactions involve inter-being, then we should realize that this trashiness will, if handled properly, become something useful. "Roses and garbage inter-are. Without a rose, we cannot have garbage; and without garbage, we cannot have a rose. They need each other very much" (Hanh, 2001, p. 57). Ask any organic gardener, or any truly masterful clinician for that matter, and you'll likely hear something along these lines.

In order to take the most therapeutic action for your most difficult clients, you need to do so from the right side of the Interpersonal Process Grid (Figure 2.1). Specifically, you can't typically take good upper-right action to help your client until you've, if only briefly, oriented yourself fully and compassionately toward the client in the lower right. You must pause to attune yourself to their wants and needs (and even their garbage) and let go of your own (i.e., defuse from your thoughts and mindfully notice your feelings). You do not want to be passive forever. You will take action. First, though, you need to find out whose needs will be met with the actions you take. That is where compassion comes in, and we must start with ourselves.

Clinician, Feel for Yourself

As we discussed in the introduction, clinical work can be hazardous to your health. In addition to run-of-the-mill reactivity to challenging client interactions, clinicians who do not adequately attend to themselves risk burnout, vicarious traumatization, and other physical and mental negative effects (Patsiopoulos & Buchanan, 2011). For the sake of prevention alone, it is important for clinicians to develop skills for self-compassion, defined as a sense of "being open to and moved by one's own suffering, experiencing feelings of caring and kindness toward oneself, taking an understanding, nonjudgmental attitude toward one's inadequacies and failures, and recognizing that one's own experience is part of the common human experience" (Neff, 2003, p. 224).

LEAN IN: CLOCKING YOUR SELF-COMPASSION

Take a stopwatch and sit in a place where you won't be distracted. Think of your role, professional activities, and efforts as a clinician. Time yourself and for a full 2 minutes, write every positive attribute, skill, or achievement that you can think of about yourself as a clinician in the space provided. Write as quickly as you can without stopping to think about the validity of anything that comes to mind.

You probably guessed the next step. Time yourself again (2 minutes), this time writing every negative attribute, action, or outcome you can think of about yourself as a clinician. Ready, set, go!

Count the number of things you listed for both positive and negative attributes and list them here:

Positive: __________
Negative: __________

What do you notice in comparing your positives and negatives? Is one list longer than the other, and what does this suggest as to your degree of compassion for yourself in your professional role? Might the length and nature of your lists change depending on whether you've just met with one of your difficult clients?

Who is doing all this noticing of the good and the bad, anyway? If you are doing the noticing, can you be any of those specific things? Is it possible to hold all of these as merely experiences, thoughts, emotions, situations that you might learn and grow from? Is there any advantage that developed over time from any of these negatives?

Take this exercise a step further. Read your lists out loud (to yourself, or even to a colleague). Don't read the items as you've listed them. Instead, read them by alternating the positives with the negatives. Read back and forth between the lists, joining each item with the word *and*. (For example: Patient *and* bored with client X"; "Really persevered with client Y *and* totally blew it with my trainee by blaming him for a premature termination.") How does your experience in your role as a clinician shift when relating to yourself in this way? Note your observations below:

____
____
____
____
____
____

A final step: Take both of your lists and sit in a quiet place. Center yourself, noting your current physical experience and your immediate context. Get present with what's there with you now. Once you are centered, look at your lists. Ask yourself: *Am I willing to hold all of these?* Instead of grabbing at or shoving away, can I simply see each item as the inevitable flow of skillful and less skillful, of the mixture of my intentions, efforts, history, seen and unseen, and the press of the moment? Am I willing to hold all of these lightly so that I'm less burdened, more free to move toward what matters most in my work?

Research on the role of self-compassion for clinicians has suggested its role as a protective factor against anxiety and depression, and has associated it with better coping and resilience, life satisfaction and social connectedness, and positive attributes such as optimism, curiosity, and initiative (Patsiopoulos & Buchanan, 2011). By means of a narrative inquiry of a group of clinicians, Patsiopoulos and Buchanan identified core themes among therapists practicing consistent self-compassion in their work, including:

- Stance of acceptance of oneself, others, and difficult situations and a letting go of high expectations (see Chapter 4).
- Stance of not knowing. Here there's a shift from a focus on one's expertise to "honoring of the client's own inner wisdom and capacity to find his or her own answers" (Patsiopoulos & Buchanan, 2011, p. 304).
- Mindfulness of present experience (again, Chapter 4).
- Attending to one's inner dialogue (defusion, Chapter 3, anyone?).
- Being genuine about one's fallibility (I call this getting real with clients, and we'll get there in Chapter 10).
- Being part of a compassionate team at work. This only validates the importance of brain-to-brain resonance. If we're around compassion on a regular basis, we're bound to develop more compassion ourselves.
- Speaking the truth to self and others, even when it's difficult to do so (also part of our authenticity intervention discussion in Chapter 10).
- Finding balance through use of self-care strategies. Whether it's yoga, racquetball, walks on the beach, or strategies from this book, active use of strategies is key to self-compassion. The shift toward a lifestyle of self-care (versus periodic use of strategies) is also important.

Participants across this study believed self-compassion had a positive effect on their work with clients. "It helped them to lower unrealistic expectations; to deliver more effective boundaries and a finer balance between client needs and counselor needs; to self-correct when necessary; and to engage in more proactive, preventative self-care" (Patsiopoulos & Buchanan, 2011, p. 306). When we let ourselves off the hook and accept the good and the bad in our work, when we hold our experience lightly, we give ourselves a chance to do our best for our clients. Our self-compassion might also serve to spark compassion in them as well.

LEAN IN

This activity is adapted from the "mirror time" intervention as described by Michael Mahoney (1991). In this activity, we'll work together to get to the heart of self-compassion in your role as a clinician. Select a time when you won't be disturbed and place yourself in front of a mirror (if one is not available, your reflection in a window will do). With your eyes closed, take a few deep breaths to center and calm yourself. With your eyes still closed, consider an invitation to open to full awareness of yourself as a clinician—all that you are and have done, effective, ineffective, well-intended, and reactively destructive. Are you willing to see what's there? When you're ready, open your eyes. . . .

- What do you notice as you first look in the mirror? What shows up first and foremost in your thoughts? What is the tenor, the tone, of your feelings?
- Look gently into your own eyes. What do you see? Notice the thoughts, evaluations, conclusions that emerge. Again, notice the tone of your emotional response.
- What urges to move, blink, speak, or shift facial expression do you notice? What does your mind do when you notice these? Can you just notice any impulses, seeing if they pass?
- Allow yourself to close and then reopen your eyes. What shifts? What shows up in your mind? Allow yourself to exaggerate and expand whatever expression you find on your face. What emerges now? How do you regard this extreme?
- Close your eyes once again. Think of your role as a clinician. Consider a recent case when you felt more than competent—one in which you believe you did truly exceptional work. Open your eyes and look at yourself. What do you notice about this person, this clinician who did this work? What does this clinician have to say? Is this person profes-

sionally perfect? Does he or she know all there is to know about clients?

- Close your eyes once more. Think of your clinical role and consider a recent case when you felt less than competent—when you believe your interventions were truly unhelpful, if not destructive. Think of interactions with clients when you know you were reactive and less than focused on the client's perspective. Open your eyes and look at yourself. What do you notice about this person, this clinician? What does this person have to say? Are you willing to let him or her remain?
- With your eyes gently open, take in everything that you've seen and experienced while at the mirror during this activity. Notice how it's all there, the worst and the wonderful. Are you willing to hold it all? Even to embrace it?
- Consider saying something akin to the following to yourself as you end the exercise: "May I learn to allow all that comes in my experience as a clinician. . . . May I learn to hold both the good and the bad with openness, and thereby continue to grow and expand in my work."

Write anything that seems important from participating in this exercise in the space below. Be on the lookout for evidence of fusion—of clenching conclusions or judgments about yourself. Watch for emotions you find yourself eager to sidestep. Write about anything you are learning about the role of self-compassion for your work. What's your frontier, your leading edge in learning to hold yourself compassionately?

Clearing the Fire Pit

As a Boy Scout, I was taught to make sure you clear the area you intend to use for your campfire of any brush, leaves, or combustible material. Only when things are cleared should you set about building your fire. It is the same for building compassion for your most difficult clients. You have to clear away the brush, the clutter of mind and emotion.

LEAN IN: CLINICAL CRYSTAL BALL

Think of your sample difficult client you've been using throughout this workbook. Cue up your three (or more) anchors. With the client firmly in mind, ask yourself: What is it, in your best professional opinion, that your client needs to do (or not do) in order to make progress, to move his or her life forward? List your top five client to-do or not-do thoughts below:

1. ____
2. ____
3. ____
4. ____
5. ____

Look over your list. These things make complete sense, don't they? This is sound professional judgment. You are highly trained and have significant experience working with these sorts of issues, right? Of course this plan is reasonable. You know this client well, and you're certain that if he or she could start doing or not doing these things, his or her life would improve.

Take a pen—the darker and thicker the ink, the better. Don't use a pencil—this needs to be permanent. Look at your top five list above and one by one, cross out each item. Pause and consider each one as you cross them out. These things are gone. I've consulted my clinical crystal ball and I've seen the future—down the tracks of your work with this client: These things are not ever going to happen. Close your eyes and use mindfulness to observe your experience of the reality that these things will never happen. What shows up in your thoughts and feelings? Do you notice any tugging toward reactivity? List what emerges below:

If you're like me when I get heavily invested in my work with a particular client, an exercise such as the one you just completed creates a fair amount of dissonance—put more bluntly, it doesn't feel so good. It hurts a bit to let go of "necessary" outcomes for our clients. These things make complete sense based on our years of training and experience. Of course clients should march enthusiastically in the direction of these changes.

But it's just your dissonance—more specifically, your drive to avoid feeling not so good about things not turning out well for clients—that gets in the way of your best, most effective therapeutic stance. It is crucial for you to learn to work from an "agenda-free" orientation, especially with the most challenging individuals. I'm not saying goals are irrelevant. I'm saying that you have to hold them lightly—on the palm of your hand, not gripped in a change-greedy fist. If you're not gripping anything, it's much harder for clients to end up playing tug-of-war with you. What we're talking about here is the importance of strengthening your perspective muscle. You can't see the clients clearly (and they won't feel like they've been truly noticed) if you're always looking over their shoulder and down the road.

Think of the most difficult aspect of your sample client's behavior. What is the one, specific thing he or she does that makes this work so frustrating, vexing, taxing? What is that most difficult behavior pattern? List it below:

What is the *cause* of this behavior? What's (or who's) to blame for it? Remember our discussion of the social psychological principle of correspondence bias in Chapter 3? This is the well-researched error that we all make in which we assume blame and intent in others—they chose to do it, or the action came out of their characteristics or (lack of) character. When we do something (like angrily shake our fist at someone in traffic), we tend to view our behavior as having been caused by circumstances, by context.

"These Boston drivers are making me crazy!" you might say to yourself after cutting off an old lady while changing lanes. "I'm only driving this way because I'm following the flow of traffic" or "I'm running late for an important meeting." The point is that we distort our perception of others and ourselves when assigning causality to behavior. We all do it and, though it's natural, it gets in the way of our best clinical work, particularly in working with clients who tend to exhibit difficult patterns of behavior.

LEAN IN

Take the most difficult behavior you listed for your sample client. Look back to what you listed as the immediate cause of his or her behavior. We're going to return to the pie chart exercise from Chapter 3, but this time we're applying it to your client. In Figure 6.1, press yourself to think less about your client's inner qualities (though these may be relevant as well) and focus on the context of their actions. What aspects of your client, the situation, the environment, and other demands and pressures (including time) may have been potential causes of the behavior? Without evaluating any, generate as many ideas as possible and write them on the pie chart. Draw additional "pie pieces" if you need to.

In the space below, describe any new observations that come to mind about this client's behavior. Look for any new frames on the behavior that acknowledge the full range of causes, as well as the way in which your client's actions were inevitable. Finish the following sentence:

"Of course [name] did what [he or she] did and things turned out the way they did because in taking everything past and present about me, my client, and the situation into account . . ."

____

____

Now, think again about this client's behavior pattern—the behavior you find upsetting or difficult to manage in some way. Do you notice any changes in how you feel, how you regard this client's behavior? Allow yourself to sit with anything that arises. I love quotes from Gandhi's work, so here's another one: "When I see an erring man, I say to myself, I have also erred, when I see a lustful man, I say to myself so was I once, and in

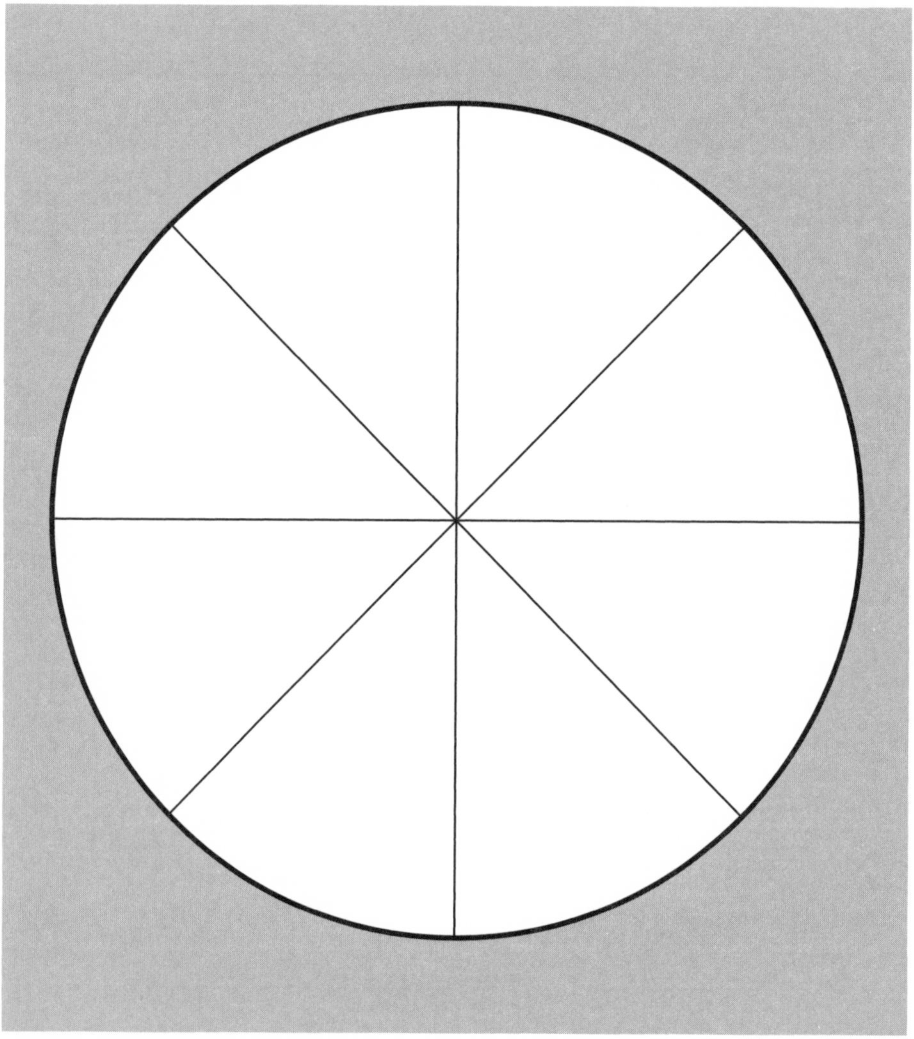

Figure 6.1 Pie Chart Graphic

this way I feel kinship with everyone in the world" (Gandhi, 1962, p. 274). Would that we, as clinicians, could clear away our obstacles to compassion in such a manner.

For your most difficult clients, until you can let go of your agendas and see the connective context of their behavior (including your own influence because of any rope pulling you've indulged in) you'll be limited in your effectiveness. You'll also be much more likely to end up creating your own Melinda Meter and blunt your compassion. You might even burn out more generally. Let's do one more brush-clearing exercise in order to get ready for building a more compassionate fire for your work.

LEAN IN

In an activity earlier in this section, you crossed out your needs for your client. You deleted them and were left with nothing to guide your work. Not so fast. Ask yourself: Letting go of what I need, what are the top five things my client *wants* for himself? Regardless of the feasibility, sanity, or appropriateness of these wants, push yourself to think of what, from your client's perspective, they might be and list them below:

1. ______________________________
2. ______________________________
3. ______________________________
4. ______________________________
5. ______________________________

Hopefully, you are beginning to let go of your sense of correctness and open to your client's perspective. That is the beginning of compassion. It is the necessary condition for relational leadership (see Chapters 9 and 10). Before moving to the next section, consider the following activities.

LEAN IN: IT'S HARD ON THE HORIZON

In this exercise, we'll look to harness the benefits of visualization for strengthening our compassion muscle. And it is indeed a muscle—compassion grows if applied when it is difficult, when effort is required. Compassion is not simply a warm feeling that comes when the situation clearly calls for it—when it's easy. The most open mind, the heart with the widest reach, is strong enough to bring all (the easy and hard) inside.

To begin, sit quietly and comfortably (though upright is best). With eyes closed, focus your attention on the natural flow of your breathing. Allow yourself to come to center. Notice, label, and allow any thoughts, emotions, or sensations to arise and fall away as we've practiced.

Now, in your mind's eye, imagine a horizon tinged with the beginnings of a beautiful sunset. Continue to allow your breath to come and go gently as you watch the play of color in imagination. The scene is warm and peaceful.

You notice a small object appearing on the horizon. It's a person, small in stature, slowly coming toward you. The warm hues of the setting sun obscure the person at first. And then, slowly, it becomes clear the person is a child. You continue to watch as the child approaches.

Suddenly, you notice that something is not right with this child. Something is significantly wrong. The child has no hair. The skin is very pale and there are dark circles under the eyes. This young child has been fighting cancer and is now standing right in front of you, reaching up. Perhaps you've known such a child. Perhaps you've known others who have lost a child in such an inconceivable way. As you look down at this child, it becomes clear to you that the child is dying. You can pick the child up if you want, but there is no stopping death.

Allow the sun to set in your mind's eye. Focus your attention on your breathing. Let any reactions—any thoughts or feelings—arise and fall. Notice and label, let them recede. Continue to follow the breath.

And again, you open your imagination to the horizon. And now the sun is beginning to rise. You feel its warmth cutting through the cold of the passing night. A new day is beginning.

You again notice a small object appearing on the horizon. It's another child, coming toward you. This time though, the child is not walking slowly but running directly at you. The child has plenty of hair, and the complexion is clear and bright. The child has run up to you and stopped abruptly just inside what you generally would consider your personal space. You feel the urge to step backward, but realize you cannot. Your back is against a wall you didn't realize was there.

The child looks up at you, parts his or her lips, and spits at you. The most horrible, vile language—terrible slurs and swearing—rip the air in front of you. Whatever would be the worst, most hurtful word to call you—the most painful label ever attached to you by another person—this child is now lashing you with it. You feel the spit sliding down your cheek. And, still looking down at this child, you see the most disrespectful gestures possible. You cannot move. You cannot look away.

You must open your mind to this latter child. The first child was "empathy easy." This new child is, obviously, "hard." Stay with this loud, unruly child. Stay very close. Lean *toward* the child. Notice the thoughts, feelings, and sensations in your body. Follow your breath and let these reactions rise and eventually fall away. You are still standing up against this empathy-hard child. If you're able, stay with the breath and allow reactions to pass. Continue in this manner for a few minutes.

Finally, the child turns and moves slowly away. The sun is now fully up, and you lose sight of the child in the distance.

Open your eyes and allow yourself to wonder:

- What is the difference in my reactions to these two children?
- For whom did compassion flow most easily?

Consider the web of connectivity in all things, the inevitable flow of cause and effect beyond our full awareness for any given event or action, and now ask yourself:

- Is one of these children truly more deserving of compassion?
- Did the second child choose to be so full of hate?
- Will an angry, punitive reaction in you really help smooth out the hate in the child?
- What might compassion do for this child?
- What might it do for you in such circumstances?

List your reactions in the space below:

____

____

____

____

____

____

LEAN IN: DEEP LISTENING

Adapted from Surrey (2005) and Kramer (2007):

- With a colleague or partner, sit facing one another in a centered, upright, comfortable position. One of you is in the role of clinician, the other is the client.
- Spend up to 5 minutes sitting quietly with eyes closed getting centered and focused. You can attend to any one object (e.g., the breath).
- The clinician opens his or her eyes (client keeps them closed) and the clinician focuses awareness on the breathing of the client. Let go of whatever arises in your own thoughts, sensations, and feelings, gently returning from any distraction to the client's inhalation and exhalation. You can silently note "breathing in" and "breathing out" to yourself (or simply "in" and "out"). Do this for at least a few minutes.
- Client opens his or her eyes and both the client and clinician lightly hold one another's gaze, but with the clinician still focusing on the client's breathing. The clinician now quietly says aloud what he or she is noting about the client (e.g., "breathing in," "breathing out," "breathing faster/slower/deeper/more shallow"). If your mind wanders, once you notice this, fall silent, return to the client's breath and continue noting its nature aloud. Do this for about 5 minutes.
- Switch roles and repeat all of the steps.
- Spend time discussing the experience together. How easy or difficult was it to tune in this deeply to the client? What, if any, obstacles emerged, and what helped or hindered your ability to return to focused attunement on the client? What was the client's experience of your listening and attunement? What did the client notice in his or her own reactions while observing your focused attention on him or her? What does this experience suggest about your current degree of attunement and depth of focused listening to your clients, particularly your most challenging cases? What does it feel like in a general way for you to focus so completely on the basics of the client's moment-to-moment experience? Write anything of note in the space below:

____

____

____

____

____

Consider the empathy-hard clients in your caseload. Might you be willing to stand up close to them? Lean in toward and truly listen to them? Are you willing to let yourself wonder how they might be suffering? Might you be able to flex your muscles of compassion? Notice that in the exercise above you stood by and allowed the child to flare at you. You ignored his behavior. There is a vast difference between rope-pulling ignoring that comes out of anger and resentment, and compassionate, attuned detachment that prepares you for truly therapeutic action. Are you interested in developing more of this latter version of compassionate response to your clients?

We've practiced the basics of mindfulness of moment-to-moment experience. We've begun to apply this mindful focus to your work with difficult client interactions. Now comes the fun part. What if you more fully and intentionally "breathed in" your clients' collective pain, anguish, anger, and despair? Break out the china and pop the champagne! Sounds like a great time, right? Why would anyone do this intentionally? . . . Maybe because by purposely taking in the pain, you are that much more able to send out that which is therapeutic. Sound like a good enough reason? The following technique is as challenging as it is old. It is simple like a climb up Mount Everest (i.e., you go up to the top and then you come down). It has the potential (applied consistently, like one foot after another during a climb) to open you up to more compassion, connection, and therapeutic action than perhaps any other mindfulness approach.

LEAN IN

Take a deep, slow breath. Once you've slowly exhaled, take another. You don't need me to remind you of the wisdom of doing this when stress descends. If you're angry, the adage is to do so while counting slowly to 10. The point is to put some space between you and your angry or stress-sparked reactions. Ask yourself: Does this really work? More specifically: Does it shift how you feel about whoever or whatever is causing your upset?

What if I asked you to take another deep breath, but to do so with the intention of breathing in the pain, upset, or unpleasantness of those around you, and breathing out an intention of goodwill, ease, and release to these disgruntled people (i.e., your clients)—even if they are the ones poking at you. Sounds silly, right? It's one thing to take deep breaths in order to calm down. It's another thing to do so and suck in others' angst, and give them all the relaxation, all the glory. You might call this nonsense.

You can also call it *tonglen*—an ancient meditation technique dating back to the 10th century and passed down from master to student across time. *Tonglen* is Tibetan for "sending and receiving" (Chodron, 2002). The technique is simple—deceptively so. When faced with pain or difficulty, one merely chooses to take in, or receive, the pain on the in-breath, and send out goodness, relaxation, ease, comfort on the out-breath. The technique is deceptive in that you will find it difficult at times to either take in pain, send out release, or both. It requires committed practice. And we'll begin with it here.

Why? Good question. Perhaps simple deep breathing has not done enough to change your experience of pain. Would you be interested in more space within yourself, more room to feel your way forward? For the practice outlined below, I'd recommend either taping yourself reading the instructions, or having a friend or colleague read them aloud to you as you practice.

STEPS FOR TONGLEN PRACTICE

1. Start with someone you feel close to—a family member, a romantic partner, a friend, particularly someone you feel quite connected to right now. Find a quiet place where you won't be disturbed for a few minutes.
2. Visualize an image that to you suggests vast openness. A clear sky. The Grand Canyon. An ocean horizon. Whatever comes to mind is fine. Center your awareness on this sense of openness.
3. Call to mind a time when your loved one was in significant pain, emotional or physical. On the in-breath, imagine you are filling your chest, your whole body, with this negativity. To make it more vivid, imagine your loved one's pain as something black, hot, or abrasive. Whatever negative sensory quality you might attach, imagine breathing this in. As you are taking this negative quality in, do it with a wish

to take the pain on yourself, to fill yourself with it. Take it in with a sense of immense space within yourself to contain it.

4. On the out-breath, imagine sending release, ease, goodness, healing, or some other open, gentle positive quality to your loved one. Attach a sensory component to the out-breath if possible (e.g., bright light, a specific bright color, cool air, warmth, a clear sky). As you send out this positive aspect, do so with a wish to give it away so that your loved one might be free of pain, and might have relaxation, ease, and so on.
5. After a minute or two of focusing on your loved one, shift your focus to yourself. Breathe in the pain, the upset, the frustration you are feeling in reaction to your difficult client. On the in-breath, take in the full measure of this negative feeling and do so with the intention to fill yourself with it. Tell yourself: "There are many other clinicians who have felt this way." On the out-breaths, send yourself the positive release, the relaxation, the healing. Tell yourself: "May I be free of this. May I open myself even further."
6. After a short time focusing on yourself, shift focus to your difficult client. Repeat the same procedure as above, bringing the client's pain and upset on the in-breath and with the wish that you might take on that pain, and that you may give the client all the release, ease, and healing on the out-breath—that you intentionally take in the negativity, and give the client your best qualities, your ability to sit in quiet and ease, so that the client might heal and change. While continuing to take in and send out on the medium of the breath, remind yourself of how many individuals are likely suffering as your client is. Also, remind yourself of how many caregivers like you are struggling with reactions as they try to help.

This technique is not about creating a specific outcome for your clients. You aren't trying to make something happen right now. It is not a form of wishful thinking, and you are not going to practice this strategy prior to a session and then expect clients to be free of negativity. This approach is more about changing something within *you*—creating more space inside, more room for movement so that you can more fully help this client (and not sacrifice so much of yourself). *Tonglen* is paradoxical in that fashion. By intentionally choosing to take in pain and give away release, you end up creating more ease for yourself and more release from that which had previously gripped you, choking off your capacity for compassionate action. It's not about being a martyr and it's not about masochism. This is a technique for creating greater compassion, especially when (and with whom) you least want to.

Tonglen is a mindfulness practice about leaning toward difficulty with your clients. If you are willing to use it regularly, you can learn to catch yourself on the verge of reactive rope pulling with your clients. You can choose to drop the rope and spark a compassionate fire in the service of your client's progress. In the process, you can melt the hard aspects of yourself, opening the space within that is the birthplace of your best work. And in the context of the budding field of social neuroscience, such practice helps develop new connections and new wiring in the brain that fosters the approach of difficulty as opposed to rope-pulling withdrawal (or attack).

Flint to Steel: Making Sparks

The more you can allow yourself to adopt an attitude of curiosity regarding your client's experience, the more effectively you will intervene. This may be intuitive for you, and you may be telling yourself that you already do this. "Of course, I consider my client's perspective every time I meet with her." Regardless of what you're saying to yourself right now, see if you're willing to simply notice what you're thinking, and do the following exercise anyway.

LEAN IN

Find a location where you can be free from distraction or intrusions for at least 5 minutes. Sit in an upright, though relaxed position, perhaps with your arms resting comfortably at your sides. Adopt a pattern of slow, deliberate breathing (diaphragmatic or "belly" breathing is best). Whatever manner of slow, calm breathing works for you is fine. Do this for at least one full minute. And now follow along with the prompts below.

Close your eyes. . . . Draw in a deep, slow breath. Slowly release it. Another deep, slow breath. Release it, and as you do, recognize that for the next few moments—you are no longer you. You did not graduate with an advanced degree in mental health. You have not been a professional helper. You do not claim specialized knowledge of how people come to be stuck in their lives and how people can go about getting unstuck. You are not sitting in the chair in your office you are more than used to—that perch which is your vantage point on the lives of those you are trying to help. That chair is empty.

Deep, slow breath. Eyes closed. You're watching that empty chair. You're sitting across from it. You are *that* client . . . the one who hits the buttons of the therapist who sits in that empty chair. Think of him or her. You are sitting in *that* chair.

What are you wearing? How are you sitting? What are the habits of movement? What are the words that tend to accompany the breaking away of eye contact? Of glances to the floor or ceiling? What are the idiosyncrasies? For now, they are yours.

Deep, slow breath. Eyes are still closed. The clinician's chair across from you is still empty. You're still in the other one. The one visited by so many people—most of whom you look forward to helping. But again you are that client. The one who hits buttons.

From this chair, what is it you most want? What matters? What do you hope for out of the next 50 minutes? Let yourself wonder. Really get curious about what you want in your life.

Do you feel that the clinician who sits in that empty chair fully gets you? Understands what your experience of life is like?

How does it feel to come in each week to talk to the person who sits in that chair about what is not working in your life? What are the blackest thoughts and feelings? The ones you actively shove away when you sit with this therapist?

Did you plan to come here each time to hit the therapist's buttons? To struggle against her? To make her feel incompetent and ineffective? To make her withdraw? To spark the same feelings in her you cannot have for yourself? Did you intend any of this?

Do you want to be happy? Do you want to be free of pain and suffering? What are you hoping to get from this person sitting across from you?

Deep, slow breath. You are you again. The helper back in the usual chair. You have your diplomas. Your specialized knowledge. Your years of clinical experience. You see that client coming into your office, sitting down across from you. Open your eyes. . . .

* * *

Take a moment and write in the space below any reactions or experiences you had while doing the exercise above. Remember, adopt an attitude of curiosity toward your client.

____

____

____

____

Did you encounter anything new about your client? With this visualization, sometimes clinicians report an increased awareness of possibilities or potential inroads for connection and collaboration with their clients.

What do you make of the agenda items, the "to-dos" or "not-dos" you listed earlier in this chapter that you felt certain about? Though you may still feel they are needed, are you willing to loosen your grip on them?

____

____

____

____

It likely took you no more than 5 minutes to complete this visualization about your difficult client. Again, what might happen if you made a commitment to carve out 5 minutes per week to consider—deeply consider—your client's experience?

Before leaving the experience of this more vivid encounter with your client, push yourself to go a step further. Ask yourself: *What is my client's bottom-line belief about himself and what he wants in his life?*

____

Hold onto this fleshed-out sense of your client's perspective. You will need to return to it over and over again. In all the moments to come in your actual interactions with this client, you will begin to pick up the rope (based on your patterning, the demands of the situation, and the surge of your feelings). If you're willing, you can choose to use the strategies we've practiced for distancing, defusing, and mindfully allowing your experience. You can orient toward your client's experience and perspective, and then you can choose to act. Only then will your actions be guaranteed to be therapeutic (though outcomes will take time and are ultimately outside your control). You will pick up the rope though. Are you willing to keep reorienting to your client? What is the alternative?

A helpful way to bundle together your understanding of your challenging client's perspective is to write a letter about your reactivity to the work. Notice your immediate reaction to this idea, and ask yourself if you'd be willing to try it regardless of this reaction. How might such an exercise deepen your understanding and perhaps increase your capacity to hold your emotions and give you more options in your work with this person? If you're willing, use the space below to draft a letter (that you will keep for yourself) to your client. Focus on authentically describing your negative experience—your reactive labels, judgments, beliefs of certainty, and the emotions tied to them—as well as what you've learned about your own scripting, any deepened understanding of the client's perspective, and finally, your hopes for the work together as things move forward.

Date ____________

Dear ________________________

____

____

____

____

____

____

____

Sincerely,

Your Signature: _________________________

What do you notice about yourself, and about your client, after taking a few minutes to write this? What has happened to your emotional experience of the client? To your thoughts and beliefs about the client and your ability to help? In the past, have you been looking at the client, or merely at your thoughts and feelings in reaction?

___

___

___

Fanning the Flames: Using Compassion to Move the Work Forward

Of course your clients are difficult. As we're seeing in our exploration, there is always a whole host of reasons inside and outside both you and your client that lead to these patterns. And where will the tugs-of-war lead? What will be the outcome then? You're learning that you can take your clients very seriously without buying into what they are saying or doing (remember you're getting great at using defusion, perspective strategies, and mindful awareness). You're working to drop the rope. You're looking more fully at your client, from that person's own perspective. You are increasingly curious and open to possibilities.

LEAN IN

Cue up the anchors for your difficult client. Fix the person firmly in mind. Mindfully notice whatever shows up—thoughts, sensations, or images. Ask yourself: *What is this client teaching me?* What am I learning here? What opportunities do these pulls at the rope provide? What is a new nuance or detail about the client that I have somehow missed along the way?

___

___

___

Now, with this open perspective in mind, review what you listed earlier in this chapter that you believe the client needs, and what the client might want and his or her own bottom-line beliefs.

Ask yourself: How can I use this? How might I show this client that I see what matters most to him or her? How can I let the client know that I value any differences between us? List any ideas that come to mind:

____

____

____

What you just wrote was the beginning of compassionate action. You've conjured ideas for communicating a greater, more contextual, relational understanding to your client. What might happen if you followed through on any of these ideas?

Now that you're working to let go of your focus on outcomes, on what you think the client needs to do, and now that you've considered the client's perspective, ask yourself, where is the possible overlap between what I think the client needs, and what he or she wants right now? What are the directions we might head together? These directions are the compassionate values that will guide your work together. A compass doesn't give you a destination; it gives you a true reading as to direction. In what directions, based on your thorough consideration of yourself and your sample client, might you go together?

Values are continuous. They regenerate across time. They pull you forward without your thinking about it. Personally, I value being a loving father (I don't usually have to convince myself to enthusiastically play with my toddler despite the evening's workload facing me). "Loving father" is a direction, a value. "Amassing $100,000 of college savings for my daughter" is a goal (and an intimidating, sleep-disrupting one at that). Goals are important in life generally, and in clinical work specifically. Here, we're focused on values informed by your compassionate stance toward your client. Perhaps it is "authentic expression regarding themes of loss" or "understanding the impact of anger." These are directions that perhaps you and your client can agree are valuable.

What are the possible shared values for your work with your sample client? Consider the full context of your and your client's perspectives.

____

____

____

It took the passage of time, and work with other, similar clients, for me to put my Melinda Meter away. I hope you return to the exercises in this chapter often. Again, you will pick up the rope with clients. Compassion is not a mountain summit where you get to hang out indefinitely. Clients, context, and your own patterning will pull you off from time to time. You can climb back up though. Remember the opportunity of difficulty. Remember the attitude of curiosity. Remember to lean toward what's hard about your clients. With mindful attention and effort, you can reach the peaks more readily.

LEAN IN

Let's broaden things out beyond your one sample difficult client. Think back across all of your work as a clinician thus far—all of the challenging clients you've worked with. Pick at least five with whom something really negative occurred during your work—and for the purposes of this activity, ideally something undesirable that happened during your interactions with the client. List these five clients and a brief, one-sentence description of the negative event:

Client 1: ____
Client 2: ____
Client 3: ____
Client 4: ____
Client 5: ____

Now, looking over these negative situations, spend time with each one, thinking how this event actually led to changes, shifts, and unexpected happenings that ended up being to your advantage, perhaps to the client's, and maybe others as well. What were the unanticipated ripple effects that you could not possibly have foreseen at the time? If you're having a hard time recognizing the benefits of this negative situation, tuck this exercise into the back of your mind. Notice if something occurs to you later. Our perspective on the good and the bad of our work (and lives in general) is extremely limited. Such judgmental labels are of our own mental creation. The work is what it is, and we (and our clients) benefit from our steadfast acceptance of this, and from our trust in the inevitable flow of behavior and experience toward what is necessary based on the conditions of the moment.

Client 1: ______________________________
Client 2: ______________________________
Client 3: ______________________________
Client 4: ______________________________
Client 5: ______________________________

We've put away Melinda Meters, climbed mountains, and started fires. In Chapter 7, we explore what to do with ourselves when the road gets especially precarious with clients. What should you do when you've strayed far beyond frustration, boredom, or dejection? How are you to handle the extremes of rage, despair, shame, hopelessness, fear, and desire arising in the midst of your interactions with clients? Sounds fun, right? Take a deep breath, let your mind chatter away as it's so fond of doing, and take a step (or better yet, flip the page) forward anyway.

MAP CHECK

Take a moment and review what we've covered in this chapter. What was one aspect, one piece of content, that resonated with you—sparked your interest, curiosity, or even angst in some way?

____

Why did this matter to you? What makes this worth writing about? Worth your focus and effort? What is the gravity that this carries for you and your work?

____

What is one specific action you can take within the next 24 hours related to this issue that feels as though it would be important and has the potential to move you in the direction of what matters?

____

≺ CHAPTER SEVEN ≻

Beware of Falling Rocks

Navigating the Most Precarious Reactions in Clinical Work

PERHAPS YOU'LL choose to skip this chapter. Maybe you just happen to be *that* clinician who has never experienced the far reaches of reactivity to your clients. Please consider yourself exempt and proceed with all due haste to the next chapter if you've managed to elude rage, disgust, despair, desire, or abject apathy in your work.

Or . . . you can join the rest of us just for the heck of it and read on anyway. "But I've never felt that intensely about a client. That's just not me," you might be saying. "That wouldn't be professional." Humor me—you might find something of use here regardless.

If you're standing on this side of the "extreme line" with me, believe me, it's not just the two of us. We're in good "bad" company. Estimates vary, of course, but the literature suggests that therapists are not the calm, composed, Mr. Rogers-sweater-wearing (and fashion-foolish) lot we might appear (or wish ourselves) to be. In one study, three-quarters of practicing therapists reported significant personal distress at some point within a 3-year period (Guy, Poelstra, & Stark, 1988). We cannot help but be deeply affected by our work. "All therapists working with survivors of trauma experience pervasive and enduring alterations in cognitive schema that impact the trauma worker's feelings, relationships, and life" (Harrison & Westwood, 2009, p. 204). In their survey of 7,000 therapists of diverse orientations and career stages, Orlinsky and Ronnestad (2005) found that 17% of clinicians reported a pattern of "disengaged practice" (defined as some "stressful involvement," but not much "healing"), and 10% reported "distressing practice" (not much healing, and more than a little stressful involvement). These are merely the statistics of those willing to report their distress. As we've discussed repeatedly, willingness is key to self-management of reactivity, and is not automatic, even for those trained to help others face their unhelpful reactions.

And it's not just intense negative emotion impacting the preponderance of therapists—intense positive affect can also get in the way. More than 84% of therapists become sexually attracted to a client at some point during their practice tenures (Pope, Keith-Spiegel, & Tabachnick, 1986; Rodolfa et al., 1994). Mr. Rogers may have maintained equanimity at all times in his peaceable television neighborhood, but our offices can sometimes seem to breed intense reactions—for our clients, and for us as helpers. Writers of books on managing reactivity are no exception. . . .

* * *

My 12-year-old client's tantrum that day had the feel of the cartoon character the Tasmanian Devil as he whirled through my office. "I wanna call my mom now!" he yelled. I'd told him that making a call at that moment was not an option—that he needed to calm down first so that we could solve whatever nuance of unmet expectation or perceived social slight was afflicting him.

Samuel lunged for my desk and the phone sitting atop it, beginning to dial frantically. My embarrassment-prone mind was thankful I was alone in the group practice that evening. No colleagues to witness my incompetent management of my bipolar disorder–diagnosed boy client. "Come on buddy," I said. "Let's talk this out. There's no need—"

"Shut up asshole!" he yelled. I stepped forward and puffed myself up in an attempt to create a human bubble around him—a bubble that seemed about to pop at any second. I said that he was "making the person who cared for him very nervous." Why I felt the urge to speak of myself in the third person was almost as notable as my desperate offer to give him some of my sandwich if he'd please simply calm down. "Fuck you!" he screamed. "I'm calling her now!"

And then I did it—I reached and unplugged the phone jack from the wall behind my desk. Samuel's fury ignited into desk shoving and a flung chair. I called 911 from an adjoining office and had the paramedics take him to be screened for admission to a psychiatric inpatient unit.

In stark contrast to his swearing and yelling during his tantrum in my office, Samuel lay like a discarded mannequin on the gurney inside the ambulance the entire short ride over to the hospital. The paramedic who sat with us in the back tried to get Samuel to answer a few simple questions during the ride: "What's your birthday? What seems to be the problem today? What medication do you take?" but he did not respond.

I looked away and out the back window. I wanted to watch anything but this boy's face. It was reddened and tight from the malicious mix of sadness, fear, and anger squatting behind it. I'm not sure if I remember accurately that Samuel's eyes were welling with tears during the ride to the hospital. It may very well have been my own clamped-off crying that my memory pasted onto his face. I do remember how he wouldn't look at me as we rode to the hospital, the adrenaline-strangled silence inside the ambulance in stark contrast to the siren's wail. The only question he responded to was, "What seems to be the problem today?"

"Ask him," he said flat and raw as a cancer diagnosis. "He's the one that called you." Samuel had indeed crossed a threshold, and he certainly needed to go to the hospital. He had trashed my office and made me feel as trapped and powerless as he did. It took a firm tongue biting in the ambulance to block the good cry I would save for that evening's glass of bourbon. He needed the hospital, and I felt I needed a new line of work.

LEAN IN

Above is an example of just one situation eliciting multiple extreme reactions in me as a clinician. What situation or client of yours arises? Call to mind a time when you experienced very significant reactions (e.g., hate, rage, fear, apathy, hopelessness, disgust, desire). With whom have you done a dance of suffering? How might you describe the situation now? Take a few moments and, without censoring or editing, write out your thoughts about the situation, what happened, how you felt, and how you think and feel now looking back on it:

____

____

____

____

____

* * *

So again, if you've been doing clinical work for a while, you've likely done the dance of suffering—you've raged (at least inside), numbed out, lashed out, despaired, or given up. It's here that you'll need to review our discussion of self-compassion (Chapter 6). In order to help your clients, you must help yourself and learn to hold your most extreme reactions. Yes, you'll need to be accountable for your actions—holding does not mean ignoring the ramifications of your reactivity for clients. It means acceptance, not absolution, and it means flexible action in the direction of what matters most in your work. From clients like Samuel above, I learned the (inevitably) hard way that a self-compassionate, proactive, skillful holding of extreme reactions helps buffer ill effects, helps repair ruptures in the therapeutic relationship, and enhances one's healing presence.

It has increasingly seemed important in my own practice to remember the sentiment expressed in a quote attributed to poet Walt Whitman—"I may be as bad as the worst, but, thank God, I am as good as the best." This chapter is no call to passivity regarding the far reaches of what we feel and do as therapists. All that is great and all that is gory is there in our clients, and in us as well. In this chapter we take a big bold leap in the direction of skillfully always being what we already are.

Steps to Self-Respect: An APPALLing Method for Your Reactive Madness

Speaking of skill, if you're going to improve in your ability to manage the worst that shows up in yourself in the midst of work with clients, you'll need to put together everything we've covered in the book to this point. You've learned to walk with application of mindfulness, with defusion and perspective taking, to articulate the values underlying your work. So now that you've learned to walk, it's time to run. Before reviewing the major areas of extreme clinician reactivity, let's put together a basic stepwise routine for self-management of each. Think of these steps as your go-to calisthenics routine for self-management of the "biggies" of reactivity. Let's briefly go over the steps, and then delve into the particulars of applying them within the specific domains of experience.

Step 1: Awareness

Begin with open, fully awake, mindful tracking of whatever arises in the moment of interaction with the client (or after). At the first flicker of intense feeling that you notice, bring in a breath and clear out a large space within yourself. What is your own personal image of vastness or expansiveness? Perhaps it's the Grand Canyon, or maybe a clear, cloudless sky—whatever it is, conjure it as you bring in a first breath on the heels of that clenched feeling we all get as the emotional wave builds. What is the energy coming through your sense experience? What is here in the "now" of your thought process?

Things happen quickly in session. The intensity of some reactions can surge seemingly without warning. Here, you're stepping back to have a seat in the front aisle of the theater of mind you typically identify with. You're sitting back just far enough to see the screen instead of simply being the character "Reactive You." Are you willing to take a deceptively simple breath and open your eyes to what is happening within?

Step 2: Pause for Perspective

You're willing to look and now you're nudging yourself to step back a bit further. This is where you'll look to use techniques of defusion (Chapter 3) to deliteralize your thinking. Instead of *being an idiot*, you're "having the thought of being an idiot" for doing or saying whatever you've done or said in session. You might use other perspective strategies we've covered to get distance on yourself (e.g., labeling the errors in your perceptions, such as correspondence bias). Remember, the mere mental act of labeling your reactions has been shown to reduce them. As you step back in these first seconds, you're seeing the forest and not just the reactive tree that's falling on you.

Notice (in case you haven't already) that this stepwise acronym APPALL is itself a cheeky defusion strategy for the grim seriousness of our most intense experiences as clinicians. As when we first talked about defusion in Chapter 3, this is not intended to belittle the suffering we experience—that's real; it's meant instead to create a helpful dose of psychic distance. Of course, you're not going to tick off the steps of what's most appalling in any given intense moment in your work, but you will, with practice, bring them to bear. I don't have to list the steps for bicycle locomotion like I did when I was 6—I just get on and ride.

Step 3: Acceptance

As we discussed in Chapter 4, with acceptance, we're not resigning ourselves to the client's behavior and our jaw-grinding reaction. Instead, we are leaning into what is. And when our client has relapsed yet again and we find ourselves sinking back into a deflated, hopeless silence, or when they've lashed out and we've emotionally shoved back (or closed off) yet again, we are making a conscious choice to say "of course" to the situation and its implications—the client's actions and experience, our thoughts, emotions, and behavior—the whole shebang.

A quick rendition of an ancient Sufi story . . .

There once was a poor farmer who decided to change his fortune by putting his every resource toward the purchase of a stallion he intended to breed. The stallion was strong, beautiful, and fast, promising greatness in his offspring, and suggesting future wealth and glory for the farmer. Many of the neighbors were intensely jealous. But not long after he took possession of the stallion, a storm's winds broke the fencing and the stallion ran away. Upon hearing this, his neighbors chided him, saying, "You were so foolish to spend everything and put all your hopes on that stallion. Isn't it terrible?"

The farmer replied, "Good? Bad? Who knows?"

Time passed and eventually the stallion returned, having joined with dozens of fine wild horses, all of which ran promptly inside the farmer's newly repaired enclosure. The farmer was now rich with this herd, and, together with his only son, tended them and prospered. The envious neighbors stood at the fence watching and said to the farmer, "How wonderful for you! Now you are rich beyond compare! How could the gods have blessed you so?"

The farmer replied, "Good? Bad? Who knows?"

One day, while tending the horses, the farmer's son fell and shattered his leg. His leg healed poorly and he was left crippled and disfigured. The neighbors hung their heads in mock sympathy. "How will your son ever make a life for himself now? How will he ever find work or marry? How terrible for you!" they said, secretly reveling in this turn of fate.

The farmer replied, "Good? Bad? Who knows?"

After a time, the country found itself at war. The government sent agents to force all young men into the army, and a likely early death in battle. When the military officers entered the farmer's house and saw the state of his son's leg, they let him be, moving on to the neighbors' homes in search of recruits. The grief-stricken neighbors who lost their sons to the ravages of the war came to the farmer. "How lucky you are that your son was injured. How generous the gods have been to you by sparing him."

You can guess his response. And so it continued for the farmer and his neighbors—him resting in unclenched equanimity, his neighbors gripped by the intensity of their reactions. Note the contrast between them. As the farmer maintained his stable stance on a foundation of acceptance despite the circumstances, his neighbors' well-being changed direction like a chaotic wind. Whom do you most resemble when your reactions to clients are at their most extreme?

In this third step, we continue to stay open as we breathe and step back from our thoughts, and as we do, we lose the evaluative labels (i.e., the good and the bad) and drop the stories we tell ourselves—the narrative judgments we impose. The client is not horrible or even difficult, and neither are your reactions—everyone simply *is*. Here, we breathe it all into the vast space we just opened. And the more we practice, the more we realize there's always room for more. And speaking of vast open spaces and stallions, it's here that we ride the emotion rising inside us in those seconds after an exchange with our client. If we're willing, we can choose to lightly hold the reins of this wildness and sit (or stand) as it moves along on its own. And most horse rides (or plastic horsy merry-go-round rides for that matter) last far longer than the span of most emotional currents—so long as we don't act to spur things into a full-blown affective gallop.

As clinicians, and as run-of-the-mill human beings, we benefit from learning to let go of the Supreme Court justice in our heads—the evaluator passing judgment and telling us how to frame every occurrence in our work. Though we're highly trained and very smart (at least I am), we're actually pretty stupid (okay—me too, I guess) when it comes to having complete understanding of all the variables determining even the simplest events in our daily lives. And just when you thought you had a firm conceptualization of your difficult client, you should remember how you can't even be absolutely certain as to exactly why that jerk cut you off in traffic this morning, or why you decided to have just one more doughnut.

Our vision for all the contingencies of every happening within and around us is myopic at best, completely blind at worst. So it behooves us to follow suit with the farmer in the story. We simply do not know what is good or bad with certainty because what is bad in our work, and in our foregoing actions, may turn out to be the seed of significant growth and positive change. At the time, I regarded my impulsive decision to drop out of law school as horrible judgment and a failure. Then again, that failure led me to open a psychology text in a bookstore, sparking a lifelong passion, and ultimately leading to the words I'm tapping out on my keyboard at this moment. We have to open up to our inevitable ignorance in order to encounter and benefit from new possibilities most readily, and we must do so by parting ways with our evaluative knee-jerking.

To summarize: With this step you're basically answering a simple question—What circumstance, what emotional reaction, is here now? And once you answer, you follow with a simple reminder: "And is it good or bad? . . . Who knows?"

Step 4: Look

You're aware. You're breathing. You keep stepping back (and you will need to keep stepping back—Do you pump the pedals on your bike just once and end up all the way on the other end of town?). Now, you're looking out and away. No, you're not looking for *that* destination, that outcome.

Besides, it's simply too far away, and you've learned time and time again that gluing your eyes to the horizon only leads to more frustration when "it" doesn't emerge. You also end up missing the inconvenient aspects of the terrain along the way—you end up getting thrown off.

Once the riding is well underway and you're able to relax a bit into the rhythm of the situation (as uncomfortable as it may be), now is the time to get your bearings. What is this trip really about? What matters about this work? There's something that gives my interventions meaningful direction—What is it? Perhaps it's about helping clients move boldly toward their fears of intimacy. Maybe it has something to do with assisting them in not numbing out and turning away when they're getting overwhelmed. Maybe it has more to do with you than the client—that you want to consistently move in the direction of taking appropriate risks, of having a creative impact on others, authentic connection, of letting yourself be with, as opposed to striving after. Whatever it is, it will be a value (see Chapter 2), a direction guiding your ongoing actions, and less of a goal, or a designated end point. If it's a value, you'll feel something as well. It will matter. What is it in this open, aware, breathing, as-is moment? What stirs you and spurs you to move the work forward despite how intensely hard this moment is? We're not typically used to connecting with our core values in these reactive moments. At first, it feels downright unnatural. Practice, practice, my friends. And a dose of patience as well. Because without all the foregoing, it's very hard to . . .

Step 5: Leap

And now that you've clicked on with open awareness, have begun to create distance from rigid, reactive thoughts, and are allowing emotion to show up as mere energy in your system, and now that you've glanced in the direction that your values would steer you toward, you're ready to move. You're "leaping" with action consistent with your clinical values. Typically, your leap will be toward the right side of Figure 7.1.

It's only been a dozen or so seconds (though from the length of this section, it probably seems like you'll need days, not seconds), and you're making your move. The client is waiting and watching. Or perhaps the client

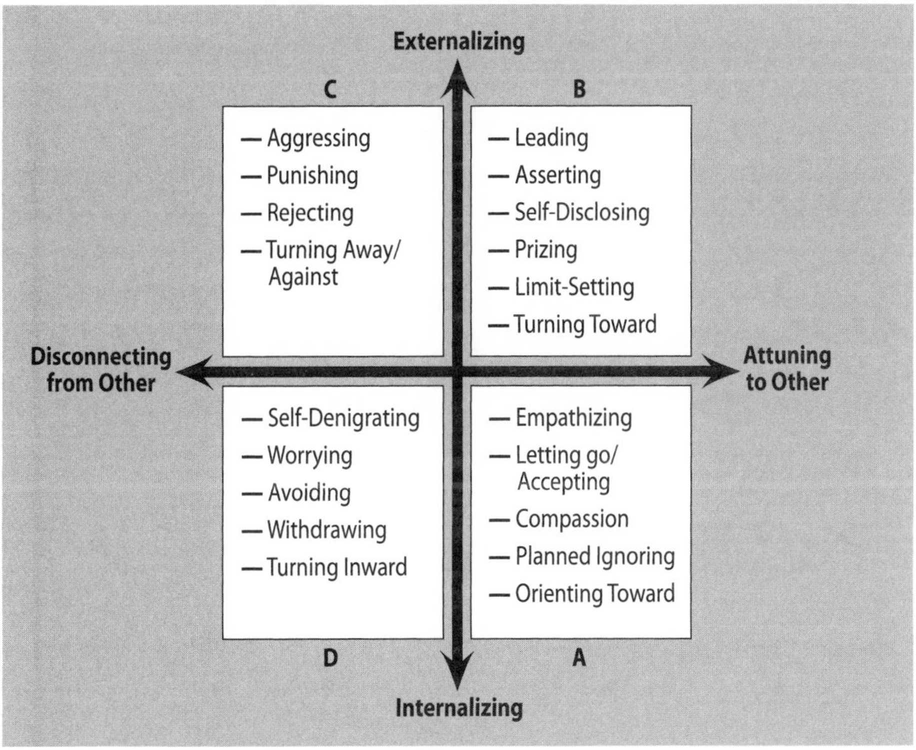

Figure 7.1 Interpersonal Process Grid

hasn't stopped and is still doing whatever it is that's sparked this moment in the first place. There's no right action to prescribe here because every moment of interaction has a snowflake's uniqueness of variables. There's no "insert action A into session moment B" instruction to follow. Don't go looking for it because you won't find it—or if you do, it will likely fail.

What's right is what follows and flows from what you've already done in these seconds. If you're Aware, if you've Paused for Perspective, and if you've Accepted what is, and have Looked toward the values guiding you and the work, then the Leap you'll take should be fairly clear (we'll discuss this in much more detail in Chapter 8). Instead of the fear-bred stumbling, the self-righteousness, the cold clinical withdrawal, or the outright nastiness (all on the left of the grid), you can move toward compassionate words or gestures, a necessary limit on the client's behavior, an artful waiting until the moment clears and the client is ready. You will do what makes the most emotional and clinical sense.

Am I saying that technique and treatment plans don't matter? Is mere clinical intuition and hunch enough to get the job done (well and ethically)? No. Of course your training, technical expertise, and facility with evidence-based treatments are critical. If you haven't had riding lessons and don't know your way around the animal, no matter how willing and open you are, you're going to end up eating cactus. What I'm saying is that when it comes to effectively managing your experiences of rage, despair, apathy, and fear in reaction to clients, you will fare much better in using these treatment tools if you're handling yourself internally with greater skill.

Remember, let yourself be APPALLed:

- Awareness . . .
- Pausing for Perspective . . .
- Acceptance . . .
- Looking toward values . . .
- Leaping into action . . .

LEAN IN

Before leaping into exploration of specific extreme clinician reactions, it seems important to pause for a moment. Sit where you won't be disturbed for a few minutes and close your eyes. As we've done throughout the book, settle into a centered space by noting the happenings and sensations in your body, as well as the immediate environment. What's here? Note the tone of your emotions, and gently touch thoughts that arise, merely noting their presence. Now, settle into the following meditation. Center yourself and consider . . .

- Why you came to this work in the first place . . .
- And what your intentions are when meeting with clients . . .
- And that you have suffered inside and outside of your interactions with these individuals—at times, intensely so . . .

- And you don't want to suffer, and that is why you've reacted as you have . . .
- And you are now willing to explore and hold it all . . .
- Because this—this entire situation with you and your work—matters a great deal . . .
- And there is no telling exactly where it might lead . . .

Open your eyes and note whatever seems important from the experience. How are you regarding the "is-ness" of what's been most painful about your clinical work?

____

____

____

None of us wants to suffer. And when we do as a result of our work, we and our clients deserve a new pattern. Let's look into that.

Managing the Samurai Within: What to Do With Rage and Disgust

There is a Zen parable in which a powerful samurai warrior came to the Master in search of the secret of life.

"Tell me the nature of heaven and hell," demanded the samurai.

The Master sat calmly and slowly looked up at the samurai whose armor was gleaming in the morning light. The Master smiled. "And why should I tell a despicable, worthless, ant of a man such as yourself?" he said. "What makes you—a lowly worm—think you deserve to know of such things?"

With a swift swirl of rage, the warrior withdrew his sword and held it above the Master's head, poised to strike down this thin, grizzled man who dared insult him.

Just before the samurai could bring down death on him, the Master pointed up to him and said, "That's hell."

The samurai dropped his sword and wrung his shaking hands. He could not believe that in a flash of anger he had almost been willing to murder a defenseless holy man. Tears dripped onto his intricately carved armor. He was fully aware of this man sitting before him whose words had, in a mere moment, taught him about the extremes of his impulses.

"That's heaven," said the Master.

* * *

In this story, a warrior's rage was just beneath the surface, easily stoked by a few simple words from the Master. Heaven and hell are the ready creations of our story-loving minds. As clinicians, we are storytellers just as much as anyone else. What we say to ourselves—how we frame a client—determines whether we end up hating or helping. Let's explore a practice for addressing the extremes of reactive anger during clinical interactions.

LEAN IN

Sit where you won't be disturbed and center yourself as we've practiced. After you've noted your surroundings, your body and breath, cue up a client toward whom you've experienced significant anger. Perhaps you've even hated working with this person. As we've done previously, with your body and mind centered, see if you can identify a few descriptive anchors that make this person and the behavior vivid. Hold these anchors in mind and allow the person to become as vivid in your imagination as possible. Now, let's walk through the steps to get you APPALLed by this client.

Step 1: Awareness. Breathe in slowly. . . . Open space around this client in your mind. The session is now happening at the edge of the Grand Canyon. Or perhaps a brightly starlit sky opens up above you as the person does whatever they've done that sparks so much anger in you.

Step 2: Pause for Perspective. Another breath. . . . What are you thinking? What thoughts are you having? Use defusion to stand clear. See them moving across the open space you've created. What's the emotion that's beginning? Give it a label as you exhale. Breathing in, note the thought you are having. Breathing out, touch with a single word to label to yourself whatever shows up emotionally (e.g., breathe in . . . "My mind is telling me this person is a hopeless addict who stole from me." Breathe out . . . "Touching disgust for him").

Step 3: Acceptance. Another breath. . . . Of course the client did this. Of course it's highly aversive to you (e.g., "I'm telling myself that I worked so hard for this guy, and this is how he treats me. Of course I'm disgusted by him because the work is stalled and I'm telling myself it's all his fault"). What is in this moment? Lean toward it. Catch any labels and breathe as you consider making the choice to say "don't know" and let it be in order to see what might happen.

Step 4: Look. "The direction that matters most to me in my work in general, and with this client in particular, is ______________________ ______________________." What feels most important about what you want to be doing in moments like these?

Step 5: Leap. What are you willing to commit to doing right now? What right-sided action will you take? List it here: ______________________ ______________________. (And do it now—or if the action requires the client's presence, take a step toward it by doing something in this moment to solidify your commitment. Schedule it, make a call to a colleague and publicly declare your intentions, whatever gets you moving instead of spiraling in anger and angst.)

In order to get out of anger hell with your more challenging clients, you'll need to cycle through these steps again and again. Practice makes patience. Your therapeutic samurai sword is better off in its scabbard anyway.

No Flinching: Dealing with Fear and Avoidance

Early in my clinical career, I was intent on being the best therapist this side of Freud. Siggy would have nothing on me, and I would prove it. I bought myself a pager and told my clients they could contact me day or night and I'd levitate them out of the muck of their suffering like some sort of psychotherapeutic Jedi knight. A client—I'll call him Tim—who presented with a diagnostic toss-up between narcissistic and borderline personality disorders was more than willing to take me up on my offer.

He'd page me at two in the morning and claim suicidal intent, only to come in the next day to the clinic and blame me for not being smart enough to give him solutions to his problems. He yelled at me, called me a "fake," and paged me just as I was drifting off into an apprehensive sleep only to tell me how much he needed to meet.

I got to the point where I was clipping my pager to the waistband of my pajamas and keeping it on vibrate so that it woke me and not my wife. Even if it wasn't Tim, I got jumpy whenever the pager rattled.

And then he did try to kill himself with an overdose of medication. "If I want to die, there's nothing you can do to stop me," he said in our first session after his discharge from the hospital.

I was edgy with my wife, slept poorly, was late to sessions with Tim, obsessed over my session notes for when I'd get sued for malpractice, and found myself white-knuckling my chair during sessions. The guy scared the crap out of me. Some Dr. Freud I turned out to be. If I'd had an analyst's couch like his in my office, I'd have crawled under it. The case was bigger than me. This client had called my egoistic bluff.

Managing fear is not rocket science. And the psychological science is clear—you have to move your way into and through it via exposure. I never really had the chance to do so with Tim. He dropped out of treatment suddenly. I worried—mostly about myself—for awhile. I was afraid he'd actually kill himself and I'd be held responsible in some way. With time, that fear gave way to regret that I hadn't done more earlier to get on top of things within myself. Maybe you can fare better.

A caveat: It's fairly obvious, but bears stating regardless, that if a client is overtly threatening you with imminent harm, it is not the time to practice mindful acceptance-based self-management. Fear originally evolved in us for a reason (i.e., saber-toothed tigers and the lot) and therefore you need to take the baring of teeth seriously, listen to your brain's alarm bells, and immediately act to protect yourself and others (see Chapter 11). Again, this is a mere restatement of what you already know, but without it, I'd feel remiss. I can imagine the complaint: "But he didn't say anything about threats and dangerous behavior from clients." I regret enough about my work with clients like Tim. I don't need to regret the lack of this reminder to you as well.

But let's assume it's not threatening behavior from a client, but instead behavior, or a pattern of interaction, that unnerves, overwhelms, and overall spooks you in some way. It's a pattern you find yourself shrinking from. Let's practice managing this sort of thing.

LEAN IN

Center yourself once again. Cue up a client toward whom you know you've experienced significant fear. Focus on someone you have found yourself avoiding in some notable way. Identify a few descriptive anchors that make this person and the behavior vivid. Hold these anchors in mind and allow the person to become as vivid in your mind's eye as possible.

Step 1: Awareness. Breathe in slowly. . . . Open space around this client. . . .

Step 2: Pause for Perspective. Another breath. . . . Notice thoughts. . . . Use your chosen defusion technique: ______________________. Breathe in the fear-laden thought and breathe out space-giving perspective. What is your one-word label for touching what's happening? What helps you see the whole situation, and not just the isolated behavior of your client? What's the big picture?

Step 3: Acceptance. Another breath. . . . What *is*? . . . Of course. . . . Lean toward the fear as you breathe in, creating space for it as you breathe out. Drop the judgment. Let go of the story. With fear present, mindful focus on a specific object can be helpful due to the mind's pull toward erratic and anxiety-exacerbating thinking in such moments. Fixing your focus on a specific point can help steady the mind until fear begins to subside. Try counting breaths (without controlling them), or repeating an acceptance-themed phrase to yourself (such as "I'm riding this").

Step 4: Look. "The direction that matters most to me in my work in general, and with this client in particular, is ______________________ ______________________." What feels most important about what you want to be doing in moments like these?

Step 5: Leap. What are you willing to commit to doing right now? What right-sided action will you take? List it here: ______________________ ______________ (and do something now). In particular, look to do things that turn you in the direction of what you've feared about the client, what you've been avoiding, and do them. If there's a conversation that needs to happen, a limit that needs setting (like no more 3 A.M. pages), then have the conversation and set the limit (see Chapter 10). If you have been afraid of the emotional intensity of a particular client, or of the feelings of incompetence the work elicits, find ways to be with the intensity, or redouble efforts to connect with your hopeless client.

Fear is the "easy" extreme in clinical work—easy to conceptualize, and easy to *not* work on at all.

Mindful of Venus: Ending the Dance With Desire

Just as you don't need much by way of reminder to not tolerate (and merely internally manage) threats from clients, you also don't need a lecture on not having sexual contact with them either. And yet, as you may also be aware, the literature has been clear that this obvious ethical and perhaps legal fence is regularly breached, and therefore deserves our attention. Among male psychologists responding to a survey, 6% reported having had sexual contact with a client (.6% of female psychologists endorsed/acknowledged contact), with 80% of these respondents admitting repeated contact (Holroyd & Brodsky, 1977). These surveys surely underreport what is a difficult-to-acknowledge pattern of behavior. Obviously, letting attraction for a client culminate in actual sexual contact is destructive to everyone involved. The focus of discussion here is what to do with desire itself, in all of its forms, as it manifests for clinicians within their work.

Let's just get it out there: As much as reactivity is universal among clinicians, so is "desire." It's just not talked about as much (for obvious reasons linked to fear of others' scorn). Research suggests though that more than 84% of therapists (again, likely an underestimate) become sexually attracted to a client at some point during their practice of psychotherapy (Pope et al., 1986; Rodolfa et al., 1994). Here are some other notable findings in the literature:

- In a small qualitative study of therapists, all six participants reported sexual or erotic feelings toward clients within therapy, and also experienced feelings of shame and embarrassment (Rodgers, 2011).
- In a sample of predoctoral psychology interns or trainees, only half disclosed their feelings of desire or attraction for clients to their su-

pervisors. They also indicated that "desire" included both physical and interpersonal or emotional aspects (Ladany et al., 1997).

- Supervisory input and appropriate training was viewed as important, and often insufficiently accessed and offered in addressing clinician desire as it manifests with clients (Ladany et al., 1997; Rodgers, 2011).
- A sample of clinicians agreed on the inappropriateness of boundary violations with clients at the extremes, and yet expressed more variability of opinion regarding fantasy, flirtation, and physical touch with clients. Minor boundary violations were viewed as precursors to more serious behavior (Martin, Godfrey, Meekums, & Madill, 2011).

As a field, it appears we have not done enough to bring the issue of clinicians' management of desire out into the open. Mostly out of shame and anticipated derision, we ignore the elephant of attraction that shows up in our work—attraction at physical, emotional, social, intellectual, and even spiritual levels. With regard to the physical, "our hormones do not differentiate which members of the opposite sex are off limits. So we try to ignore our needs for intimacy, for sexual contact, for friendship with clients" (Kottler, 1993, p. 86).

A mere repressive, control-oriented response to clinician desire simply won't work. As therapist and author Jeffrey Kottler goes on to say, "there is usually a theme of 'stifle yourself' juxtaposed with encouragement to be authentic" (1993, p. 88). And there's the bind—clinicians are trained to be open and connected to clients, but to shut down and disconnect from the common, human pulls toward connection at all levels. We must go beyond moralistic "just say no" admonitions and face desire head on, learning to manage it, and managing even to learn from it.

LEAN IN

Think back across the span of your clinical work—all the clients you've worked with over time. Let yourself mentally acknowledge the clients toward whom you experienced feelings of desire of some sort. What shows up in your thoughts and feelings at this mere recognition? Ask yourself: How willing am I to lean toward and learn from these experiences? How willing am I to begin exploring them with colleagues and supervisors I trust? What shows up for you at the suggestion of doing so?

Again, mere denial of desire is a significant piece of the problem. We need to open ourselves and each other to how to best manage attraction before clients' boundaries are dashed and before we do significant damage to those we agreed to help.

LEAN IN

Take any of the clients from your past for whom you've experienced desire and cue them up in your mind once you've centered yourself. Allow yourself to review how desire manifested in you, and what you did or might have done. Instead of our normal practice in this book of working to create distance from our experience, here allow yourself to fuse as tightly as possible with the experience that emerges. Let the story play itself out. Follow the desire where it leads. Allow the movie to happen.

Take a deep, slow breath. Clear your mind. Think of your image of vast open space.

And now, let your mind gravitate toward thoughts and reactions to everything that might result from your continued fusion with this desire. What are all the actions and consequences that could possibly occur? Allow yourself to brainstorm as many possibilities as you can and list them below:

What is the "cost" of the sum total of these actions? What is lost and what will this mean for you, the client, and your work?

____

____

____

How typical is it for you to process these experiences as you have thus far in this chapter? Isn't it a tad odd for a trained, competent, compassionate clinician like yourself to delve into this aspect of your experience? And notice that as well. . . . Your mind is likely running around like it's on fire right now. Let it burn. You won't get better at managing your extreme reactions, and desire is more likely to get in the way of your work, without this brutal honesty and willingness to sort through it, learn, and expand your self-understanding.

When I was in training there was little (if any) discussion of desire. Group supervision with fellow graduate students (my friends and colleagues) as well as a faculty supervisor (whom I respected and hoped would regard me similarly) was the model of training. Needless to say, a difficult topic felt impossible in such a context. I can't stress enough how important it is to begin discussing these experiences (and all inner reactions to the work) with others. Don't stop with your self-explorations here in this book. Do yourself and your clients a favor and give the elephant a solid kick in the shins.

Before leaving desire behind, let's do a final practice. Here, instead of the past, we'll take a look at a current (or at least very recent) client. And speaking of leaving desire, a quote from French novelist Marcel Proust is relevant. In his multivolume novel *Remembrance of Things Past,* Proust (1925) wrote that "we do not succeed in changing things according to our desire, but gradually our desire changes." You won't likely change the client or aspects of yourself that initially sparked the attraction to emerge, and yet you can, with practice, learn to allow the desire to dissipate, to have less impact on the work. As author and meditation teacher Sylvia Boorstein has noted, "waiting around allows us to see that the desire itself is just mind energy. . . . If we recognize it as just an energy, we realize it's not an imperative to action" (1995, p. 78). So let's hurry up and wait a bit.

Let's have a go at letting go of the "mind energy" of desire arising during interactions with our clients.

LEAN IN

Center yourself once again. Cue up a client you know you're overly drawn toward (again, use a broad definition of desire to include emotional and intellectual in addition to physical pulls—the main criterion is that the desire alters your boundaries such that your work with the client may suffer). Focus on someone you find yourself thinking or fantasizing about, and talking about and behaving toward in a manner that suggests blurriness in the boundaries of the work. Identify a few descriptive anchors that make this person and his or her behavior vivid. In particular, focus on the aspects or characteristics that most readily elicit the attraction reaction in you. Hold these anchors in mind and allow the person to become as vivid in your mind's eye as possible.

Step 1: Awareness. Breathe in slowly. . . . Open space around this client. . . .

Step 2: Pause for Perspective. Another breath. . . . Notice thoughts. . . . Use your chosen defusion technique: ________________________. Breathe in the attraction-laden thought and breathe out space-giving perspective. What is your one-word label for what's happening? Work to get distance from what is showing up in your thoughts and emotions.

Step 3: Acceptance. Another breath. . . . What *is*? . . . Of course. . . . Lean toward your experience as you breathe in, creating space for it as you breathe out. Drop the judgment. Let go of the story. Accept the energy of the attraction, while simultaneously letting go of the narrative that stokes the fire. . . . Let the energy be and watch as it changes on its own. . . . Try to merely note this energy without following after it too closely. You're dispassionately riding the wave versus passionately letting it wash over you. Watch the thoughts and physiological reactions as they emerge as mere passing things (like clouds or particles of dust). Watch for any signs of it changing on its own.

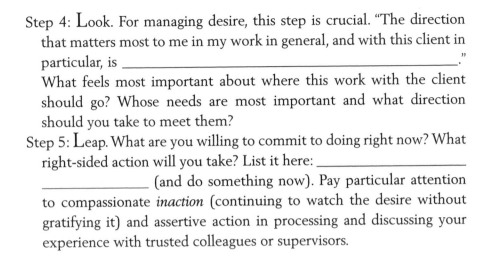

Step 4: Look. For managing desire, this step is crucial. "The direction that matters most to me in my work in general, and with this client in particular, is ____."
What feels most important about where this work with the client should go? Whose needs are most important and what direction should you take to meet them?

Step 5: Leap. What are you willing to commit to doing right now? What right-sided action will you take? List it here: ____________________ ______________ (and do something now). Pay particular attention to compassionate *inaction* (continuing to watch the desire without gratifying it) and assertive action in processing and discussing your experience with trusted colleagues or supervisors.

Ideally, you will consistently practice getting APPALLed by the desire that shows up in you. By working proactively with these feelings, you will prevent damaging boundary violations, and perhaps learn important clinically useful information regarding patterns of action and reaction between you and your clients. One key in doing so is to remember self-compassion and to not beat yourself up for experiencing these thoughts and feelings. Desire can lead to a great deal of self-flagellation—a topic to which we now turn.

Out of the Hole: Managing Shame

You would think I would have learned from what Kurt Vonnegut said about failure that day in graduate school. Alas, just a few short years later, toward the end of my training, I made a fairly egregious mistake. I was working in a youth correctional facility (for boys who had committed fairly serious violent, sexual, or drug offenses). I was both the individual and group therapist for one particular inner-city boy who presented for his first therapy session in stereotypical streetwise fashion. He denied ever having raped a much younger female cousin a handful of years earlier. He sported self-carved tattoos and wore his jeans as slack as he could without guards giving him grief about it.

But in that first individual session, for whatever reason, this "thug"—this tough guy who refused to admit what he'd done (and it was well documented, and he was required by the courts to complete our treatment program in order to be released on time)—broke down and began crying. He told me about how his mother was battling cancer and things were not looking good. He said that doctors had said she was likely to die while he was still locked up. I chalked his opening up to my skill as a budding therapist.

I took the credit and decided I'd push him to the next level in our following session. "So if you want to go home to be with your mom as soon as you can, you need to own up to what you did to your cousin. You need to talk about it in group," I said. From how he slumped forward and looked down at the carpet, I felt a surge of something wrong. I knew I'd messed up. He told me I could go do something not so nice to myself.

Instead of worrying about this young client of mine in those moments after our session, I focused on myself. I walked to my supervisor's office for some sort of absolution. Supervision often had a sort of confessional feel for me in those days. "It's good you recognize your mistake with him," said my supervisor. I felt I deserved a public flogging, and this guy was praising me. I received no reprimand. My supervisor looked at me and said, "He was real with you, so maybe you should think about being real with him."

I walked this boy to a bench outside the school building where we both had a good view of the razor wire–topped security fence in the distance. "I screwed up when I tried to make you talk about things by bringing up your mom," I said. I remember the words coming halting and hesitant; how they should when you are finding your way over new ground. "It was really wrong for me to take what you had the guts to tell me and try to use it against you." In psychotherapy, in trying too hard to be right, the therapist sometimes misses the mark; sometimes the therapist pierces the client.

What makes us feel ashamed (or incompetent) in our work? One study found that therapists felt the worst in reaction to resistance from clients, as well as their lack of appropriate management of countertransference (Sandell, Ronnas, & Schubert, 1992). Basically, if we feel shoved around and blocked by clients, or if we're not managing ourselves well, shame can set in. For some, there might be a vicious cycle of ruminating about errors and incompetence that further impairs clinicians' ability to effectively navigate the situation with their clients. Impaired interpersonal problem solving has been demonstrated experimentally for people who are already dysphoric and are prompted to ruminate about their actions (Lyubomirsky & Nolen-Hoeksema, 1995). When we get stuck in our heads poking at ourselves for mistakes and at the client's resistance to our valiant efforts to help, we can make tough situations worse. We suffer, and so does the work.

As Kurt Vonnegut told us that day while I was in graduate school, we will all certainly fail. It doesn't mean that we should mire ourselves in shame, and further bog down our potential to intervene effectively. That would be APPALLing (sick of this yet? . . . At least you'll remember it). Mindfulness and acceptance skills can again be useful. We need more flexible thinking as to our blameworthiness and we need to take committed action in the service of the values guiding the work.

LEAN IN

Center yourself once again. Cue up a client you worked with when you know you experienced shame. Focus on someone you have blamed yourself for underserving—someone you've kept yourself on the hook for. Identify a few descriptive anchors that make this person and his or her behavior vivid. Hold these anchors in mind and allow the person to become as real in your mind's eye as possible.

Step 1: Awareness. As we've practiced, breathe in slowly. . . . Open space around this client. . . .

Step 2: Pause for Perspective. Another breath. . . . Notice thoughts. . . . Use your chosen defusion technique: ________________________. Breathe in the shameful thinking and breathe out space-giving perspective. What is your one-word label for touching what's happening?

Step 3: Acceptance. Another breath. . . . What *is*? . . . Of course. . . . Lean toward the shame as you breathe in, creating space for it as you breathe out. Drop the judgment. Let go of the story. Let go of blame and intent. Yes, you did what you did. It had ripple effects. . . . *So now what?* How is it helping your current work to lash yourself? What are all of the things that went into causing you to act as you did? Think of everything that went into that situation with your client. Were you as aware of things then as you are now? Of course your perspective was more limited at the time.

Step 4: Look. "The direction that matters most to me in my work in general, and with this client in particular, is ____________________ ____________________." What feels most important about what you want to be doing in moments like these?

Step 5: Leap. What are you willing to commit to doing right now? What right-sided action will you take? List it here: ____________________ ____________ (and do something now).

The self-management steps are the same for each extreme reaction. The situations and the content of the interaction with your clients, as well as the specifics of your patterning and theirs, are quite distinct. The overall process of what ideally happens inside you to manage the reactions is the same. It all boils down to a more flexible emotional and cognitive response that opens up possibilities instead of further hardening the moment into a spiral of negativity between you and your clients. Obviously, these are the very same skills we would like to see develop within our clients.

You may not be a mindfulness or acceptance-based clinician in what you technically offer your clients, and yet it's my conviction that the best interventions flow out of a mindful, accepting stance within you as a person. You don't need to claim an engineer's expertise to ride a train, but you do need to trust in the mechanics and the physics that drive the thing forward on the rails in order to get where you are heading. It's similar with your work—mindfulness, perspective, acceptance, and valuing are skills that you don't have to explicitly preach to your clients, but your work will roll forward if you assume their relevance and apply them as your internal fuel.

Hope for the Clinical Flatliner: Arising From Apathy

My client, Jill, was one of the saddest sacks I've ever worked with. That's how I regarded her before the end of our time together—a sad sack of do-nothingness that depressed me almost as much as she depressed herself. This woman came religiously to every appointment (until she precipitously dropped out of treatment) and seemed to have made a religion of malaise. My toddler's whining pales in comparison to Jill's endless bloodletting and bemoaning in each and every session.

Over the year or so of the work, I went from compassion, to confusion, to complete fusion with thoughts of her as hopeless and beyond not just my, but anyone's, ability to help. "I can't do it!" she'd wail. I'm not sure how many times I watched her sob in session in the recounting of the smallest of life stressors. Her dog snubbed her one day over a lack of treats in the house, and you'd think a car had run the pooch over.

I found myself numb in response to her expressions of pain. Even worse, I found her pain annoying. "Suck it up," went my mind's chatter. "Do something—anything—to help yourself already."

Then I went into session one day with a plan. I would motivate her to reach out to her estranged half-sister and merely say hello. Maybe just call during the day when her sister would be at work and leave a brief but pleasant voice mail on her machine. My client would certainly have the time to do this since she hadn't held a job in over 10 years. With no advance notice of my plan, I plopped the phone book down in front of my client.

"Today, we're going to call Edith," I said. "Actually, I'm looking for you to call her. That's your task before the end of today's session. We'll do it and see how it makes you feel."

Jill burst into tears. After a few minutes of blubbering, she looked at me from behind her wadded tissues. "You do it. . . . I can't."

I pressed her, and felt confident in the plan. Her depression would not lift if I merely empathized with her. The literature was clear that she needed to start taking action within a cognitive-behavioral model of change. That was Jill's best shot.

In reality, this plan was really my own best shot . . . at getting Jill out of my hair. And it worked. She never came back after that session.

Clearly, I was struggling with Jill. My empathy, due to the barrage of Jill's low mood and lack of agency, gave way to apathy. And not being willing to face my reactions, I defaulted (in full fusion fashion) toward a shove that at some subconscious level I knew would drive her out of my office. Apathy is perhaps the hardest extreme reaction to manage (at least for me). I was highly shaped by friends, family, teachers, and supervisors for high-wire achievement. To dwell in do-nothingness was unfathomable. Clearly, my reactions were a great defense—not so much against outside forces as against what I was unwilling to have within.

Once a supervisor asked me what the opposite of love was. I said, as most everyone would, that, of course, hate was the answer. "No," he said. "It's indifference." Relationship research has shown that patterns of withdrawal from one's partner are predictive of divorce (Christensen, 1990), and psychologist John Gottman (1999) lists "stonewalling" (withdrawing from interaction) as one of the "Four Horsemen" (along with criticism, defensiveness, and contempt) of the poor and at-risk marriage. While contempt and overall negative emotional reciprocity are the best predictors of divorce, apathy isn't anything to dismiss. When we don't care, we don't do the work that needs to be done to improve a difficult situation. We, as clinicians, can't afford apathy. Let's perk up this Debbie downer of a section with a bit of practice.

LEAN IN

Here we go—last time for this chapter. Center yourself again. Cue up a client toward whom you know you've experienced significant apathy. Focus on someone you found yourself giving up on, or not caring how the work turned out. Identify a few descriptive anchors that make this person and his or her behavior vivid. Hold these anchors in mind and allow the person to become as vivid in your mind's eye as possible.

Step 1: Awareness. Breathe in slowly. . . . Open space around this client, around yourself as you've sat, distant and disengaged, with this person. . . .

Step 2: Pause for Perspective. Another breath. . . . Notice thoughts. . . . Use your chosen defusion technique: __________________________. Breathe in the dark, thick, or perhaps heavy thoughts you have about this client and the work, and breathe out space-giving perspective. What is your one-word label for touching what's happening in your interactions with this person? What conclusions have you drawn about your client, the work, yourself? How can you see these as the conjuring of your ever-babbling mind?

Step 3: Acceptance. Another breath. . . . What *is*? . . . Of course. . . . Lean toward the apathy as you breathe in, creating space for it as you breathe out. Drop the judgment. Let go of the story. Take in whatever feelings coagulate around this apathy—give them physical qualities (e.g., hard, dark, bland, gritty, gray, deathly silent, dark). Breathe them in and breathe space in among, around, and through them. Notice any impulse to shove them away, and instead allow them to reside as they are. Watch what happens as you continue to breathe.

Step 4: Look. "The direction that matters most to me in my work in general and, despite my current feelings, the one I'd most want to head with this client in particular is ______________________________ ____________________." What feels most important about what you want to be doing?

Step 5: Leap. What are you willing to commit to doing right now? What right-sided action will you take? List it here: ____________________ ________________ (and do something now). Are you willing to do something despite any screaming from your mind to do nothing?

I'm betting you're aware of psychologist Martin Seligman's (1975) research and writing on the concept of learned helplessness. Here, using the strategies we've been practicing, we're looking for a pinch of learned hopefulness when our work with clients seems most dismal and lacking, when we've all but given up.

As you practice with these skills and work with any apathy arising in your professional doings, I have found it helpful to remember to hold all outcomes lightly. As we've discussed, focusing exclusively on goals for your work can breed apathy when nothing seems to be panning out. In addition, our focus on outcomes can, at times, get in clients' way. "In the absence of attachment to results, the therapist creates an atmosphere of acceptance within which the patient can increase understanding of his or her own behavior, of Self, and way of living" (Kopp, 1977, p. 102). Remember: Good? Bad? Who knows?

You can't control outcomes, but you can control what you focus your mind on. How can you define success from within the frame of your process (versus content) with clients? Instead of "resolving my client's depression" as the marker for good work, how about telling yourself, "Anytime I lean in toward my urge to give up, and yet do something to try to help anyway, and help my client to lean in and try as well, I am successful in my work." Do you see the connection with values, as opposed to goals, here? The former is focused on content and outcomes that can't be controlled. The latter is process or ongoing directed action that can. Apathy dissipates in the face of clinicians who are willing to continually loosen their professional identity into a process perspective. So go forth and adjust your "Success-o-Meter." I dare you to give Kurt Vonnegut a nudge to roll over a bit in his grave. You can do so if you're willing to keep failure at bay by refusing to fuse with apathy-breeding definitions of your worth as a clinician.

A final pointer: Apathy requires close monitoring in one's role as a clinician. It is here (as with all of the more extreme reactions) that it's crucial to seek out and maintain supportive contact with supervisors and colleagues (I'd recommend both). As we've already discussed, clinicians have underreported the degree of distress and despair resulting from their work. We are mere mortals and are just as (if not more) susceptible to the spirals of depression as any other professional group. We need others who hold us with care and compassion to willingly hold up mirrors to our functioning and help us awaken to the implications of our reflected pain. We cannot abide the far reaches of our work alone.

* * *

With the conclusion of this chapter, we end our discussion (but hopefully you're just beginning your regular practice) of the skills for internal self-management of reactivity in the midst of clinical work. Before embarking on the second portion of the book and its focus on in-the-moment, what-to-do skills for building alliance and intervention effectiveness with clients, it's important to do one last bit of internal work. We need to become grateful.

Research has explored the role of cultivating one's experience of gratitude in well-being and overall functioning. People who regularly experience and express gratitude are more likely to report increased subjective well-being and life satisfaction (Froh, Sefick, & Emmons, 2008; Krause, 2006). Gratitude also may prove important in maintaining interpersonal bonds, with data suggesting that romantic partners who feel appreciated and show appreciation of each other are more committed and responsive to one another (Gordon, Impett, Kogan, Oveis, & Keltner, 2012). Perhaps it behooves us as clinicians to do what we can to cultivate appreciation for our clients, even those who press us against the sharpest edges of our experience. What might happen if we intentionally rest in gratitude, and how might it buffer and lift us up when the worst shows up in our reactions?

LEAN IN

In a quiet place, spend a few minutes centering yourself as we've practiced. Move from inside your body to touch what is there in your environment, and then back inside to your thoughts and emotions, witnessing what is there in this moment. Once you've centered, move gently through each of the following objects of focus:

1. A person with whom you are deeply connected who has helped or given to you in some way. See his or her face and allow yourself to connect with the feeling of appreciation and gratitude. Try to let go of thoughts and stories and merely feel the gratitude. Let it emerge.
2. A colleague or friend who has recently helped or given to you. See the person in your mind's eye and connect with the feeling of gratitude. Let it build within you. Don't force anything. If the feeling of gratitude arises—great. If not, merely note your appreciation.
3. A client with whom you've formed a strong alliance and have done important work recently. See this person and your recent exchanges. Consider how this work has benefited the client, and how the opportunity to meet together has benefited you. As before, allow yourself to access the feelings as much as possible. Wish the client continued growth and positive change.
4. A difficult client with whom you've struggled—when the interaction has been difficult, perhaps even resulting in extreme reactions in you. Before you get tangled and fused with stories and judgments about

this client and yourself, consider whether there are aspects of this client, your work together, and you as a professional and a person that you (even in a small or indirect way) can acknowledge appreciation for. Again, is this work good or bad—Who knows? Can you be grateful for something this client has taught you, or something about yourself that has been revealed that will benefit you and your work in some way? How might others have benefited from your interactions with this client? Notice your mind gravitating toward any of the bad thoughts, conclusions, or consequences and gently come back to your review of what can be appreciated. Take the time to generate as many possibilities as you can. Write them down. Connect with any gratitude that arises, and if none does, accept this as where things are at the moment, and ask if you are willing to keep working to cultivate it.

Wish all the people you've connected with in this exercise their own experience of well-being and gratitude. Wish them safety, success, and release from any suffering. Wish it for yourself as well before ending and returning to tasks at hand.

I would recommend returning to this practice as regularly as possible. Carve out time daily if possible, or at least weekly, to plant seeds of gratitude, even for your difficult clients, and for yourself after you've been reactive and flooded by the work. This is not mere Stuart Smalley–style positive thinking. This is the hard yet fruitful work of someone who is willing to extend the borders of practice as broadly as possible. There is courage in entering the world with a daily dose of gratitude. The world may not initially agree with your stance, but it will feel the impact. The ripple effects can't possibly be apprehended, though they can, and hopefully will, be appreciated.

MAP CHECK

Take a moment and review what we've covered in this chapter. What was one aspect, one piece of content, that resonated with you, that sparked your interest, curiosity, or even angst in some way?

Why did this matter to you? What makes this worth writing about? Worth your focus and effort? What is the gravity that this carries for you and your work?

What is one specific action you can take within the next 24 hours related to this issue that feels as though it would be important and has the potential to move you in the direction of what matters?

≺ PART II ≻

Effective Use of Reactivity Management Skills to Enhance Clinical Work

≺ CHAPTER EIGHT ≻

Knowing When to Hold 'Em and When to Fold 'Em

The Role of Timing in Effective Intervention

I WAS INTENT on beating out my academic rival for top-dog status during our senior year of college. This other guy—a 17-year-old child prodigy international student—and I were neck-and-neck for valedictorian laurels heading into the fall semester. I needed a plan to pad my GPA and give myself an edge. The clouds parted one day there in the mountains of northeast Tennessee and the academic gods shone down with the answer: "Go forth and take tennis!" Instead of loading up on yet another challenging English or history course, I'd backhand my way to top honors. I could not claim genius with the idea; it was divine inspiration.

Unfortunately, my timing was off. In both the mechanics of actually playing tennis and my decision to intervene with an "easy A" course, my actions were faulty. Long story short, the written tests were "unfair" in their pickiness regarding the rules of the game (note my blaming of the coach). The ball machine was a relentless juggernaut of shame leading me to want to chuck my racket toward the far court where my erring return shots often landed. (Do you see any acceptance-related issues here?) I left class often feeling like that player whose arthritic grandmother could best him in straight sets. (Where was perspective-taking intervention when I most needed it?) The prodigy ended up with the valedictory double asterisk next to his name on our commencement program, and I had to settle with just one asterisk next to mine. I was so focused on my failure that I almost missed the import of the moment when my rival walked up to me, diploma in hand, brushed his tassel aside from his face, and told me that he admired my mind. The prodigy not only had a leg up on me with .0001 of a grade point, he, at a mere 17, had a developmental edge in compassionate, right-sided action as well.

I didn't realize I'd just had a lesson in timing, and that I would need to keep learning about it in order to get anywhere close to decent in my clinical work. Another lesson came some years later in graduate school during a supervision session. My supervisor, an unassuming man who had the magnetic power that comes from inner calm and consistent focus on others, watched me patiently as I talked. I was recounting recent sessions with clients when I'd felt stymied. I was telling him ad nauseam about how I was falling short of the expectations I'd set for them, the therapy, and ultimately myself. I remember the relaxed gaze he had for me that afternoon. My recollection is that this was his default—he made compassion look automatic, somehow easy to manifest in the muscles of the face, the receptive focus of the eyes.

My supervisor was silent until I sat back and looked out the window of his office. It was as if he somehow knew which moment was required for an intervention. It was as if he knew I needed to exhale fully before I'd be able to breathe in what he had to offer. He slowly leaned forward toward me, held up a hand, and balled it tight into a fist. "I wonder whether you need to always be like *this* with yourself," he said, his fist shaking ever so slightly in the air between us like something coming alive on a tree branch, something wriggling free of its cocoon.

And that was all he said that I can remember of the conversation. I'm sure we moved on to other things, continuing our processing and planning of my upcoming sessions, and yet I was left with the ripple effect of his perfectly timed gesture. I indeed needed to work (and still do, though I'm better) on letting go of controlling the outcomes of my work.

How do I know his intervention was well timed? Because it resonated with me then, helping me to experience myself and the unhelpful process I was locked in and was not fully aware of, and also because it resonates for me even now. It sparked new, creative connections for me. I regularly tell colleagues and trainees of this experience. It was one of those interventions that rolls gently to your feet, and then ironically explodes like a perfectly placed compassion hand grenade. How did he know the "when" of this piece of supervisory handiwork? Why is this even important for us to discuss?

LEAN IN

Circle any of the following statements that sound familiar to you—that you've noticed yourself saying or thinking about your interactions with clients:

"I think I was 'off' during the session today."
"The client and I seemed to be missing each other."
"That didn't go as well as I'd hoped it would."
"Well, that was sure a disaster!"
"The client completely threw me today."
"I was scrambling in session—I had no idea what to do next."
"I'm working hard to come up with what to do or say with this client."

Ask yourself: How do I know *when* to intervene? Take a moment and write a few sentences describing your current model for managing the timing of your actions during interactions with clients. What are your choice points, and how do you determine them? Don't worry about how valid or articulate your model currently is. Just write what shows up as your current paradigm.

____

____

____

Now ask yourself: How concerned am I by the thoughts/statements I circled above that show up in my work? What are their implications, along with my current model of intervention timing, if they continue as is? How workable are they?

1	2	3	4	5
Not Workable		Somewhat Workable		Very Workable

Based on your sense of the feasibility of your timing-related thoughts, how willing are you to work toward a new model of managing the "whens" of your work? I'm only asking because this is no small task. How was it for you learning to ride a bike? Did the timing come easily? Now you're older and more stuck in your ways. You'll have to be willing to catch and interrupt old habits and adopt new patterns. Still interested? Note your degree of willingness to work on your model of intervention timing:

1	2	3	4	5
Not Willing		Somewhat Willing		Very Willing

The Air We Breathe in Session: A New Model for Regulating Clinical Timing

Let me be perfectly honest with you before we embark on a new understanding of intervention timing. This model is unpatented—it's brand, spanking new and untested. It fits with my own clinical experience, and my best understanding of the work of colleagues and trainees, but it's shiny and right out of the box. And like all new products, it may have some kinks to work out. Why then am I proposing that you, kind reader, adopt my newfangled concoction? The answer is simple: In all of my research for this chapter, I found very little, next to nothing actually, in the research literature (or clinical and practice writings for that matter) on understanding and honing one's skills for intervention timing in clinical work. There were a few references (that we'll consult in a moment), but I was struck by the lack of attention to the topic. Not surprising considering the lack of hands raised when I ask workshop participants if they've ever had specific timing-related training.

We wouldn't want our surgeons to have poor timing skills when things go awry on the operating table, so why should we be content with leaving our skills to the whims of sentiments such as "you pick it up through experience" or "good supervisors help you learn it"? Of course these are true, but what if our experiences and our supervisors teach us poor models of when? How will we improve? How will we even know our timing is off?

Think about it—if your interventions are consistently poorly timed, clients won't necessarily give you feedback (because they either won't care to tell you, will be too put off, or will vote with their prematurely terminating feet—remember my depressed client and the phone book intervention? It took years for me to realize that my timing may have been a central factor). We need a system for monitoring our interventions, and we need skills for managing feedback loops so that we can—in true Kenny Rogers gambler style—"know when to hold 'em and know when to fold 'em." Let's begin with a brief overview of this shiny new model (more of a metaphor, actually).

What if your home's thermostat was not regulating things appropriately and your furnace kicked on at all the wrong times? What would the atmosphere of your household be like? How conducive would the environment be to completing the tasks at hand in your home? I'm betting that if your thermostat was out of whack, you'd be highly motivated to get it straightened out. A call to a technician (or a handy older brother like mine) would rise to the top of your to-do list. You need your thermostat to know the "when," the timing, of intervening to keep the temperature in your house within reasonable, livable limits. You need the same homeostatic, self-regulating control of timing in your clinical work as well.

I've already apologized for my metaphor addiction, so please permit me a further indulgence. Figure 8.1 summarizes the metaphor I'm proposing for you that will hopefully, with consistent application, assist you in improving your intervention timing. As you can see, it's a summary of all we've covered thus far. When clients pull, poke, avoid, attack, and self-destruct before our eyes, in true furnace fashion . . .

- They pump the air of heated experience into the room with us. . . .
- The difficult moments resolve, and the stuffiness recedes with our use of perspective and emotional distance-giving filters. . . .
- As well as skill for willingly opening our vents wide and being with our experience as is. . . .
- As well as for channeling, via thoughtfully laid ductwork, our experience (and our energy) in the direction of the guiding values of the work.

Thermostat	Mindfulness-based attending/tracking
Furnace/AC unit	Client difficult behavior
Air	Clinician experience (thoughts, feelings, sensations)
Air filter	Defusion/perspective skills
Air vents	Willingness/acceptance/"being with" skills
Ductwork	Guiding values

Figure 8.1 "Clean Air" Metaphor of Intervention Timing

While this is a metaphoric mouthful, it basically boils down to developing habits and skills for monitoring the here-and-now of clinical interactions—taking in what is in a flexible fashion and using mindfulness and perspective-taking skills to determine when to intervene.

This is what we've spent the first portion of the book covering—the inner skills of clinician self-management. We've worked on laying down the mechanics of a well-ventilated, open-air office. The rest of the book covers what we do after we've managed ourselves internally—once we're more skilled at breathing in what the furnace sends our way. And in order to act to help address the client's own furnace and get it in fine working order, we need to know when to connect with it—when it needs an intervention. We need a system, a thermostat, for our sense of clinical timing.

Help! My Thermostat Is Busted! (or, the Barriers to Good Clinical Timing)

Imagine you have a rather scattered, befuddled colleague, Dr. Oliver Theplace, and he's coming to you for a consultation. He's looking for your input regarding his work with a particularly difficult client. You smirk a bit as Oliver describes his client because you've been here before with him—he tends to repeat the same patterns with a number of clients and, for some reason, he likes coming to you for feedback. Like it or not, Oliver Theplace finds you helpful. "Where did you learn your intuitive sense of what to do with these trickier clients?" he asks. What Oliver has not been trained to understand is that the wheres and whats of the work are less relevant to getting unstuck than a good sense of when.

Instead of getting mired in a discussion about yourself and your training, you move the conversation forward with Oliver. You pause a moment, center yourself, and look directly at him. "So tell me about this client of yours." Though you have any number of your own clinical concerns to attend to, and even though there's an irritating nasal whine to Oliver's voice, and despite his fingernail-on-chalkboard tendency to say "yeah" in agreement before you've even finished a thought, you focus on what he might hope to take away from the consultation. You think about Oliver's clients and how his learning more about the junctures in his sessions when he might intervene will likely lead to dramatic improvements in his work. You listen for the obstacles to good clinical timing.

Obstacle 1: Theoretical Gridlock

Oliver leans back in his chair and scratches his chin in a show of intellectual confidence. "Clearly, my client has been intermittently reinforced throughout her life by her loved ones, and even her previous therapist, for her self-injurious behaviors." Oliver nods in response to his swelling certainty. "Therefore I have very consciously and consistently refused to reinforce her attempts to get my approval of her attention-seeking behavior during our sessions. . . . And therefore, because I'm not giving her the reinforcement she has been shaped to expect from others, she's reacting with an extinction burst of acting-out behavior during our time together."

Is Oliver wrong? Is his training as a behavioral psychologist leading him astray? Larson (1980), in a survey of practicing therapists, noted that while they tended to align with a single theoretical perspective, 65% acknowledged endorsement and integration of aspects of other orientations in their practices. This willingness on the part of clinicians to be influenced is key. Oliver is not necessarily inaccurate—it may indeed be useful to conceptualize his client's behavior in terms of contingencies of social reinforcement. The problem is that once he's hit the nail on the head with this conceptualization, he tends to see every situation, and every similar client, as a nail deserving the same theoretical hammer strike.

In the language of Acceptance and Commitment Therapy (itself an offshoot of traditional behavioral psychology), Oliver has experientially fused with his theory—he is a behavioral psychologist, and his client is exhibiting maladaptive behavior due to schedules of reinforcement. This rigid identification with theory creates risk for problems and ruptures in the therapeutic relationship. Oliver will be more likely to label and categorize his client's behavior versus engaging it, being moved by it, and responding authentically and with well-timed intervention. I'm not saying theory is bad. Theory should inform the work, but the work should not be made to conform to it. What makes more sense while hiking in the wilderness? To consult the map, but then be willing to shift course based on the lay of the land, or to plunge headlong into a river's raging rapids just because the map indicates it should only be a quaint, meandering stream?

This is no plea for vacuous eclecticism. Being grounded in a particular theoretical orientation adds depth and richness to one's understanding of human functioning, as well as providing a range of techniques informed by this understanding. Throwing the theoretical kitchen sink at clients runs the risk of leaving you listless and inconsistent in your work—too quick to shift to another approach in search of an effective silver bullet—and it may leave both you and the client highly frustrated and confused. By all means, hold a perspective, but just hold it; don't give it a death grip.

Obstacle 2: Drowning in Floodwaters

Your feckless friend, Dr. Theplace, has called you once again for a consultation. His ranting on the other end of the phone leads you to pull the receiver away from your ear, turning Oliver into a chipmunk's squawking. "I can't believe this client," he says. "She showed up late—again—and then had the gall to blame the fact that I charged her for a recent no-show on her inability to pay her rent, her eviction from her apartment, and even her suicidal thoughts! Can you believe her?"

You breathe slowly, again centering yourself. You connect internally with what matters most about what you will say in response. Before you can say anything, Oliver breaks in once again. "She got me so worked up that I couldn't think for the rest of the session. I'm also waking up at night thinking about what she said about suicide. She did attempt once, you know." Oliver pauses and sighs heavily. "The topper is that this particular session was being observed by one of our postdocs from behind the mirror. She works with the head of my clinic, so I can just imagine what he's thinking about me right now. Might as well kiss my hopes for the assistant director position goodbye!"

Your colleague tells you that during this particular session with his client, he ended up spending the majority of the hour assessing suicidality and insisting on the client's collaboration in creating a contract for safety. Eventually, the client agreed to call a crisis hotline if she was becoming flooded and unstable. Oliver watched his client leaving and remembered that they never really discussed the issue the client initially raised about the no-show charge. "Oh well," he told himself, "we'll get to that after this crisis is over."

Bottom line? Oliver struggled with his timing in this session due to factors creating a state of emotional flooding. Ultimately, the low-road structures in the brain that we've discussed (e.g., the amygdala, insula) became overactivated, leaving the high-road areas of the frontal cerebral cortex unable to direct his in-session behavior in a more ideal (and mindfully timely) fashion. Research into the neural basis of animals' ability to anticipate is just beginning, but suggests that a number of interacting systems work together to generate our anticipation of events in our environment. According to neuroscientists Michael Antle and Rae Silver, "anticipation likely involves learning and memory, reward and punishment, memory and cognition, arousal and feedback associated with changes in the internal and external state, homeostatic processes and timing mechanisms" (2009, p. 1643). In a nutshell, much of our mental hardware must link up in order for us to effectively intuit when to do what we hope to do well.

Our clinician in this example was also ruminating a great deal during and after the session with his client. Research has linked rumination (repetitious, preoccupied thinking about negatively perceived events and persons) with impaired interpersonal problem solving (Yoon & Joormann, 2012), and that even trying to use a strategy such as distraction after a period of rumination leads to less effective solutions. Oliver appears to have fused with negatively charged thoughts and interpretations of the client and potential outcomes (e.g., the client committing suicide); he was therefore less available (i.e., mindful) during the session, missed opportunities to intervene regarding the client's upset over the money issue, and arguably overintervened regarding the client's risk of self-harm.

Oliver appears to be suffering with fusion with thoughts of his incompetence and inability to manage his anxiety in reaction. Do you sense this fusion as well as experiential avoidance underneath his statements? Oliver holds rigid beliefs about his client. He cannot accept what's showing up emotionally in his client, and ultimately in himself, and is unwilling to make and sustain contact with his experience, unwilling to get flexible distance on his thoughts and emotions. He is stuck in rigid thinking and is paralyzed as a result. A quote credited to Napoleon Bonaparte seems relevant: "Take time to deliberate, but when the time for action arrives, stop thinking and go in." Few historians would call leaders like Napoleon ruminators (although they may question his values).

Let's add the fact that Oliver feels under the microscope in this session due to having a postdoctoral fellow observing his work. Social psychological research has thoroughly documented the negative impact of being observed (and perceiving oneself as being evaluated) on performance (Liebling & Shaver, 1973). Poor Oliver—the deck was certainly stacked against good timing for him in this situation. He needs your help to get things on track.

Obstacle 3: Preaching What You Don't (and Shouldn't) Practice

This obstacle is fairly intuitive, and yet is tripped over by clinicians with some frequency. It boils down to attempting to intervene outside of your skill set. It would be my attempting to practice as an early developmental specialist, or conducting an inpatient therapy group with women struggling with bulimia. Obviously, it is tough to have a sense of when to intervene if you're swamped during the interaction with excessive frontal lobe musings of what you're supposed to be doing.

While I'm sure it makes complete sense to you not to intervene completely outside your training and experience, it happens nonetheless that we, as clinicians, meet with one of our clients and the conversation strays into roads less traveled. I'm reminded of my high school physics teacher's story (thanks Mrs. Colwell!) of the frog in the heating pot of water—that a rapid shift in temperature (such as any suggestion that you take up a dramatically unfamiliar arena of practice) prompts Kermit to leap to safety outside the pot. On the other hand, if the temperature is very gradually increased (i.e., you slowly drift toward interventions and clinical topics outside your purview), no such leaping necessarily occurs, and our green friend ends up cooked.

Imagine the following: You begin the session with an agreed-upon task of role-play practice in developing the client's assertiveness skills. After the first couple trials of practice, the conversation shifts toward how assertiveness is tough in many domains, not just at work with the client's boss. You then begin practicing assertive responses in other situations, such as telling the client's pushy and enmeshed mother that 2 months is longer than what the client had envisioned for her "brief visit." This is all well and good—until the client raises concerns with his wife. "I can't seem to connect with her." And so practice shifts toward more direct self-expression to her as well. Notice the temperature gradually rising in the work? Before long, the client is talking about his erectile dysfunction and you've turned to your computer to help him search Wikipedia for ideas and methods for how to improve his sex life with his beloved. Yes, I'm being a tad dramatic, but you get the point (and perhaps you recall a time or two when you strayed into less trammeled areas yourself).

Timing requires you to know what you're doing, and know it well. If the interventions you're offering aren't overlearned in the sense of being highly practiced and familiar to you, then not only are you straining the ethical boundaries a bit, but your brain's going to be so busy trying to think through what you're doing that your poor inner CEO won't be able to keep up. Both the content and the timing of the interventions will suffer.

Think of it this way: How good was your timing in shifting gears in your parents' car when you were first learning to drive? And even if you've got the gear shift in that old Accord down pat, don't plop yourself behind the wheel of an 18-wheeler expecting to be the king or queen of the road. You need sufficient training and applied practice of a given intervention toolbox to bring your tools to bear with effective timing.

Obstacle 4: The Therapeutic Insanity Defense

Ring, ring! It's Oliver Theplace calling again. Now he's telling you about his angry client. "He just won't fill out the exposure monitoring forms I'm giving him. How am I supposed to help him get on top of his anger if he won't give me something to work with?"

There's little therapeutic sense in belaboring an intervention, and expecting it to eventually work, when there is sufficient feedback from the client that it is not working. (Remember Einstein's definition of insanity?) Of course, you need to avoid changing course with the slightest obstacle, but drilling a client when reactions show that the intervention will simply not take suggests more about our own (fused) resistance than any on the part of the client.

Good intervention timing is therapeutic skill released in a fully apprehended and mutually meaningful context. It's being in the right place (i.e., stage of the work and readiness for change—remember Prochaska and DiClemente's [1982] stages model from Chapter 2) at the right time in the interaction (a "moment of meaning" that I'll describe in a moment) with the right response (a skillfully delivered action that resonates with the values guiding the work). No small feat. It's going to take some practice to get these "rights" right.

Consider this example from a study by Daly and Mallinckrodt (2009) in which peer-nominated effective therapists were interviewed as to their clinical approach to working with adult clients presenting with high "attachment avoidance" in their relationships. Coding of interview responses suggested two timing-related themes of these therapists' treatment conceptualizations. For these clinicians, "the initial pacing and timing may involve gratifying some of the client's needs either for distance or closeness until the therapeutic alliance is strengthened" (p. 558). Therapists indicated that with these interpersonally disrupted clients, strategic timing in managing the therapeutic distance between themselves and clients was important in helping these individuals reshape their models for connecting and communicating effectively with others. The authors referred to the dance between these expert therapists and their clients. The metaphor is apt because that's just what good dancers (and good clinicians) do when, with good timing, they move toward one another.

Oliver Theplace is all over the place on the dance floor. He keeps stepping on his clients' toes with his damned self-monitoring worksheets. He needs to practice reading the cues and considering the short- and long-term contexts of his therapeutic interactions and take in the feedback he receives in order to get things moving again.

Going With the (Air) Flow

You've likely come across Mihaly Csikszentmihalyi's writing at some point on the psychology of "flow" ("the sense of effortless action" and full engagement) in one's life activities (1997, p. 29). It's that experiential quality of (as the word indicates) flowing into and through one's actions without a sense of "should," "must," or "would rather be eating bonbons." To return to our thermostat metaphor, the air is just (you guessed it) flowing well through the system and it's getting to where it needs to go, and action is experienced as optimal, effective, and worthwhile.

In our work with clients, particularly with the tougher characters in our caseloads, our good timing for the work is more likely to emerge in these in-the-moment states of engagement. Long before Csikszentmihalyi's studies, therapist and author Sheldon Kopp commented that "when the therapist does the best work, he or she does not experience trying to change the patient, or even doing psychotherapy. The therapist *becomes* the Work. The therapist *is* the psychotherapy and it all just seems to flow" (1977, p. 21). Values (ductwork in our metaphor) are what channel, focus, and energize this state and facilitate timely aeration in the consulting room.

LEAN IN

Check back in with the values that sit at the center of your work as a clinician from the discussion in Chapter 2. Take a moment and write in these compass headings—these directions, or ongoing actions on your part—in the space below.

____

____

____

Think back to times when you were working from any of these values—when your intervention flowed in that particular direction. What was your sense of the passage of time? How self-conscious were you? Were you more likely to be fused or defused in the quality of your inner experience? Were you connected with your sensory and cognitive experience as is, or were you tripped up and ensnared? Note your thoughts below:

____

____

____

As Csikszentmihalyi's (1997) research indicates, people acting in flow are receiving immediate feedback as to how they're doing, are experiencing their skills as fully committed to the challenges presented by a given situation, and find their attention and energy fully focused and engaged. Sounds like what we need more of in working with challenging clinical interactions, don't you think? That's what or (more appropriately for this chapter) *when* we're aiming for with our clients. Mindful connection with the moments of the work and monitoring of consistency or inconsistency of these moments with values facilitate the flow that makes for masterful timing.

Better yet, the air really gets blasting into the room when the values are mutual with our clients. They need not be (and typically aren't) identical, but I'm recommending that in order to facilitate flow and to decrease the likelihood and degree of destructiveness, of alliance ruptures, consider directly discussing the creation of shared values for treatment with clients. Do so at the outset of the work, and revisit them often. Again, values are not goals (specific outcomes). They are the meaningful directions with the potential to energize the work (and to facilitate well-timed interventions). As we'll discuss, they are a big part of the thermostat for deciding the when of things. For now, consider the following (and create your own) questions for use with clients in eliciting mutual values:

- "In thinking about our work together, when we see it going well, what does that look like? What are we each doing across our times together?"
- "When we sit here together at our final meeting, how do we want this to have gone? What, specifically, will we have been doing that will have mattered?"

- "Where are we heading in our meetings? What direction do we want our conversations to go?"
- "When things are hard, or when we're stuck during our interactions, what, specifically, will be important for each of us to be doing?"

These are just ideas. Strive to keep these conversations from growing stale. Don't rest with trite or socially desirable responses. Dig and root around a bit (though don't hammer them à la Oliver from above). Let the client know (through your own energy and curiosity) that you're really invested in co-creating the work. You'll know values are sprouting in the air between you when there's energy to the talking. You'll sense the flow beginning.

Setting Your Process-o-Meter

Enough hypotheticals and what-not-to-dos. Let's get to the recommendations for developing more effective intervention timing in your work. As has been the case for the entire book, mindfulness skills are the core of what makes for good timing. Knowing *when* to do *what* comes down to a firmly, yet fluidly, developed habit of regularly conducting mindful scans of oneself, the client, and the interaction during each session. Regardless of your specific theoretical or technical penchants, good timing requires that you are consistently scanning what is and simultaneously entertaining specific questions in order to inform the best points during which an intervention is warranted.

Consider highly acclaimed actors, musicians, tennis players, and conductors—just about any performance profession where you must do things with good timing in order for the performance to come off well. If John McEnroe had never developed exceptional timing—a mindful sense of each moment on the court—would I be writing about him today? What separates Alan Gilbert of the New York Philharmonic from the conductor of your town's thrown-together Fourth of July brass ensemble? Many things perhaps, but impeccable timing derived from complete mindful absorption in the now, along with spacious awareness of the full context of the players, the audience, the intent of a given piece—that is certain. Let's give some timing practice a try.

LEAN IN

Find a ball (a tennis ball would be ideal—I'd recommend against a bowling ball for reasons that will be obvious in a moment). Practice standing in place, holding the ball at about waist level, and tossing the ball about 2 feet up into the air (i.e., shoulder height). Try to keep your hand in place (i.e., don't bring your hand up to grab the ball) and let the ball fall back down toward the same hand as you open your palm to catch it. Do this over and over until you have it down. Easy, right? You could probably get so practiced with this that you could let your mind drift to other things—your taxes or perhaps the global warming crisis. Whatever it might be, your timing in throwing and catching the ball comes readily.

Now (and I'm sure you anticipated this), continue throwing and catching the ball in the same manner, but do so while walking around the room you're in. Notice anything? What happens to your timing in those initial moments after the shift in task?

If you're willing, try any or all of the following variations: tossing the ball with one eye closed or standing on just one leg, or while walking backward. Try tossing the ball higher into the air. Or maybe give it a shot after a full minute of jumping jacks (go ahead, stand up and give yourself a bit of cardio).

Now, I don't recommend actually doing it, but imagine trying to maintain your ability to catch the ball while rapidly climbing a flight of stairs, or while crossing the street, or when someone is yelling in your face.

What's the point here? Other than having a nice physical break from the tedium of reading for the purposes of professional development, there is value in considering that your intervention timing varies according to the lay of the land—as conditions change in your interactions with clients, it's important for you to recalibrate and shift your rhythm and perhaps even the nature of your therapeutic actions. Though your ball tossing may have been a piece of cake while standing flat-footed next to your desk, it's likely to hit the floor when the client throws something unexpected at you. You need the benefit of mindfulness skills to improve your ability to more accurately appraise the when of things.

Now that you're perhaps wishing I were there with you so that you could test your timing in pitching the ball at my head, please feel free to have a seat so that we can proceed.

In conducting brief (several seconds is often all that's needed) mindfulness scans during interactions with clients, there are key questions to practice answering. You need not consider this an exhaustive list, nor should you feel compelled to check off each question during every scan. With practice, my experience is that creating an open, investigative, curious space within oneself leads to the right questions, as well as the most workable answers. Try it out for yourself and see (and we'll practice doing so in just a moment). First, the W questions:

- Where is my body right now (e.g., think posture, gestures, fidgeting, distance from client)? Where is energy showing up in my body?
- What is happening right now? What are all the variables contributing to this interaction? What else could be influencing this? (Look for alternatives and missed variables.) What is not being said or done? What stage of change (remember Prochaska and DiClemente's [1982] work, Chapter 2) is the client at relative to readiness to alter coping and patterns of behavior? What might I do right now and with what purpose? What is my plan based on what's arising in this moment and the goals and values guiding the work?
- Who is at fault right now? Who is affecting the other and how? Who will have their needs met by the reaction I'm considering? Who is this person across from me—including all moments and situations and not just this one?
- Why intervene now and not later (in the interaction, at another time, or at no time altogether)? Why would an intervention matter to this client? . . . to me?

Taking a moment to mentally (and emotionally) answer any of these questions, even in the midst of challenging exchanges with clients, allows for a gap in which you can derive more effectively timed interventions. Clinical work is not typically a race (unless you're doing crisis intervention with riders during the Tour de France). We can afford a handful of seconds to scan what's happening and make more informed, and mindfully centered, decisions as to the when of our work.

Here's the thermostat in brief. You might notice the thematic and technical overlap between these 3 Ls below and the APPALL steps in Chapter 7. Just as with managing your more extreme reactions by learning to become "APPALLed," you are again practicing creating inner openness, mindfully leaning into emotions, connecting with your guiding values, and taking informed action to address the concerns of the moment. The metaphor isn't really important (it's there as a memory aid). Indeed, the trick is to practice this basic sequence of awareness, connection with purpose, and committed action until the metaphor and the acronyms drop away. Do so consistently and I'm betting your timing will be quite a bit more refined. These core mindfulness-based strategies help you know *when* because they're helping you take in what's there in the room as fully as possible and integrate this with the direction you've already pegged as important for the work. It really is like riding a bike—your teacher's words fall by the wayside as you just pump the pedals, tilt yourself to and fro, and work the handlebars. You just ride. Another way of saying it is that you just learn to . . .

- Listen . . . with curiosity and flexible, defused openness to your thoughts and emotions as they arise during interactions with clients. Lean into your emotions and any reactive thoughts. Allow them. Dispassionately notice them. Use defusion and mindful, attentive awareness to simply listen to them without picking them up. Breathe . . . listen to the echo of old emotional patterns. Listen to your body and the energy that the emotions bring to you. Let the energy rise and fall on its own like waves in the few seconds while you're pausing. Listen for evidence, for clues, of the full context of the situation. Here's you asking the where, who, and what questions from above and pausing for answers (possibly even saying these simple words silently to yourself—a self-querying mantra of sorts). Again, you need not run through the whole list—just breathe for a handful of seconds and get curious about hearing a larger perspective.

- Look . . . You've stopped to listen for a moment and have a larger sense of the space of the interaction, the client, yourself, and the tasks at hand. Now, check in with the values that guide the work. Bring them into this space you've created. Ask: Why intervene now? Notice any urges for rope pulling on your part. Mindfully breathe in and connect with these values. Are you about to act in a manner consistent or inconsistent with them? Here's where the thermostat knows to kick in or not . . .
- Leap . . . You've given yourself time to stop and look, you've listened to your thoughts and emotions without following them—now is the when. You can leap—take action in the direction of the values that guide your work with this person. You can now proactively lead the relationship, whether it be with compassionate "prizing," process intervention, a limit on the client's behavior, and specific techniques (e.g., an exposure, role-play). Consult Figure 2.1 and, with what you've gathered from your listening and looking, make your best in-the-moment choice as to where exactly you'd like your behavior to land on the right side. With a stance of attunement to the client, do you want to lead with outward action, or go inward to deepen your compassionate focus?

The idea is to develop the habit of regularly pausing internally to conduct a 3 L scan resulting in a more planful and timely intervention. Even (and especially) with our most difficult-to-work-with clients, it's possible to connect with our experience, as well as our most passionately held values, in order to guide our actions as clinicians. As we'll now practice, we should aspire to the ideal suggested by Vietnamese Zen master Thich Nhat Hanh (1992) in that we should look to "make flowers out of the garbage" in our clients, and in ourselves. As he explains in his writings (and as we've discussed), we are always connected with our clients, mutually influencing one another through the inter-being of things. Any flower eventually wilts and becomes garbage, and garbage eventually becomes soil that becomes a flower (Hanh, 1992). We can, if we're willing, make what I like to call "moments of meaning" (MoMs) out of the most charged, vexing, stuck junctures of the work. Recognizing the beauty of the energy of these sorts of "bad" interactions is what allows for the perspective granting expert clinicians the timing to intervene in the direction of full-blooming change.

Here's how you'll know a MoM has emerged in your interactions with clients (I like this acronym, because I happen to find a lot of MoMs with my own mom). You'll feel that flow that Csikszentmihalyi describes. These MoMs, these flow experiences, are excellent signposts or markers of good timing. When you're feeling challenged, focused, engaged, attuned, and energized, and when the work feels important (i.e., consistent with values), you are in an ideal time zone for offering input to the client. The alliance is strong, and you (and, due to reciprocal influence, possibly the clients as well) are psychologically open. These are the moments you might recognize when you find yourself on the edge of your seat, drawn forward and into the interaction. Look, better yet, feel, for them and let them inform you about the fundamental question of when.

In addition to describing the sense of flow you experience as a signal of the timeliness of your interventions, author and clinician Sheldon Kopp emphasizes the importance of watching the engagement in clients as a barometer for intervention timing. "If the intervention is correct, and the timing is right, the therapist's work serves to restore and promote resumption of the patient's full participation in that process. . . . Direct confirmation from the patient comes in the form of new and fresh material of many kinds" (Kopp, 1977, p. 118). When we lean in and intervene, and when the client responds with rich material and a sense of engagement, it's a good sign that your moves have hit home. When both clinician and client are vibrating, not unlike a well-struck musical chord, then the timing is likely right.

System Check: Timing Practice

A quote often attributed to 60s rocker Jim Morrison seems relevant to our discussion: "I think of myself as an intelligent, sensitive human being with the soul of a clown which always forces me to blow it at the most important moments." Though Morrison arguably showed amazing musical timing, his cadence for life skills more broadly is questionable. His thermostat may not have been working well in the areas that might have helped extend his life and his musical impact. Here, we begin the never-ending path of practice to tweak our own inner homeostatic controls. Let's work on our "whens" so we blow it with our clients less.

LEAN IN

Create a centered space for yourself through mindfulness of breath, body, and thought. Once you are ready, cue up a recent difficult interaction with a client. Aim for an interaction that carried a great degree of emotional intensity for either you or the client, or one that left you with any of the timing-related stuck thoughts from the beginning of this chapter. Choose any moment of "stuckness" you can recall and imagine rewinding the film of this interaction, editing it with your implementation of the 3 Ls and the W questions, and replaying the movie. What would your moments of mindful scanning reveal?

Listen: ____

Look: ____

Leap:____

As you imagine editing the session with this scan, this thermostat check, what might have rippled out? What might have shifted in your intervention timing? In the flow of the interaction?

____

____

____

LEAN IN

Either take the same sample interaction from above or choose another from the same client, or another client altogether. With a colleague, take turns role-playing the interaction (at least 10 minutes in each role in order to give yourself sufficient time and material to work with). Practice conducting mindfulness scans at varying intervals. When first beginning this practice, try giving some sort of sign (such as a raised hand) to your "client" that you are pausing to scan the moment. Though you obviously won't do this in actual sessions (unless perhaps you're an EMDR clinician), it will give you more space for practicing the scanning steps more fully. Once you've practiced a bit, shift into more real-time scanning. After each participant's turn in the role of clinician, give one another feedback on the experience of intervention timing. Consider the following questions to help with this feedback loop:

- Were there any points during the interaction where you, as the client, felt disengaged or in any way displaced by my behavior?
- What specifically was I doing that you resonated positively to? That led you to feel disengaged or displaced?
- How did the pace and flow of the interaction feel to you? Did it flow, or were there parts that were disjointed or didn't work for you in some way?
- Did it feel like our conversation was moving in a meaningful direction? Why or why not? Any ideas as to what, specifically, I might have done more or less of that would have made for more forward movement?
- What is your sense of what my intentional behavior was during the interaction? What were my interventions and how did you receive them?
- Based on my behavior in this interaction, would you be more or less willing to rehire me for the next session?

As you do the hard work of learning to refine your sense of intervention timing, it will help to integrate feedback loops whenever possible. Without regular and rich input on the effectiveness of when and what you're doing, you end up repeating the same errors, doing damage to the alliance, and increasing the odds of difficult interaction patterns. As we end this discussion of timing, let me throw in a few feedback-related recommendations:

1. *Play historian with yourself.* After difficult (as well as ideal) interac-

tions with clients, conduct a brief chain analysis of everything that happened in time sequence. Social workers are trained to do this via "process recordings." Here, you're gathering a sense of the ebb and flow of the interaction. Looking over your chain analysis, ask yourself at what junctures the timing was on or off. What were the markers, the aspects of you, the client, and the situation that set up good versus poorly timed intervention on your part?

2. *Record and review your work.* With client permission, video and audio recordings of your sessions can be extremely useful in improving your timing. This was a significant component of my own early clinical training and I found it invaluable in learning to monitor the interaction for choice points for intervention. Colleagues and supervisors can also be useful in providing feedback on your recorded work (and yes, you can push through the initial anxiety of being on display). Watching or listening to yourself work can provide immeasurable benefit in increasing your perspective on clinical intervention. In a sense, by observing your work in this way, you are creating the metacognitive experience of your thoughts, feelings, and particularly your actions that mindfulness skills (the observing witness) provides in the moment.

3. *Your best feedback is sitting across from you.* All too often, we seem to forget that our clients have a wealth of perspective on the work. We tend not to leave out comment card boxes in our offices. (Though is that really a bad idea?) Why not ask the clients themselves how they experienced the interactions? What's their sense of what worked or didn't work regarding the content and timing of our interventions? Take any of the processing questions from the last Lean In exercise above and consider posing them with clients. I would recommend inviting them into a feedback conversation first (in order to make sure you have their consent and they don't feel pressured). What you may find is that the authenticity and immediacy of these feedback conversations can breathe a lot of life into the alliance. It is this aspect of authenticity in the work, and how mindfulness-based strategies can enhance it, that we turn to in Chapter 9.

4. *Now is always the time to practice your timing.* Don't restrict yourself to your clinical work in terms of learning to improve your relational tim-

ing. Mindfully track and scan all of your important interactions. How would you answer the W questions and how would you listen, look, and leap during challenging moments in your personal connections? While you shouldn't look to do a lot of professionally informed intervening in your closest relationships (ask my wife for her opinion on this), it does help to at least monitor the when of your interactions from time to time. You might learn more about your own patterns that influence your professional interactions.

* * *

So what do you do, what leap might you take, if the client is acting in an off-putting or self-defeating way (but not sufficiently violating to call for limit-setting)? And what do you do if the relationship (to use Pirsig's freight train metaphor) has derailed? Maybe you have done or said something contributing to a rupture in the relationship and the work will be impaired without direct intervention. These are the moments when clients pull away from you. It's when they raise their defenses and won't readily bring them down again. The interaction begins to feel stale and artificial. The person of the client is absent, though the body is in the chair across from you. Or maybe the client isn't showing up at all. All the defusion and mindful noticing on your part will do nothing unless you do something now to reengage the client. These are the times when the person of the therapist is crucial. This is when authenticity is called for. In Chapter 9, we will explore how best to use the here-and-now of your interactions with difficult clients. The more you are willing to engage the client with whatever shows up between (and within) you, the more you will be able to demonstrate the leadership to move treatment in a positive direction.

MAP CHECK

Take a moment and review what we've covered in this chapter. What was one aspect, one piece of content, that resonated with you—sparked your interest, curiosity, or even angst in some way?

Why did this matter to you? What makes this worth writing about? Worth your focus and effort? What is the gravity that this carries for you and your work?

What is one specific action you can take within the next 24 hours related to this issue that feels as though it would be important and has the potential to move you in the direction of what matters?

≺ CHAPTER NINE ≻

Relational Leadership, Part 1: Getting Real With Clients

The Critical Role of Authenticity in the Therapeutic Relationship

PHILOSOPHER Martin Buber (1958) made an interesting distinction between two basic types of human interactions that are important for our work with clients. He wrote of interactions that are more of a transaction—you communicating with someone but without much of an authentic connection. He called this an "I-It" relationship. These tend to be our interactions with clerks in stores, waitstaff, and others who are more roles than real. The "Its" are more akin to cardboard cutouts than people with emotions, wants, dreams, and suffering.

And then there are the "I-Thou" exchanges, when a communion occurs between the authentic aspects of each person. Obviously, these are the interactions that matter most to us personally, and are likely to have the greatest impact professionally.

LEAN IN

List below experiences that come to mind (personally and professionally) when you are clear within yourself that I-Thou has occurred, when there was a communion of sorts between you and the other person.

____

____

____

____

____

Looking over these experiences, notice what shows up for you right now. How do you regard these people? What are your thoughts and feelings? List below as specifically as possible what you and these others did that may have facilitated these experiences.

____

____

____

Chances are, you listed things such as "talked honestly," "sincere," "communicated respect," "I felt that he completely understood me," "completely focused on the other person," and so on. I'm also betting that you've experienced I-Thou interactions with people who admitted error after having hurt you in some way. When the therapeutic alliance ruptures, it can often be because the clinician (consciously or not) went too far with an interpretation or intervention, pushed when he or she should have waited, or didn't engage enough when the client really needed it. Remember, our social brains are constantly processing each other's emotional intentions in milliseconds. We're wired to attend to these messages. Your clients, even your most difficult ones, are aware when you are not acknowledging mistakes. The relationship suffers and so does the work.

In Chapter 7, I told the story of an adolescent client of mine with whom I made a significant error in trying to leverage him to talk about his past offenses. This has always been my best personal example of the power of a "one-down" intervention to authentically connect with a client and address a rupture in the treatment alliance. You may find it useful to spend some time generating your own example from your work.

LEAN IN

Think of a time in your personal life when someone who mattered to you authentically took responsibility and acknowledged the impact of his or her behavior on you. Recall how this felt and how it impacted your relationship, your own willingness to engage the person. Comment on this below:

____

____

____

Now, think of a recent exchange with a difficult client in which you may have pushed or missed the client in some way, possibly rupturing the relationship to some degree. Note below what evidence you have that this may have been a rupture. What happened for the client and for you right after all was said and done?

Now, ask yourself and note below how you might directly take responsibility for your action with the client. What might you do or say? What might get in the way of doing so? Can you admit your error without placing any expectation on the client? List your reactions below:

LEAN IN

How *real* are you? The following self-assessment activity gives a general sense of your willingness to be authentic, especially when it's tough to do so. This is not an empirically validated measure with sound psychometrics. It's a brief self-quiz regarding your overall approach to authenticity in relating to others. Think of it as a *Cosmo* quiz with a legitimate purpose. Rate each item as to your general perception of willingness to engage in the action described.

1. When it's clear I've wronged someone, I readily admit it even though it might be embarrassing or lead to other negative consequences to do so.

1	2	3	4	5
Not Willing		Somewhat Willing		Very Willing

2. When I'm feeling something strongly, I tend to express myself despite the opposing views of others whose opinion I value.

1	2	3	4	5
Not Willing		Somewhat Willing		Very Willing

3. I'm clear with others about how I think and feel about them in the moment when these experiences occur for me.

1	2	3	4	5
Not Willing		Somewhat Willing		Very Willing

4. I express *into* people rather than past or through them because it's important for me to have them connect with me around what matters.

1	2	3	4	5
Not Willing		Somewhat Willing		Very Willing

5. When I'm feeling vulnerable, I openly express myself despite the risks.

1	2	3	4	5
Not Willing		Somewhat Willing		Very Willing

6. Despite urges to avoid a difficult interpersonal situation, I do or say what is necessary.

1	2	3	4	5
Not Willing		Somewhat Willing		Very Willing

7. When push comes to shove, I speak from the heart.

1	2	3	4	5
Not Willing		Somewhat Willing		Very Willing

Add up your responses to these items. Again, there's no normative sample for comparison, but subjectively, I'd argue that if your total score was 21 or higher, you generally value exhibiting skills indicative of authentic expression. Consider your score your "authenticity baseline" and return to it later after you've been working for some time to implement the skills and strategies discussed in this chapter (and throughout the book). It *will* be interesting for you to note any changes in your self-assessment over time. Clearly, there are times for passionate revelation of one's perspective (even in treatment), and there are certainly times when this is not appropriate (see below on self-disclosure). And yet I'm arguing that authenticity, by and large, is a useful stance for clinicians to assume in managing the trickier interactions in clinical work. Let's explore the rationale in greater detail with a clinical example.

The Ins and Outs of Working With the Here and Now

A colleague recently consulted with me about an exchange she'd had with a difficult client. My colleague is a school guidance counselor who was having a very challenging interaction with a parent of a high school senior who was about to graduate. My colleague felt that the student was not ready to graduate and would need another year to receive more special education services. To put it mildly, my colleague and the client's mother disagreed. "But he's worked so hard," said the mother. "He's been looking forward to this for so long." And then this mom unleashed on the clinician. "Why are you working against me on this? You're not doing your job. It's your fault if he's not ready to graduate."

Apparently, this had become somewhat of a pattern with this parent—calling up my colleague and verbally unleashing on her as well as other members of the school staff. This clinician decided to intervene regarding the process with this mother—the here-and-now "how" of the interaction. The following is a reconstruction of my colleague's response:

"I'm wondering if I can ask you a question about our conversation today. . . . [Mother pauses briefly in her rant and says okay.] It's clear how much you love your son because of how powerfully you're feeling right now. Do you notice, though, how loud you are and how much you're directing your anger at me? I'm not sure, but it feels to me like you'd like me to simply agree with you despite our previous discussions about the things your son would need to get done in order to graduate on time—things he hasn't done."

My colleague described how the mother's demeanor shifted rapidly. While she didn't say, "Hey, thanks for pointing that out! I was really out of line," she did slow down, lower her voice, and was able to have a more focused discussion. She still disagreed with the decision not to have her son graduate, but she did shift in how she directed her anger.

Though we could spend an entire book exploring the nuances of process intervention with clients—using the here-and-now of the interpersonal moment to create opportunities for social learning about communication and emotional patterns—we will focus on a brief overview of skills. Here, I will give a summary of the work of many others who have developed relational psychotherapy interventions (Levenson, 1995; Safran & Muran, 2000; and Yalom, 1995, to name a few). For our purposes, we are exploring how mindfully engaging the dynamics of the exchange between you and your clients, how holding up a mirror to the client and your behavior and reactions can help lead the client toward more effective and authentic relating with others. Process work requires clinician mindfulness and self-management. Attempts to intervene at the level of in-session process without mindfulness are unlikely to be very unhelpful and, at worst, may spark more rupturing in the therapeutic relationship. Implemented with good timing (as we discussed in Chapter 8), process intervention can do much to dissolve the most difficult of ropes tangling up the work.

Consider the following hypothetical clinical situations:

- A depressed client who typically withdraws into self-loathing statements and crying whenever you point out positive things she has done.
- A lonely, isolated man who talks of women in very derogatory, blaming ways (and, by the way, you're a female therapist).
- A physician currently on trial for malpractice and suffering from frequent panic attacks who tends to correct your grammar, criticize your wardrobe choices, and arrive late to session.

In reviewing these scenarios, ask yourself: How would I tend to react? What would the pull be for me? (Review our work on your emotional patterning from Chapter 5.) In addition, ask yourself: Would any of these behavior patterns require that I set a firm limit with the client? What if you've already tried to address the patterns and they persist?

Here is a key question to ask yourself for determining whether process intervention and exploration might be helpful for these difficult client patterns: Is the client's behavior significantly self-defeating and is it a reflection of a pattern that somehow blocks authentic communication between us and therefore inhibits the client from making progress in treatment?

If other interventions do not appear appropriate, and if you answer "yes" to this question, then process work might be helpful for a particular situation. Process work requires that you are already practicing everything we've discussed thus far: You're aware of the influence of your own patterns; you work to defuse from unhelpful thinking; and you're mindfully aware and accepting of your own emotional reactions. You accept the inherent mutuality of influence between you and your clients. You work to lean in toward what's difficult. Now, you're ready for process intervention.

LEAN IN

Cue up your anchors for your difficult client. Make the person vivid in your mind's eye. What is a specific behavior pattern the client exhibits in session that meets the criteria in the question above? List it below:

____

____

How have you responded to this pattern in the past? What was the effect of this?

____

____

We'll return to your client in a minute. Now, let's review the guiding themes of process work and a model for intervention steps. All good process intervention rests on a foundation of themes (Figure 9.1). The figure (adapted from Safran & Muran, 2000) is not necessarily exhaustive, but is

	Process Domains		
	Perspective	Emotion	Action
Process Themes	1. Here and now focus	5. Empathic, yet willing to mirror what is happening in the interaction	9. Feedback is specific and concrete (not global or character based)
	2. Collaborative ("we" and "us")	6. Interested, curious, engaged	10. Tentative and emphasizing subjectivity ("This is just my take, but I'm noticing—")
	3. Focus is awareness, not change (no outcome focus)	7. Openness, willing to explore patterns	11. Persistent, but not hammering client (knowing when to leave things be)
	4. Creation of new, authentic experiences vs. explaining or interpreting to client	8. Confidence, presence	12. Willingness to appropriately self-disclose (not self-indulgent; focused on client)

Figure 9.1 Process Intervention Themes and Domains

meant to capture the orientation of a clinician who is effective at increasing process understanding and learning for clients.

LEAN IN

In order to begin internalizing these themes, review the therapist statements below. What process intervention theme is the therapist overlooking or mishandling for each? See the key following the exercise for suggested answers (you will likely find that multiple themes might apply for many of these).

A. "So, instead of avoiding talking about your pain, what might you do differently from now on?" ______________________________
B. "Who in your life used to use this angry tone with you?" ______ ____________________
C. "So let me tell you how what you just said reminds me of a time

when I was in college. You'll like this, it's pretty funny. . . . " ____
____

D. (*Client is pounding the arm of the chair as he or she often does when angry. Client is yet again withdrawing into a sullen, nonresponsive state.*) "You're having a hard time. . . . Yes . . . I can see that." ______
____

E. "This dropping off in your voice is part of a larger tendency in your life to avoid asserting your needs to others. Sounds similar to you as a little girl feeling dwarfed by your controlling mother, doesn't it?"
____

Key: (A) 2, 3, 10; (B) 1, 4; (C) 2, 12; (D) 5, 8; (E) 1, 4, 10.

The overall goal of good process work is to increase the authenticity of the communication between you and the client. To the degree the client (and you) can learn to directly and honestly relate to one another, impasses and ruptures can be successfully navigated. Ropes will be dropped and the goals and values of the work can be pursued. Clients will be less likely to drop out of treatment prematurely, and your risk for burnout is greatly reduced. If the client agrees, the patterns of communication may become a focus of treatment in and of themselves. If so, process work can become a centerpiece of your intervention toolbox.

I've always struggled to have a concise sense of exactly how to best conduct process work with clients. It's inherently subjective and elusive stuff, and seems very intuitive and fluid. Therefore I think many clinicians give it little credence. Again, however, as I've hammered at you for this entire book, communication and self-disclosure are inevitable. Process is an inherent part of every clinical interaction. Just because it's difficult or a bit slippery does not mean that we, as a field, should not continue to refine, scientifically study, and enhance our skills for here-and-now work with clients. Especially with your more difficult clients, process work is crucial.

So, bearing all of the themes listed above in mind, here is a basic frame, a sequence of steps for conducting a process intervention. It is an I-Thou OFFER of possibility and authenticity you are making to your client.

Observe the Pattern

Let the client's behavior play out repeatedly before you hold it up to him or her. Otherwise, the client will likely be defensive and you won't have the credibility of prior experience to help him or her see the pattern. You also want to be as clear as possible that this is indeed a pattern inhibiting the work and the client's progress. And a big piece of this first step is to observe the pattern mindfully—using skills of defusion and mindful awareness that, by this point, you're quite adept at! Do not even think of proceeding if you are in a reactive, tug-of-war state. I guarantee you, it will not go well.

Invitation to View the Frame of the Pattern

Process statements and interventions often spark defensiveness in people. (Remember how awkward the eye contact exercise was? The here and now can be intimidating.) It is important to have the client's permission to proceed. "Is it okay if I let you know something I'm noticing going on right now?" or "Are you open to discussing something that's happened here in the room?"

Point to the Pattern and Its Adaptive Function

It is here that you briefly and concisely state to the client what you have observed. It should be overt behavior and not an interpretation of the dynamics. Think of the Interpersonal Process Grid (Figure 2.1)—how has the client disconnected and gone inactive (Quadrant D) or attacked or aggressed in an active way (Quadrant C)? You are calmly, tentatively, and empathically holding this observation up to the client. "I'm noticing now that you're looking away from me a lot while you're telling me about this" or "I'm noticing your voice has been getting very loud and intense these past few minutes."

After concisely pointing to the pattern, let the client know that it has likely served a useful purpose. "It makes sense to me that looking away like this helps you feel safe in telling me all these painful things" or "Your tone tells me that this is really important to you and you want me to understand how crucial it is." This adaptive framing helps clients adopt an "of course" mentality—that they aren't intentionally looking to left-side people. They're doing the best they can, and you see that. Approaching clients from this positive frame helps them hang in with the exploration with you. It opens them up a bit more. Again, remember to emphasize how subjective your perspective is—you don't have omniscience or special powers. You're merely another human being who happens to care about helping them and has the guts to authentically communicate what's happening in the room.

Collaboratively Explore the Pattern

This is the meat of the process work. You will want to stay consistent with all of the process themes above as you walk with the client in looking at the pattern. Again, the goal is awareness, not change. To the degree that clients view you as trying to change them in this perhaps awkward, anxious, upsetting moment, they will become even more difficult and the work will suffer. You might make statements here such as:

- "Have you noticed how we tend to end up in a sort of tug-of-war when we talk about this?"
- "I'm curious about how to understand what just happened. You did X and my sense/feeling is that I should do Y. How do you see it?"
- "What do you make of how you responded just now when I said/did X?
- "Are you aware of changing the subject just now away from an upsetting topic?"
- "To me it feels as though things are very clenched, tight, for you right now. Does that make sense? . . . If you were to notice that clenched aspect somewhere in your body, where would it be? . . . If it were an object or thing, what would that tight aspect look like?" (Notice the defused quality of exploring the nature of the rigid relating pattern the client has presented.)
- "I'm wondering if you could put that experience you're having right now into words—what words would you attach to it?"

During this step, the focus is collaborative inquiry into the ebb and flow of the interaction with your client. It is very helpful for clinicians to pay attention to markers signaling that this pattern is arising. What was the client doing (even in terms of subtle nonverbal behavior) just before this pattern started? What were you doing? What was the content of the discussion? The anchors you've been using to cue your sample client to awareness are likely candidates to signal that a pattern ripe for process work is at hand.

This step requires a great deal of mindfulness—a detached, curious, willing stance. If you remain open and interested, clients may very well perceive this and open themselves more as well.

Reveal Your Experience of the Pattern

You are part of every pattern of interaction with clients. Acknowledging your experience helps clients see their behavior more clearly. The authenticity of a real human exchange (the I-Thou aspect) in which you are willing to let clients see how you are influenced by them will open them up to learning. You might say things such as:

- "I'm sitting here feeling a bit stuck myself. My mind is telling me I should try to fix this for you, but somehow I have the sense that wouldn't be helpful. What's your take on that?" (Notice the defusion here—"My mind is telling me . . ." Notice the tentative approach and the collaborative involving of the client.)
- "Right now, it feels to me like you've got one end of a rope and I've got another and we've spent the past few minutes yanking back and forth. How has it felt for you?"
- "I'm not certain, but it feels to me that when I've tried to move closer to you during this conversation, you've pushed me away by pointing out things I don't understand. How do you react to that? . . . [Later] Again, I just told you how painful that sounds, and I felt a sense of shoving from you when you said I have no clue how complicated things are at home."
- "I want to let you know that I've been feeling a bit restricted just now—almost as if it would be precarious for me to say too much or else it might trip something for you. What's your take?"
- "I have the feeling that I've been pushing pretty hard at you today. I'm wondering if you're sensing that."

- "I want to say that I really feel as though you've taken a huge risk in here with me today. I'm really noticing it based on what you just said and how willing you were to say it even though it looked like it was really hard to do."

In this last step, you reaffirm the reciprocal nature of the therapeutic relationship. You emphasize the sense of "we-ness" that the client has probably been lacking in certain aspects of his or her life. By expressing your partial ownership in the here-and-now of the session, you are giving your client a sizable dose of authenticity—some of the most healing medicine in your therapeutic arsenal. You are not befriending the client. You are not (and should never) reveal your deepest vulnerabilities and insecurities. It is a planful and strategic self-disclosure of your in-the-moment experience, and it is highly attuned to the client's needs.

Notice that you're not prescribing any process homework, and you're not asking clients to compare notes on how this in-session pattern plays out with others in their lives. If they bring this up as fodder for discussion, so be it, but you're not going there yourself. To do so would be to focus on change—an outcome—instead of increasing their awareness of the pattern. The trick here is to trust that with highly attuned exploration, awareness will facilitate choice and change.

LEAN IN

In order to begin applying the themes and steps of process intervention, take the hypothetical situations below and generate your own process intervention responses:

1. A depressed client who typically withdraws into self-loathing statements and crying whenever you point out positive things she has done. (In response to your observation that the client has shown a lot of perseverance in her job search) "Yeah, well, I'm such a damn idiot. It's no wonder I'm having to look for a job . . . again."

   ____

   ____

   ____

2. A lonely, isolated man who talks of women in very derogatory, blaming ways (you're a female therapist). "And I have to tell you—that bitch of an ex-girlfriend of mine needs to wake up and realize that she's the one who screwed up our relationship. Women are morons for not realizing how good they have it."

   ____

   ____

3. A physician currently on trial for malpractice and suffering from frequent panic attacks who tends to correct your grammar, criticize your wardrobe choices, and be late to session. "It's 'you and I,' not 'you and me' if you're trying to talk about both of us in the same sentence. . . . I'm guessing psychology programs must not grade for grammar."

   ____

   ____

LEAN IN

Now return to your own sample client. Cue up the anchors (this should be getting pretty easy for you by this point) and visualize the specific difficult behavior pattern the client exhibits. Does it meet the criteria for a process intervention? If so, lay out your ideal process intervention below. Remember, you are making an OFFER (observe, frame, function, explore, reveal) to the client—you are not hammering or trying to change the client in the moment, and you are very mindful of your own experience.

_**O**____
_**F**____
_**F**____
_**E**____
_**R**____

What might your client do that would lead you to *not* use a process approach in a particular situation? What might be happening for you with regard to this client that would preclude a process intervention?

Hopefully, this section provides you with food for thought regarding process work. Your confidence in process work will come primarily from your actual interventions and subsequent processing with colleagues or in supervision. You do not have to practice from a psychodynamic orientation to use process intervention. You merely have to be willing to work in the immediate moment; you have to consider the relationship itself a viable source of learning. With a commitment to exploring process work, your skill will continue to develop because you will tend to view interactions with clients with more of a process lens. With greater skill in managing process, you will find yourself less intimidated, daunted, and disdainful of work with difficult clients.

Want to Know What I Really Think About Self-Disclosure in Clinical Work?

I had to remember to cover up the picture of my grandfather before every session with my client, John. His own grandfather, who had raised him, was dying of a protracted and very agonizing bout of colon cancer. Much of our therapy was devoted to working through grief and helping John learn to manage his daily life despite these painful and highly intrusive feelings. His grandfather had been an existential anchor for him throughout his life. John felt himself being pulled into a vacuum of sorts at the prospect of losing him.

I made a conscious decision not to let John know that my own grandfather (to whom I was also close) was also dying of cancer. I struggled with my own reactions after many of our sessions—my own pain surfacing at witnessing and focusing myself on John's. And yet it seemed important to keep John completely in the dark as to my personal experience. Avoiding disclosure of my personal and very parallel experience was, in my best judgment at the time, crucial.

And then there were the parents I've coached in recent years who have been faced with the trials of managing the behavior of an emotionally and behaviorally challenged child. One such parent, Stuart, struggled to manage his anger in reaction to his preteen son's impulsive, destructive, and sometimes aggressive behavior at home. He felt himself a failure as a father and believed that any use of "active ignoring" of his son's provocative behavior was equivalent to throwing in the towel and failing his wife (who would then have to take up the slack of intervention with their son). So his only recourse was to yell, threaten, and come completely unhinged, serving only to exacerbate things. Unlike with my client John, I spoke openly with this father about my own emotional patterning and how it had impacted me as a clinician and as a parent (the angst-avoidant theme leading to Little League and law school quittings, as well as a near-miss decision to give up on becoming a psychologist). In this case, self-disclosure made (to my mind) good clinical sense, and it was my experience that my client (and our alliance) benefited from my attempt at well-timed candor. Unfortunately, our field rarely opens up about self-disclosure. And since this chapter is focused on harnessing authenticity with clients in order to build the therapeutic alliance, it seemed important to cover.

The research is just beginning, but initial data suggest that therapist self-disclosure can not only enhance the therapeutic alliance but augment the outcomes of the work (Barrett, 2001). Increased self-disclosure in this experimental study led to reduced client symptom distress, as well as increased reports of client liking for their clinicians. But what of the clinical lore about the dragons of self-disclosure? That untoward things will arise and scorch the work if clinicians unearth their personal lives with clients? Are we to let go of our concerns and compulsively self-disclose in the service of our connections with clients?

I completely agree with Jeffrey Barnett (2011), who recommends that self-disclosure be actively addressed in psychotherapy training, and that supervisors look to model appropriate self-disclosure when possible. Such attention to self-disclosure in training and supervision (as well as in research) is sorely lacking and, as a result, lowly authors such as me must whine about it and resort to clinical anecdotes to get the ball rolling.

Thankfully, Barnett provides helpful guidelines in considering the appropriateness of self-disclosure during clinical interactions. As Barnett indicates (and as you know from your own experience—even in the course of reading this book) self-disclosure is inevitable. Wedding rings, the location and layout or decoration of your office, and even what you wear all tell stories about you to clients. There are also the slips of the tongue and even the hard-to-suppress smiles, nods, and grimaces that also disclose a great deal of your inner landscape. And then there are your more volitional disclosures—those that relate your personal experiences, history, and emotional and intellectual experience of the client. It is this latter portion of self-disclosure that we focus on in this section because it's here that the messages ring the loudest (and where you can learn not to ring the bell in the first place if that's what's called for).

Self-disclosure is a subdomain in the arena of managing boundaries in clinical work. In Chapter 10, we'll discuss limit-setting as crucial to boundary maintenance, which also includes topics such as managing time, money, personal space, and touch with clients. Ideally, self-disclosure in clinical work can be viewed as an intentional expression of personal perspective or information in the service of the work itself—it is, as Gutheil and Gabbard (1993) indicated, a "boundary crossing" (as is limit setting) in that it is a temporary intrusion meant to create a beneficial impact. This is in contrast to a boundary violation that is more impulsive, reactive, self-focused, and mindlessly rendered, which is potentially harmful. Liability concerns may lessen our willingness to offer more of what's real of us to clients.

Even if you do not invest heavily in conceptions of transference and countertransference, you do care about your clients showing up for sessions, and that they view you as a person with whom they want to work. Assuming this is so, judicious self-disclosure can be of considerable benefit, even if relationship is not at the forefront of your interventions. Again, the brain is always binding us to one another, and therefore self-disclosure is a notable tether between us.

Below are questions derived from Barnett (2011) and my own experience, for you to review with frequency such that they become an automatic filter prior to your self-disclosures with clients. Again, you won't regulate every disclosure (particularly those of posture, affect, and gesture), but you can have (and here's where mindfulness skills and the timing discussion from Chapter 8 come in) significant choice in using disclosures strategically in order to build momentum in your alliances.

- Have I considered my client's personal and clinical history relative to the potential effects of this self-disclosure (e.g., before revealing an anecdote of personal loss, is this a client whose own loss has been an unaddressed and overwhelming trauma)?
- Am I aware of the current laws, regulations, and ethical guidelines governing my work such that my use of self-disclosure can safely be considered to be within the lines?
- Is this disclosure consistent with the goals and values guiding the work?
- Is the client consenting to this self-disclosure (i.e., have I previewed the possibility of my discussing personal material to give the client the opportunity to choose to receive this boundary-crossing intervention or not)?
- If I share this, who benefits: me or the client? Will it harm the client in any conceivable way? (Think short and long term, as well as in terms of the content of the work, as well as the process of interaction with you.)
- Might the client be confused as to my role if I disclose this, such that it might inhibit the client's ability to access the work in the future (e.g., will the client feel as though he or she needs to avoid or hold back in order to protect my feelings)?
- Am I approaching this client, and my expressions or disclosures, in a markedly different fashion than I do with my other clients? What might this suggest?
- Will this information enhance the trust and authenticity of our therapeutic relationship?
- Am I fully considering the client's identity (e.g., racial, ethnic, cultural, religious, sexual orientation, disability status, gender) and unique clinical and personal history, and the potential ripple effects, for this particular disclosure?
- Would I be willing to share this disclosure with my colleagues and supervisors? If not, what does this suggest?
- If I waited a few minutes, would I still want to disclose this?
- Am I fully comfortable with this disclosure? Will I regret it later and how it might impact the work?

Obviously, you won't have time to review all of these questions prior to every juncture of possible self-disclosure in your clinical interactions (unless you want to carry a clipboard around and risk the impact I had on my client from my training days). Again, these questions (along with others that you and your colleagues might generate) are meant to be the mesh of a filter that you've constructed and practiced in advance. With repetition, these questions (and their answers) will likely arise in your awareness during your moments of reflection in session. Again, this is another reason why mindfulness is a cornerstone of effective clinical work—the few seconds you use to step back and conduct a mindfulness check-in will afford you the opportunity for these questions and their answers to come to mind. You will then make better, timelier, and clinically indicated decisions as to what of yourself to share, and what should remain clattering about unnoticed inside your mental closet.

Your difficult client may particularly benefit from self-disclosure. What are you most likely to do when poked, prodded, and challenged by a client? You tighten, withdraw, attack, and otherwise defensively constrict yourself in reaction to the client's maladaptive and displacing behavior. Doesn't this make sense? And how likely are you to choose to self-disclose in these moments? Feels like you're opening yourself to further attack, doesn't it? And it's just this sense of vulnerability you're hoping the client will allow, isn't it? (A willingness to be open in order to attempt a new, more adaptive pattern.)

Instead of doing a defensive dance with clients, self-disclosure (sufficiently answering the questions above) can model the authenticity that the therapeutic relationship, and the client in particular, needs. It's tough to debate someone's personal experience. It's not easy to negate someone's authentically relayed feelings. Clients enter therapy with an inevitable power imbalance in the relationship. And those clients who are most difficult are often the ones most sensitive to this discrepancy, perhaps sparking at least some of their more challenging presentations. As quoted in Barnett (2011), clinician self-disclosure allows for "increased visibility [that] allows the marginalized client more power in the relationship than she would have with a less forthcoming psychotherapist" (Vasquez, 2009, p. 407).

LEAN IN

Cue up your anchors for your difficult client. Mentally review your recent interactions. Look back at session notes if need be to refresh your memory as to the content and process of these sessions. What, if any, junctures were there for self-disclosure on your part? What would the purpose, intended result, and possible effects of any disclosure have been? What impact might this disclosure (and others like it) have on your alliance with this person? Are there any aspects of yourself, your past, and your experience of the client that you would definitely not want to disclose? Why? Take a few minutes to comment below. If possible, review your responses with a colleague in order to elicit feedback and compare notes on the colleague's standards and experiences regarding self-disclosure.

____

____

____

____

____

We need not be open books with our clients, but clients benefit when we're willing to at least give them the more authentic, enduring, and cheat sheet–worthy aspects of ourselves. In today's world of information leaks, we should not leave our clients to the whims of Internet searches to learn about us (and believe me, they *are* searching for you online). Whether you're a behaviorist or a Freudian, let clients see the person behind the diploma and technobabble on occasion. Test it and see the results for yourself.

Sit-Down Comedians: The Role of Humor in Therapeutic Interaction

It's not every day that Hollywood makes a movie about you, so when it happens it must mean you've done something noteworthy. In 1998, Robin Williams starred in the movie *Patch Adams,* the true story of a physician who was also an amateur clown. In the movie, Adams goes to medical school and is appalled at the cold, clinical distance between his colleagues and their patients. Instead, Adams offers patients healing mixed with a heavy dose of humor, and the patients appear to respond. Once he has become a doctor and has opened his own clinic based on his more patient-centered brand of health care, Dr. Adams has to defend his approach against a medical establishment that misunderstands and belittles his methods.

In real life, Adams and his colleagues founded the Gesundheit! Institute, a holistic medical community that has provided free mirth-filled medical care to thousands of patients since it began in 1971. For Dr. Adams, "gesundheit" is not just something you casually and politely say to someone when they sneeze; it's something engaging and reframing that you offer to others to help them heal. The idea is simple: Humor connects us, binds us together, and creates a space for change.

It might be hard to take a professional argument seriously when its proponent is talking from behind a big, red clown nose. We don't have only Patch Adams's perspective on the matter, however. As Adams alludes to on his Web site (www.patchadams.org), a sizable research literature supports his basic argument for the healing role of humor. While a systematic review of this research is beyond the scope of this chapter, studies have consistently supported the role of humor or laughter in reducing stress (Lefcourt, Davidson, Shepherd, & Phillips, 1995; Martin & Lefcourt, 1983; Nezu, Nezu, & Blissett, 1988), and humor has even been linked with physiological changes associated with improved health outcomes (such as increased immune function and blood pressure reduction) (Berk et al., 1989; Kamei, Kumano, & Masumura, 1997; Martin & Dobbin, 1988).

It appears that humor not only makes us feel better—it actually helps us heal better too. It strengthens our immune system, speeds our recovery from illness, and buffers us against disease. With all of these positive effects, it's little wonder that we find ourselves drawn to people who possess a strong capacity for humor. Like comedic pied pipers, we're lulled by the emotional and physical balm their humor provides.

Graham (1995) suggested that subjects who were rated as having a higher self-reported sense of humor, and who then interacted with others believing themselves to be more moderate in the humor department, were more likely to create positive effects in a 30-minute interaction. Partners of participants with a high sense of humor were more likely to report a reduction of uncertainty experienced during their interaction than partners of individuals with a low sense of humor. People who are more comfortable at self-identifying with humor may help ease social interactions, disarming the anxiety arising from not knowing what to expect. Humor makes things familiar and safe, and it gives people a place to start learning about one another. In addition, Graham's data showed that partners of participants with a high sense of humor were significantly more likely to report a desire to engage in future interactions with these people. Clearly, we're drawn to humor, and this research suggests that we are at least in part because funny people mitigate our anxiety; they make interactions more predictable, and they open us up to new possibilities. Humor reduces what Graham calls the "social distance" between us.

Forget what all the research data suggest about the positive effects of humor, and rely on your own experience. Think across your entire clinical career thus far—all of the clients you've worked with over time. Think about all of the clients you've shared laughter with at some point during the work. Consider those clients with whom there was smiling, quipping, puns, or just pure laughing at the raw reality of what emerges in the room. Ask yourself: How did this work turn out? In general, how would you assess the alliances with these clients, as well as the outcomes of the work, relative to other clients? What does this say about the possible role of humor in clinical interaction? Part of an authentic therapeutic interaction is the willingness to share laughter. And with your most challenging clients, your willingness to break the ice (or cool the flames) with some jocularity might do wonders for the health of the work.

Here's an important caveat: Many students, trainees, and clients have told me that I look like comedian Conan O'Brien . . . but I'm not Conan. I have my moments, but I'm certainly no comedian and my clients do not show up hoping for a rib-tickling monologue or onslaught of one-liners. Humor has a role in therapeutic interaction when it increases the authenticity of the connection, when it increases the tethering of brain to brain in the service of healing and change. If you're trying to be funny, reacting with sarcasm, or quipping in a way that makes light of the client's situation, the alliance will most likely suffer. Instead, authentic, well-timed (using all of the recommendations on timing from Chapter 8) humor can help connect you and your clients to the universal, human aspects of pain and struggle. Humor equalizes and opens, and you don't need to have the comedic talent of Robin Williams or Bill Cosby, you merely need to be willing to risk an honest moment in which you discard your pretense of expertise and let yourself just be a person.

LEAN IN

There's no training to be had here in developing skill in using humor in your work. Instead, take a recent interaction with a challenging client. Visualize yourself pausing in the interaction and opening to an observation, a side comment of mild self-deprecating disclosure, a wry quip over something funny that the conversation sparked in your mind. What emerges now as you imagine yourself doing this? Do you notice any reactions in yourself at even attempting to imagine?

____

____

Are you willing to risk such a moment even if it were to fall flat? What might happen if you continue to do so from time to time in your work with this person from a place of honesty, of authentic willingness to reach out to share?

____

____

Again, you're no comedian, you're a clinician. The key question is whether you're willing to use humor to sow the seeds of authenticity in your work with clients—even the really tough ones.

Stacking the Deck Instead of Resting on a House of Cards

A very wise supervisor of mine once said that it is one thing to praise clients for doing the work of treatment, for changing things in their lives, but it is altogether different to "prize" the client. As we leave our discussion of relational leadership with difficult clients, I want to emphasize the need for expressed attunement to these individuals who might not seem to deserve it—the empathy-hard in our caseloads.

Think of times when people have praised you—sometimes you like it, and sometimes it leaves you feeling patronized. Prizing goes beyond any sense of hierarchy or being the well-adjusted expert and is more about the authentic relationship. It's a reminder to us as clinicians to let our clients occasionally (and perhaps often) see that we, as people, really value what we see them doing—as if their efforts to change are a gift we've happened upon. Though we don't want to attach strings to our clients (again, we're all about rope dropping) and make them feel emotionally indebted to change for us, it is important that you see them and care about what you see.

In my work with kids, the common phrase is, "catch them being good." It is noticing when the child is doing something well and letting the child know you see it. Prizing goes beyond this. It lets clients know not only that you see something good they are doing, but that it matters to you. There's a risk, though, for clinicians who frequently prize their clients, even their difficult ones—they end up looking forward to their work, doing it for the sake of doing it, losing track of time during sessions. Sounds precarious, right? Prizing is a decision to give to both the client and to yourself.

LEAN IN

Think of your sample difficult client. What is at least one aspect of this person that you can prize? How might you demonstrate this to the client at your next session? Are you willing to commit to doing this?

____

____

Prizing can become a habit. It contains a measure of gratitude toward the client for being willing to risk so much in coming to work with you. It takes a fair amount of effort at first, and will fall away unless you stick with it. How might you prompt yourself to hang in with prizing? Would it help to discuss this with a colleague? To provide a cue for yourself inside your office (maybe an object that you place in clear view that has meaning only for you)? What is your plan for fostering a prizing approach to your work?

With all this authenticity and prizing we've been discussing, it's tempting to forget that sometimes clients need us to do more than connect. Sometimes their behavior requires a response that they may not like or want in the moment, but nonetheless the viability of the work hinges on it. In the next chapter, we mindfully and compassionately turn toward the client and manage the interaction directly and assertively. Our clients, particularly the difficult ones, require this aspect of leadership.

MAP CHECK

Take a moment and review what we've covered in this chapter. What was one aspect, one piece of content, that resonated with you—sparked your interest, curiosity, or even angst in some way?

Why did this matter to you? What makes this worth writing about? Worth your focus and effort? What is the gravity that this carries for you and your work?

What is one specific action you can take within the next 24 hours related to this issue that feels as though it would be important and has the potential to move you in the direction of what matters?

CHAPTER TEN

Relational Leadership, Part 2: Ditching the Bad Behavior Manager

AT THE BEGINNING of Chapter 4, I told you about Teddy at the therapeutic day school where I work. I described how he pushed my buttons and yanked that old pattern about wanting to avoid conflict and emotional intensity out of me. In order to kick off our discussion of what to do to lead the treatment relationship forward, how to structure and move things in a better direction when the client is still in button-pushing mode, I thought it might help to reveal a bit more from my "failure folder" regarding how not to lead. Here's a snippet about my work with Teddy, a boy with significant mood and behavioral issues.

How to Be a Bad Behavior Manager

And by "bad" I don't mean the client. I always saw Teddy first thing in the morning. His fuse usually had more length early in the day. It also had always been my philosophy to get the hard items out of the way up front. Whether it be test items or unruly kids, get them taken care of first and then the rest would be easy. Teddy was that impossible test item crushing my confidence. "One of the toughest kids we've had," I once heard a coworker at school say of Teddy. "A real heavy hitter."

Trying to have Teddy open his mouth to describe his feelings was a dental impossibility. At least teeth give way with sufficient leverage and time. Not once did he end up crying as a result of in-session buildup. He never asked to speak to me, revealed his honest worries, or let me wander with him into a thicket of nervous questions. It all stayed confined behind his clenched teeth. There was something emotionally ancient about Teddy—a wordless, reptilian reactivity.

Once, I stood at the small write-on board mounted on my office wall. I knew I needed to hook Teddy quickly with this problem-solving strategy. I had the narrowest of windows for getting him to work on anything. He sat in my desk chair, swiveling back and forth.

"Okay, buddy. Let's take that thing that happened yesterday in the classroom. Remember?"

He didn't answer. Of course not. I kept wishing he'd suddenly snap out of it and want the help I was offering. I wanted him to take an episode from the previous day and process it with me. Processing was intended to be therapeutic. It was supposed to lead a kid from being emotionally stuck and in the dark regarding behavior to the light of reason, but sometimes, it was more an opportunity for therapists to feel on the ball, regardless of anything sinking in for the kid.

"I don't want to talk about it," Teddy said. He yanked my keyboard onto his lap and started tapping away at it randomly.

"Teddy, please put the keyboard down. We're not going on the computer just yet."

"Sorry, sorry," he said. It was a hiccup of sorts, an involuntary reflex when an adult pointed out some transgression and Teddy was in an okay mood. He was hoping to happen upon the password to unlock my computer. I always locked it before going to pick him up for sessions. I had learned that lesson well—if Teddy got access to my computer, there was no processing to be had. He'd be lost to the intoxication of Internet shooting games and fantasy basketball Web sites.

I took a step toward him as he sat at my desk. "So what was up with the whole situation in your classroom yesterday?"

He grabbed up the keyboard again.

"Teddy—"

"Sorrrry," he said. Just once. Not the usual pop-pop of contrition. His voice drew out the word, as if wringing it.

I turned toward the board and drew a big circle around the first part of the problem-solving strategy I wanted Teddy to learn: *S—Say the problem.*

"Okay, buddy—can you read what it says here next to the S?"

I watched his eyes glance up quickly at the board and then flit back to my computer screen. "What's your birthday?" he asked me, his fingers poised over my keyboard.

"We're not using my computer yet, Teddy. We've got 10 more minutes before we can have reward time." His pounding of my keyboard intensified.

"What's the S for here?" I asked, pointing to the board. I'd become my astronomy teacher in high school whose lectures were completely ignored. Mr. Herranston's droning about nebulas and parsecs were light-years away from our own kid agendas. More keyboard tapping and more ignoring from Teddy. I thought, no matter what, this kid will do therapy today. A kid as impulsive and unsuccessful as he'd been in school and with other kids was in desperate need of solid problem-solving skills. I wondered if Teddy had any inkling how much he needed this; how he needed to know the "STEPS." It was one piece of a well-researched curriculum (Kazdin & Weisz, 2003) for teaching kids to manage themselves. I was in the mood for change whether Teddy was or not.

S—Say the problem
T—Think of solutions
E—Evaluate your options
P—Pick one
S—See if it worked

That day in therapy, more than 2 years into my time with Teddy, I was exhausted and far past frustration with him. This kid needed to do some work. He had no clue how close he was coming to being sent to a residential placement. Each time he blew off another therapy session and another attempt to help him, he, the adopted kid from Ukraine, was playing Russian roulette with his future. And his mother wasn't helping. During weekend visits she let him roam and plunder their neighborhood like Genghis Kahn. Buying him scratch-off tickets and letting him fire pellet guns at his friend, and call her a bitch in the check-out aisle at Walmart. I had to step in. I needed to keep things from exploding; my Beaver Cleaver quietude required it.

Teddy was going to learn the problem-solving STEPS that day. I was immovable about making him a flexible thinker. Teddy wasn't answering, so I told him his problem was that he'd screamed at his teacher when she told him he had to stay in from recess to do the math worksheet he'd ripped up and thrown on the floor. He ignored me and asked what my wife's name was. "Put my keyboard down," I said, and I reminded him therapy was not play time. His face twisted and I was met with a caveman's grunting.

I told him to look at the board. He grunted louder. I asked what the S was for. He turned away from me toward my computer, literally jamming his fingers into the keyboard like a rabid pianist. I asked again. He was doing therapy, by God. He was going to tell me what the S was for. This kid was not going to fail. Not with me. And then he told me. He yelled as he pushed back from my computer, "Stupid!"

I capped my marker and looked at this boy who'd been born in a Russian orphanage, had been neglected and ignored for the first few years of his life, and who now struggled to risk loving anyone, including his adoptive mother. I looked at this boy who'd failed and been expelled from every school, who was convinced he was retarded and who sometimes, even though he was 12 at the time, peed the bed on occasion. It was no coincidence he had never had a sleepover with a friend, that he had so few friends. I stood over him, convinced he needed more than I could give, more than our school could provide. I was certain he was refusing to help himself, and I felt my voice dying, my therapeutic lung collapsing.

Be a Pattern Breaker

Okay, here's your chance. You've been biding your time this entire book, and you've been very nice about it. You've patiently and diligently heeded my prompts and thoughtfully responded to my questions. I've probed and prodded you and perhaps on occasion you've been a tad irritated, or at least you've regarded me with a head shake and a "this guy can't be serious" smirk. Well, here you go. Take the preceding section—this real situation (though, of course, altered and edited to protect confidentiality)—

and rip it to shreds. I've asked you to look hard at the blemishes and imperfections marring your work—now go ahead and point out mine.

LEAN IN

Review the vignette above and assign my reactions to my young client to a quadrant on the Interpersonal Process Grid (Figure 2.1), noting them in the margins. Also circle any thoughts, or inner dialogue, I appeared to be experiencing that might have been exacerbating my negative experience. Imagine you had my mind (scary, right?) and write in the margins any ideas you have for defusion or perspective-taking strategies that might create some distance on these thoughts. Circle any negative emotions and note any mindfulness strategies that you think I might have benefited from (if I hadn't been so caught up in forcing things with my hapless young client).

Wow, you really can be cruel when you want to, can't you? You must think me the worst therapist in the history of the profession. So, you noticed a "few" things I might have done differently. At the time, my tendency was to beat myself up for my failure to reach this particular client, to help him (and myself) move forward in the work. Here's the trick though—let me summarize all that we've covered thus far about the inner work of managing difficult clients: Of course I failed with him. Patterns, old mental and emotional habits, lack of perspective and tools for experiencing things differently with less rope entangling—all of it made for a failure to adequately connect with this kid inevitable.

And with all my reactivity to this boy, one other aspect of my failure was the difficult time I had setting appropriate limits with him. Either I pushed too hard or (as was generally the case because of my avoidant scripting) not enough. Without a rope-dropping light touch regarding my inner experience of this client, I either yanked too hard or ran the other way. As relationship researcher and psychologist John Gottman (2002) has suggested, we have three alternatives in reaction to left-sided (in terms of the Process Grid) negative client behaviors—we can either aggress/reject (Quadrant C), avoid/withdraw (Quadrant D), or self-disclose/lead (Quadrants A and B). In this chapter, we're learning how to earn good relational "grades" with our difficult clients. Growing up as a student, As and Bs were the only acceptable grades. No pressure for you (and of course you'll fail time and time again as I do), but we should all aspire to ongoing attunement with our difficult clients, and active leadership of the therapeutic relationship. We want to foster a therapeutic attachment and strong alliance. We want to break the patterns in ourselves and our clients that block progress and positive change.

LEAN IN

Think of a time when you struggled to provide sufficient structure and containment to the client's behavior. The client poked, pressed, denied, subverted, and in some way acted out with you during the work together and you failed to manage the situation well. Think of the Process Grid—where did your reactions fall? What did you do (or not do) and what were the consequences for the interaction?

____

____

____

Think to yourself: What might have happened if you had applied some of the strategies we've discussed thus far for managing your experience of this client? What possibilities for proactive intervention and leadership of the interaction might have emerged subsequent to using them?

____

____

____

Consult the values you specified in Chapter 2 that guide your work as a clinician. Emblazon them on the inner surface of your skull because, ideally, they are always present for you. If not, here's a quick tidbit that might help. If you indeed adopt the stance of a pattern breaker, if you're willing to be a clinician who interrupts unhelpful patterns within himself and is open to helping difficult clients do so as well, then you're the sort of clinician who creates positive ripple effects. Unworkable emotional and interpersonal patterns have momentum, often decades of it. Though the going is rough (particularly in the beginning), your willingness to break patterns for the betterment of the work and the client is something more than noteworthy—it shakes things up, creating a seismic shift in a new, positive direction. It's what I call clinical honor.

Lost in the Mail

As we've already learned, it is impossible not to communicate when we're interacting with clients (or anyone for that matter). Communication, intentional or not, is a biological inevitability. Before exploring strategies for actively intervening with clients' difficult behavior, it's crucial that you consider the messages you think you have sent to clients with your reactions versus the messages they actually receive. Sometimes (if not often), the real message you intend gets lost in the mail.

LEAN IN

Cue up your anchors for your difficult client, or select another client with whom you experienced significant conflict, when things were tense and charged and it felt like a lot was at stake. Once you have the client in mind, allow yourself to just notice the images of the moment-to-moment exchange that come to awareness. You might imagine it as a movie clip played in slow motion. Don't try to force the memory to surface. Let it come to mind spontaneously.

Sit down in a quiet place where you won't be disturbed for at least 10 to 15 minutes. Take out a blank envelope and a blank piece of paper. Taking the envelope first, write across the front and back of the envelope the specific external actions you displayed to the client during this particular event. If you were angry about the client not keeping an agreement, write out how you "used a sharp tone," or how you "reminded her of how she's done this before," or that you "looked away and abruptly changed the topic." Whatever your overt actions were, list them.

Now, taking the blank piece of paper, think to yourself about what the real message was you were hoping the client would receive. What was the intent behind your actions on the envelope that you were hoping the client would internalize and respond well to? What was the feeling or need behind that? What was the unspoken expectation you were hoping the client would respond to? Perhaps it was for the client to notice how frustrated you've been with where the work is going. It might have a lot to do with worry or fear. Perhaps you were deeply concerned for the client and were just trying to ensure he or she finally got on the right track. You'll likely find that these deeper messages relate to values of yours that have been blocked or gotten stuck in some way. Whatever the deeper message that was surrounded by your behaviors, write out on the sheet of paper your best sense of what these intentions and feelings were.

Put the letter in the envelope and seal it up.

Clear your mind. Center yourself with a brief period of mindful focus on your breath. When you are ready, hold the envelope in your hands. Imagine that you are not you anymore. You are the client—the one you experienced the difficulty with. You have just received this letter in the mail. Read what's written across the envelope—all these interventions projected at you. Read the words slowly and deliberately, perhaps even saying them out loud to deepen the processing.

In your role as the client, what is your impulse? What do you want to do with this envelope? Notice any thoughts or reactions that arise. If the envelope contains any significant pushing or pulling, anything with a tug-of-war feel to it, it's a safe bet you're noticing yourself less interested in what might be inside. You may toss the letter aside as junk mail altogether.

Wonder to yourself how much your client may have disregarded your "letters"—the true messages—because of the emotional and behavioral graffiti all over the envelope.

Leadership in clinical work involves looking deeply into the perspective of a client, appreciating all the internal and contextual factors driving the behavior, understanding and allowing one's own understandable negative or painful reactions, and . . . setting limits, implementing structure, and providing guidance anyway. Clinicians who work most effectively with difficult-to-manage clients do so from a simultaneous balance of compassion and what I call "presence"—being firmly rooted in one's own and the client's perspective and acting to protect the values guiding the work. This presence is a set of skills—cognitive, emotional, and behavioral—that we'll now discuss and practice together.

Clients won't know how far they can push things, and they might just be overwhelmed by all the open space around your therapeutic stance unless you're willing to build some fences. Though to some people it might sound contradictory, setting limits and boundaries in clinical work with difficult clients is indeed a very compassionate thing to do.

Building Fences: The Importance of (Compassionate) Limit Setting

Ask any parents, and they'll give many examples of their kids testing them, pushing buttons, and misbehaving in order to get something, avoid something, or just for the heck of it (or so it seems). Homework delay tactics, chore dodging, jealous sibling tattle-taling, I-want-pizza-for-dinner-and-because-it's-liver-I'm-tantrumming—most parents have ridden this merry-go-round of mischief. Ask any parent and, if they're in an honest mood, they'll admit to their occasional (or frequent) cave-ins—the avalanche of avoidance that leads them to let kids have what they want. It's difficult to set consistent limits on children's problem behavior. And yet, it is so important that parents do so. It is also crucial that we do so as clinicians with our clients when they act in ways that are significantly detrimental to them, the therapy, and to us personally. Of course, we should not regard our adult clients as kids. Adult status doesn't preclude, however, the need for proactive responses to inappropriate behavior in session. But how do you know when a client's behavior calls for a limit?

In the space below, give your own list of the client actions and the situations that would ideally call for clinician leadership—setting a limit or providing structure for the client's behavior.

____

____

____

____

I spend a significant portion of my professional time coaching parents in managing their children's problem behavior at home. For parents I work with, it is tempting for them to think a particular infraction of the rules is no big deal and not worth a pitched battle that disrupts the entire household. "Johnny didn't really mean it," and "besides, I don't want to get the whole house into an uproar." For many parents, the day has already been far too stressful. "I just need to relax. I can't handle this right now." Yes, it's true that parents should pick their battles. There's no need to pounce on kids' every misstep. Correct—children's feelings and perspectives are important, and must be acknowledged. "Because I said so!" should be stricken from the parental vocabulary. Remember, though, it is also true that kids are sending messages with their noodginess and ne'er-do-welling—"I'm anxious," "I'm physically revved up and can't calm down," or "I'm upset and don't know what to do with it" are common themes.

Our difficult clients are sending us their own messages with their problem behavior. They are telegraphing their pain. Our tug-of-war, knee-jerk reactions send messages as well. Without intending to, we send messages to clients such as:

- "I don't want to deal with this."
- "You cannot be contained."
- "You're on your own figuring out how to deal with your pain."
- "I'm going to prove you wrong."
- "People in your life will get out of your way and bow to your whims and desires."

As clinicians, we must ask ourselves what messages we ultimately want our clients to learn about how best to handle their pain. What do we want them to remember about how we handled our own?

How to LEAD as a Clinician

You're not looking to control your clients. You are not your clients' parent. Clinical leadership is focused on a sense of empathic vigilance—keeping treatment on the path consistent with agreed-upon goals and values for the work. We've spent the book thus far dealing with your own reactions that can take the work astray. Now (and only now) are you fully prepared to deal with the client's behavior. To set limits and structure on client behavior without orienting fully to their perspective, and without gaining defused distance and perspective on your own experience, will lead to situations similar to those of some parents I've coached:

- "You're grounded for a month!"
- "You will never see that boy again!"
- "Why do you have to do it? Because I'm your mother, and I said so!"

Instead you want to LEAD: Four steps to follow to ensure you are building fences around behavior that create the necessary safety, and what researchers Schneider, Cavell, and Hughes (2003) refer to as a sense of "perceived containment" for the client. Compassionate limit setting creates a space for clients to pause, learn, and realign their behavior with the values guiding their lives. Due to the wave of angst clients can unleash, proactively setting limits requires courage. In order to set limits (or manage boundaries, if you prefer that term) in a nonreactive way that benefits the therapeutic relationship, the work, and you as well, consideration is also important. I like the word *consideration* because it implies thoughtfulness, a willingness to look at the broader context and take action for the betterment of everyone involved. Though it may be a firm fence you erect with a client, there's a warmth there as well (notice I said warmth, not electrification).

One last thing before we discuss the steps to effective limit-setting with clients: Let's take a brief look at what not to do. Consider the following limit-setting statement from a clinician to a client who has been coming to sessions high on cocaine. See if you can locate the problems with this clinician's limit and its delivery.

> At the very end of the session as the client is getting up to leave, the clinician says, "Oh, Jim, I need you to know that it's clear to me that you're using once again, and that doing so is an attempt to avoid the work we've been doing around your anxiety."
>
> Jim, the client, hovers at the doorway with his hand on the knob. "So what? I don't give a shit."
>
> *cont'd on next page*

> *cont'd from previous page*
>
> "What you're doing is unsafe and I may have to take action to have you committed later today. You're not making sound decisions for yourself."
>
> Jim rips the door open, and turns to glare at the therapist. "Go ahead and try it, asshole! See if I ever pay your bill."

I'm sure you agree that this hapless clinician's limit was poorly set with this client. Here are three key principles this clinician violated:

1. The limit should be appropriate for the context.
2. The limit should be clear (specific about the client behavior involved as well as the action the clinician will take).
3. The limit should be doable (i.e., you can actually implement it).

LEAN IN

Take a moment and specify how you think this limit was poorly managed in this example:

____

____

____

In this example, the clinician hesitated until the very end of the session to set the limit regarding the client's cocaine use, and therefore did not allow any time to process things with the client. In addition, the client's behavior of "using and being high during sessions" was never specified. Last, the clinician's stated action of committing the client is not even possible under his state's involuntary hospitalization statute (i.e., not a doable, or enforceable, limit). You can imagine how much work it will take for this clinician to repair this rupture with Jim (if the chance even arises).

So with that brief interlude in the land of poor limit setting, let's get to the steps for the more effective rendition. Think of the example above (and perhaps some from your own practice) as you read and consider these steps. You'll likely see where this clinician (and most others, despite our best efforts and intentions) often go awry in managing boundaries in our work.

Lean Into the Moment

It is here that you need to insert everything we've practiced thus far—all the defusing from your script-based thoughts, mindful awareness of your emotional reactions, and orienting to your client's perspective—his or her wants. Basically, you're moving toward the present moment. You're noticing what shows up in your thoughts and emotions, and you're focusing on what matters most on the letter inside the envelope to your client. Even if your client is escalating with anger, you can (if you're willing) still accomplish all of this within the span of a few seconds. Obviously, if a client is imminently dangerous to himself, others, or you, you will need to act to ensure safety (e.g., moving out of the client's way, calling for help, calling emergency services, initiating a hospitalization, bringing in other professionals to contain the situation). These situations require less leaning and more leveraging. There is little room for ambiguity, and I don't think you need this book to know the basics of why and how to intervene (that's what the crisis intervention training you've probably had was for). Here, we're focused on the less obvious situations.

Examine the Appropriateness of a Limit

After you've leaned into the moment, you then ask a couple quick questions of yourself. The answers should spring readily to mind and guide you to the next step. This is the step where parents learn to pick their battles. It is a very brief cognitive pause during which you make sure a limit on the client's behavior will move things forward.

- Is the client's behavior right now significantly interfering with the agreed-upon goals and values of our work together?
- Is the client's behavior significantly violating my boundaries (i.e., do I find myself feeling unacceptably uncomfortable)?

Actively Intervene and Set the Limit

Your answers to the questions at the last step tell you that a limit is necessary. Now, you are ready to assert structure on the here-and-now of the interaction. You are guiding what happens next, and you are setting an expectation. You are letting the client know where the boundaries are, and you're giving the client an opportunity to learn about the impact of his or her behavior on others. This step involves just a few pointers:

- Assume the physical and nonverbal stance of a leader. Sit up, lean forward, make eye contact, take on a more assertive, serious expression, shift toward a more businesslike tone of voice, and use as few words as possible.
- Acknowledge the client's "letter"—the feelings and perspective behind the behavior. Let the client know you see what's driving things. "You have every right to be angry right now . . ." or "I know you are really suffering because of what happened . . ." or "This is incredibly unfair and painful for you."
- Link this acknowledgment to the limit. You've let the client know you see his or her perspective, the emotional engine for the behavior, and you're still going to structure what happens now in session. "You have every right to be angry right now and . . ." (proceed to the next step).
- Inform the client of the "if . . . then" contingency. In as few words as you can, let the client know your previously constructed (if at all possible) cause-and-effect sequence of what will now happen in response to the behavior if it continues or does not immediately cease. I can't emphasize enough how important it is to have prepared in advance as to what your limit (or consequence) on the client's behavior will be. A key principle of any behavioral limit setting is to only set limits that you can consistently implement. Telling your client that you will no longer pay attention to threats to harm herself in session is a limit you cannot ethically and legally abide by. Using a consequence you have prepared in advance (and one that you can implement), give the client your "if . . . then" statement.

- "If you continue directing your anger at me by yelling in my face, then I will ask you to leave."
- "If you call me again at my home number, then I will need to end our sessions and will refer you to another clinician."
- "If you can't pay the balance we've agreed upon, then I will need to suspend our meetings until it's paid."

Allow for a processing gap. Sometimes, particularly when clients are emotionally charged up, their frontal lobes need a few moments to take in what you've said. Don't jump too fast with actually setting your limit. It's not a race, but then again, you don't want to give the impression that you're hesitating—that you won't follow through. Remember, clients might assume that since you're a clinician, you might be soft on setting limits. Give their frontal lobes a chance (a few seconds to a minute is enough), but don't give them the sense that you're a pushover either.

Detach and Assess

This step is crucial. You've defused and mindfully made contact with your own reactions; you've connected with the client's perspective; you've determined the behavior needs a limit, and now you've set it. Now you're in the gap while the client processes, and you're waiting to see if the client will respond (or not). Here, it's very important that you resume with defusion from negative pattern–based, blaming sorts of thoughts, mindfully notice emotional reactions, and detach from the outcome of the interaction. You cannot control what the client does next. You have merely provided an opportunity. You are defusing, detaching, and disentangling from any ropes that the client is throwing your way. You are firmly on the right side of the Interpersonal Process Grid. Here, you are attuned to the client and you are actively leading the interaction forward. During the gap, you may choose to briefly and concisely restate the limit in "broken record" fashion.

"Again, you have the right to be upset, and if you can't stop pounding my desk, sit back, and get control over your body, then you will need to leave my office."

These are the steps for right-sided leadership of client acting-out behavior. They come from a compassionate consideration of the client's perspective and the collaborative values that direct the course of the work. They are not heavy-handed because you've ensured that they are not the result of a tug-of-war. They are in the best interest of your client.

Limit setting is not about becoming a clinical executioner. You did not (hopefully) enter this field in order to drop the hammer on clients. It's not about crushing clients under the weight of professional pressure. In the same sentence that you tell a client that a behavior is inappropriate, crosses the line, and results in a consequence, you can acknowledge the truth and validity of the impulse—the real message—that spawned it. Feelings and impulses are always acceptable. Bad behavior—destructive to self and others—is not.

Very importantly, notice what is not part of any of these LEADing responses to client behavior. There is no sarcasm, debating, arguing, or lecturing. These are obvious left-sided reactions that are telltale signs of a full-blown tug-of-war. While these may be obvious, you will (in true Vonnegutian style) pick up the rope and use them from time to time. The trick here is to catch yourself and remember that it is never too late to drop the rope and use strategies we've discussed for creating space, distance, and perspective. Do so and you can spark a more therapeutic pattern of interaction with your client.

Here's another step to any effective limit. You have to be ready and willing to authentically acknowledge clients' movement in the direction of the limit. Even if they are tentative or begrudging in their actions, if they are moving toward following through, you need to acknowledge it.

- "I'm glad we're on track again. This is clearly very tough for you."
- "Thanks for taking care of this. I really appreciate the respect you're showing our work together."
- Or a quiet, simple, full eye contact "thank you."

It can be hard to acknowledge clients in this manner. In particular, it can feel like the last thing you want to do since they may have just finished directing a lot of angst in your direction. They may have done or said something very hurtful or anxiety provoking. You would be within your rights to feel as though they don't deserve such accolades from you. And yet, such an attuned response is exactly the sort of rope dropping that will get the interaction unstuck.

A final hint for any effective limit setting: *Follow through with it.* Not to do so gives a clear message to clients: The fences you erect are pointless, merely for appearances. If you tell a client you will hang up the phone, you must hang up. If you say that you will refer the person to another therapist, you must pick up the phone and do so. Whatever the limit you set—whatever fence you build—make your message to clients consistent and authentic. You mean what you say.

LEAN IN

Cue up the anchors for your difficult client. Bring to mind one of the more problematic acting-out episodes you experienced with this person. Perhaps it was a pattern of intense anger directed at you; maybe it was (as in the example above) showing up at session drunk or impaired by other substances; maybe it was some other provocative violation of boundaries; or maybe the client just isn't paying the bill. Whatever the scenario, use the space below to construct your own limit for the client's behavior. How will you LEAD this exchange with the client forward? Construct your own phrasing and specific contingency for how to best structure the client's behavior.

Client behavior or situation:

____

____

Lean In responses and strategies:

____

____

Examine the appropriateness of a limit:

____

____

Active limit-setting approach:

____

____

Detach and assess strategies:

____

____

It can be very helpful to visualize how you will lead a difficult interaction in advance of having to do so in reality. During your time of regular, mindfulness awareness rounds or check-ins with the difficult clients in your caseload, it will dramatically enhance your ability to set appropriate limits if you practice in your imagination with as much concrete and visceral detail as possible. Ask yourself how you will handle a particular client's tantrums in your office. How will you deal with yet another no-show? What will you do when the client yet again lets you know she's been researching your personal history in great, stalkeresque detail? How does it feel to imagine yourself in these situations? What shows up in your thoughts and emotions? What might get in the way of your ability to LEAD, and how will you address these obstacles?

In addition to your own contemplative rehearsals, it can also be very helpful to process your plans, and your reactions to implementing them, with a trusted colleague or supervisor. Role-play possible situations if that would be helpful. The more actual practice you have in clinical presence and leadership behaviors, the more you will find yourself able to exhibit them when clients are whipping you with the rope.

As in the clinical example above (and as we discussed in Chapter 8), timing is crucial in order to process any limits you've set with clients. Don't "doorknob" clients with a limit at the very end of the session and don't hammer them with it as soon as they walk in your door either. Whose needs are you really meeting in either scenario? It's generally ill advised to attempt a great deal of processing when the client's frontal lobe is awash in dysregulation-inducing neurochemicals, and yet avoiding the conversation altogether risks creating a "process elephant" that squashes the authenticity of the therapeutic relationship. Again, all this is why timing is crucial in our work, and limit setting absolutely requires it.

Hurry Up and Do Nothing

One of the more notable strategies in the coaching work I do with parents, and in my work with troubled kids more generally, is called "active ignoring" (Kazdin, 2005). In this approach, parents and staff members are taught to identify a child's disruptive, provocative behavior—one that functions by hitting buttons and generating a reaction. Many of the kids I work with seem to be board-certified professional button pushers. They know their caregivers hate embarrassment, rejection, threats of safety, and loss of both face and financial wellness. "I hate you. . . . I want a new mom. . . . I wish I was never born. . . . You suck as a dad. . . . Yeah, I broke the stereo, who cares? . . . I don't care if the whole world is looking. . . . I'm gonna get you fired"—and let's not forget the infinitely charming whining and incessant crying, "You don't care about me!" And they say and do these things because—simply put—it works. Eventually they get a reaction, and sometimes even a negative reaction is ample reward. A tug-of-war commences between adult and child, often with the child getting his way (or at least a delay in the homework, the trash-taking, or whatever it is he doesn't want).

With active ignoring, the caregiver turns off the attention and stops talking with, and even turns away from, the child. Even if the child increases the intensity of button pushing, the key is to keep the buttons out of reach and not respond. Only when the child calms it down and slows or stops the behavior, does the switch flip on again and engagement resumes.

Through the use of this planned response to provocative behavior, clinicians can help clients learn that certain attention-seeking behaviors are ineffective. Again, I'm not suggesting you regard your clients with arms-crossed parental condescension. What this approach does provide, though, is an opportunity in a safe, supportive environment for clients to learn new, more effective ways to connect and be heard.

But wait, you may be wondering. "I thought this chapter was about what we can do when clients are acting out? This seems passive—almost like you're letting clients do whatever they want." Active ignoring is not a left-sided rejection of the client. In fact, if done correctly, it is quite compassionate. To use the metaphor of a light switch, you turn off your engagement and responsiveness temporarily in response to a client's provocative behavior, but you're waiting to immediately turn on again when the client turns away from or stops that behavior. You are very present—you understand where this behavior comes from, and you're helping the client get feedback that can be crucial to making better connections with others. Particularly when the therapeutic relationship is strong, this strategy has the potential to influence clients for the better. It requires a great deal of perspective, defusion, and mindful allowing on the part of the clinician. A client might be shoving a great deal of provocative nonsense in your direction, and it can be incredibly difficult not to pick up the rope and react.

Therapist and author Sheldon Kopp (1977) wrote regarding a therapeutic use of distance in response to client acting-out behavior, emphasizing, as we've discussed throughout this book, the importance of immediate messages our behavior as clinicians imparts during interactions. According to Kopp, "the therapist must avoid reinforcing the patient's acting out. I do this by withholding the expected social response. . . . I must be willing to tolerate the patient's hurt and angry response to what is likely to be seen as my arbitrary, unreasonable, rude, uncaring and even hateful behavior" (p. 97). Kopp recommends that clinicians learn to embrace their own silence and to view themselves as working quite hard (in attuning to the client), even if "doing nothing." "For most therapists, talking too much is the more common error" (p. 142). Our willingness to hold our tongues, ride our reactions, and avoid reinforcing client problem behavior can often serve to create the space necessary in the interaction for clients to more fully engage their experience and make therapeutic gains.

LEAN IN

Take a client of yours (either the one you've been using so far, or another) who exhibits provocative behavior during interactions with you. Select a behavior pattern that does not meet your boundary-violating or treatment-interfering criteria for limit setting, and complete the prompts below:

What is the specific behavior? (The more concrete and detailed you can be in describing it, the better. Let go of any judgments or interpretations in your description. What does it look like?)

When does the behavior occur? What tends to be happening just before the behavior? (What are you doing? What do they tend to be doing or talking about? How do they seem to be feeling?)

What tends to happen right after this behavior occurs? What have you done in reaction in the past? What have you gleaned as to how others react? What does this tell you about what the client is looking for with this behavior?

What will you now do to actively ignore this specific behavior the next time it occurs? Does sitting quietly without saying anything make sense? Might you assume a blank, waiting sort of facial expression?

When clients first encounter this intervention, they may "burst" with even more of the behavior in hopes of eliciting a reaction. How will you handle such a reaction? How might defusion and mindfulness strategies we've discussed be helpful here?

You've flipped the switch of your engagement off during the behavior. How will you flip it on once the behavior ceases? How will you reengage the client?

It may be helpful to preview with clients that you may use active ignoring as a therapeutic stance in your work. (Hint: You might want to call it something else when talking to the client—maybe "active detachment"—so that it sounds less rejecting). To the degree they understand in advance that you may not respond to certain behaviors as a way to help focus the work and provide feedback about communication patterns, they will be less likely to respond with contempt ("Hey, you can't ignore me!"). They still may not like it, but they are more likely to understand where you're coming from. Well-timed, active ignoring can create room for shifts in unhelpful patterns in the therapeutic relationship. I would also recommend collaborating with clients around this strategy. Connect it with the values and specific goals underlying the work. Especially if clients are invested in improving their communication and authenticity skills with others, active ignoring might be a strategy they would be willing to see in session from time to time (though they may not enjoy it in the moment).

Active ignoring is another strategy that can be helpful to practice with a colleague. Taking turns presenting difficult statements and behavior to one another, practice active detachment and discuss or troubleshoot the likely outcomes with clients. Sometimes, doing nothing, creating space, is the most helpful thing you can do in response to difficult client behavior.

Tending the Fence: Integrating Skills to Manage the Therapeutic Relationship

We've discussed setting limits and boundaries with clients. We've just practiced how you might detach in order to help redirect client behavior. Let's shift gears and get our hands dirty. You've been working diligently at managing yourself, and are now making forays into managing what shows up for the difficult client. What do you do when things get really hairy in your interactions? Threats are flying, indecent proposals are made, and all manner of chaos has been flung in the direction of your office fan. What to do?

MAP CHECK

Take a moment and review what we've covered in this chapter. What was one aspect, one piece of content, that resonated with you—sparked your interest, curiosity, or even angst in some way?

Why did this matter to you? What makes this worth writing about? Worth your focus and effort? What is the gravity that this carries for you and your work?

What is one specific action you can take within the next 24 hours related to this issue that feels as though it would be important and has the potential to move you in the direction of what matters?

≺ CHAPTER ELEVEN ≻

Lost in Left Field

Managing the Unexpected, the Extreme, and the Repugnant With Clients

YOU DIDN'T NEED a degree in psychology to know Susan was significantly depressed. Her hair was oily and tangled, her clothes mismatched and baggy, as if to hide herself from the world. She slouched down in her chair across from me, her face sagging with pained weight. I smiled and told her I was glad to see her, and she glared at me, opening her mouth slowly as if requiring great effort.

"I want to die and be done with all this. I've failed at everything else, but I'll finally get it right when I off myself." She didn't cry and did not ask for help. She was all business. Her pain was so dense I could feel a piece of it stretching my stomach as if I'd swallowed a cannonball. I knew she would not accept reassurances or reminders of the obvious reasons she had to stay alive, or anything coming close to an attempt to strip her of her desire to kill herself. Ward Cleaver's moralistic lectures would indeed fall flat.

I held on to that wad of lead in my stomach, realized that it was a mere speck of what Susan was feeling, and let myself focus on what it would be like to feel myself crushed with the weight of it. After a long pause, I told Susan, "It makes sense that you want to die. You're doing the best you can to get out from under all this pain."

It was a statement that, at the time, did not feel at all risky. I wasn't saying anything she didn't already know; in fact, that was just the point—I started where she was. I started with her stuckness and reframed what her suicide attempt was actually about. I took the fact that she had swallowed numerous sleeping pills and reshaped it into an effort to heal herself of the seemingly overwhelming pain.

Susan looked at me and said nothing for a long time. We sat together in silence as she tried on this new frame for her distress. Susan was fashioning a starting place for looking at options, and slowly began doing the hard work of crawling out of the crater her life had descended into.

I'd love to claim that I've always managed such extreme situations with a similar centered, stable, compassionate demeanor. As I've already said, I've screwed up enough in the face of intense client behavior to fill many a supervisory session (or confessional booth). This chapter is less about a prescriptive laundry list of tips for what to do with the client gone wild, and is more a nudge in the direction of leaning in toward this wildness, taming the moments of difficulty in order to create openings and opportunities.

In my work with troubled kids, I've been punched, kicked, spit on, had my hair pulled, heard my brand-new blazer ripping from an angry kid's yanking, and I've even been slapped in the leg with a pee-soaked towel. While this may sound intense, I've never been physically assaulted in a way that I would consider life threatening. I've heard kids tell me they were going to do not-nice things to my person, and that my life expectancy might come into question, but I can say with certainty that I've never been threatened by a client in such a way that I knew my life was in danger. Some of you have. Although my vignette above describes an attempted suicide by a former client, I have never (to my knowledge) worked with a client who later died by suicide. Again, some of you have.

Any reader who has actually had their life imperiled by a client, or has suffered the devastation of a client suicide, has an understanding I can never claim, nor would pretend to. I've known intensity, but I must admit I don't know what some of you unfortunately do. This chapter is not meant to replace other works that are much more suited for addressing specifics of psychiatric crisis management (such as Phillip Kleespies' [2008] *Behavioral Emergencies*), or how to best understand vicarious traumatization and address its effects (B. Hudnall Stamm's [1999] *Secondary Traumatic Stress*, or Babette Rothschild's [2006] *Help for the Helper*). I am far from qualified to counsel clinicians on these aspects of managing the extremes of client behavior. This chapter is about how to use the mindfulness-based skills we've been practicing as "mindfulness in action"—how to take the inner work and translate it into increased capacity for outer behavior during and after the most intense, difficult, and extreme situations.

LEAN IN

In the space below, list the most intense, outlandish, upsetting, destructive, and downright repulsive behaviors you have either witnessed a client exhibit, or have knowledge of. Without pausing to consider each, continue writing out your comprehensive list of everything you can remember across the course of your career thus far.

____

____

____

____

____

____

Now, go back and circle any client behavior that you felt thrown by—that you reacted versus mindfully responded to. Even if it was a behavior you did not witness, what did you do, say, or think when you first learned of it? Circle all the client actions that sparked reactivity in some notable way for you.

Look over your list. What reactions do you notice even now? Allow yourself to merely watch them within yourself. Sit with them until you notice them changing in some way on their own. Once things have seemed to shift, move directly to the next exercise.

LEAN IN

In the space below, take a few minutes and write a summary of a recent challenging interaction with a client. Describe who did what, and what you make of the interaction—its importance, meaning, and possible ramifications. Focus on drawing conclusions about what happened and what the interaction suggests.

Review your writing. Look for any references to either you or the client having "done" something (e.g., "client was defensively avoidant of any experience of vulnerable affect") and edit your writing in the following ways. Go back and cross out words and write in others based on the following guidelines:

- Change all references to "client" or "you" as the clinician to the word *we*.
- Make every sentence present tense—no past or future.
- Underline every verb—what exactly are you and the client doing?

Take a moment to review these changes. How is the interaction now different? What does this suggest? How has the meaning of the exchange shifted?

As we consider the most extreme, difficult interactions with our clients, it's important to remember how limited our perspective is on what's happening—that our window of insight into all the variables leading the client's actions is extremely small. There is always a "we" and there is always the "now" of the interaction and often, particularly after the most intense behaviors, the collective, reciprocal, and immediate aspects are lost.

Meditation teacher and author Sylvia Boorstein (1995) suggests people are actually more verbs than nouns. Instead of the fixed entities that tend to solidify even more in the most challenging moments, it may help for us to step back and see the inevitable flux and fluidity in clients and us. Here's a mouthful to consider: *Your clients—even the most vexing ones—have not always been, and will not always be, what they are right now that you most adamantly don't want them to be.*

LEAN IN

Before getting too lost in philosophical flights of fancy, close your eyes and center yourself in breath and body. Take your sample difficult client, or take a client interaction that was particularly egregious. See the movie of this behavior playing itself out in your mind and notice the reactions emerging. Let yourself focus on the situation until you're completely immersed in it, until it's vivid.

Now imagine the following:

- This particular client as a newborn baby.
- This client as a young child, afraid and overwhelmed, and, at the moment, alone.
- This client failing in some way as a young adult, desperately wanting something that slips from his or her grasp.
- This client dead and buried (or in some way dispatched from life).

Come back to your breathing, and come back to visualizing this most unbelievable behavior on the client's part. How solid is it? Will things change? Might there be another stance you could take on the energy conveyed by the client's actions? And while you're at it, ask yourself: Who is noticing all of this? If you are watching all of these thoughts, images, behavior, and emotions swirling about, then can "you" be these things? Who's minding the store?

In considering the most extreme client behaviors—the threats, the using, the violence against self and others, the abuse and neglect of children, partners, and parents—you should be aiming to loosen your grip and take in the inevitability and the malleability of these situations. *Of course* the clients behaved in this way (because the intersection of their context, learning history, and biology at that moment in time demanded it), and of course their behavior will vary—these factors will inevitably change to some degree with time (and perchance, with your intervention). Though patterns may repeat, nothing ever occurs in exactly the same way and with all the same conditions as before—even slight shifts underscore the point: Change is not just possible, it is persistent. To fully experience this "temporariness" can have the benefit of decreasing the hardening that tends to come in reaction to client extremes. Let's extend this sense of the workability of extremes with another exercise.

LEAN IN

Sit comfortably and center yourself in your surroundings, body, and breath. In your mind's eye, imagine sitting with a large audience in a darkened movie theater. You're in the front row, and the room is packed with people. The film is playing on the big screen in front of you—*it's all about you.* In sequence, imagine the following scenes as they unfold. Listen for the thoughts and feelings that emerge as you watch scenes depicting . . .

1. Your most egregious mistake, transgression, blunder, foible, failure—whether it's personal or professional, let that episode play itself out. Note any impulse to look away, to flinch from the screen, and, if you're willing, watch and listen anyway. The whole audience is seeing your outrageous, unbelievable actions in excruciating detail. What's showing up for you? What's here for you as you sit and watch your greatest failure big and bold on the screen?

2. Your "best" client. . . . This next scene is about the client you always like to refer to, the one you tell stories about who makes you feel worthwhile and effective. Imagine that the scene is all about this person's most egregious action. You and the whole audience are seeing this paragon of your professional efforts mess up in the biggest of ways. Even if you're not aware of what this failure might actually have been for this person, allow your mind to conjure what it could be. See this playing out on the screen. Who is this person to you in this moment as you and the audience react?

3. Your "worst" client. . . . Perhaps it's the one you've been referring to throughout this book, or maybe it's someone you've actually avoided thinking much about until this moment. On the screen, see this person doing whatever it is your mind assumes he or she does outside your office. Notice the emotional tenor of what your mind immediately gravitates toward. What does this suggest about how fused and fixed your views of this client are? No matter how disruptive and destructive the client's behavior, how might any fusion, any rigidity on your part, perhaps contribute to the interaction in some way?

Now, imagine your worst client in the absolute best moment. Perhaps her child is being born. . . . He is standing, diploma in hand. . . . She takes a meal to the shut-in elderly man who lives down the hall.

Imagine this "worst" client in other, less desirable moments. What might the person be like at the moment of finding that her longtime pet has passed away on the carpet at home? Perhaps he sits shaking with fear in the seconds after a car accident that has left him injured. Maybe her hand covers that of her dying parent in a silent, darkened hospital room. Whatever you're aware of that's occurred for this poorly behaving client, or whatever your mind can create, see it happening vividly on the movie screen in front of you. And now realize that these moments, both the "best" and "worst," are not mere movie scenes—they have, are, and will occur for this client.

What happens for you in attempting to imagine your most difficult clients in this way? Does your mind push back at the notion of softness or empathy for such people? Some of our clients behave in what can be referred to as a morally repugnant manner. They demean, violate, offend, abuse, you name it. Are you supposed to simply wrap a pretty emotional bow around them in your mind and flash them an enthusiastic smile while they're whipping you with a pee-soaked towel or maligning your very existence? Because you're a clinician, are you supposed to just absorb whatever they do with blind, mute, and dumb acceptance?

The most effective management of these trickiest of moments has little to do with mere silver linings and reflective listening mantras. As we've discussed before, acceptance of client actions does not entail condoning them. You don't need to clap your clients on the back and give them a hearty thumbs up, but it may indeed help to assume that the energy of their actions comes from the confluence of their unmet needs and outclassed skill sets. *It just is*, and railing against the reality of it is like shaking your fist at the sun for being so bright.

Managing moral repugnance also requires that you assume the inevitability in yourself. At times, your own unmet needs and outclassed skill sets come to a head in the air between you and the client. Instead of self-flagellation, you (and the client) benefit from a compassionate creation of space and supports for yourself. There is no room in our work for helplessness and ongoing victimization. Punching bags are meant to take and absorb an endless barrage—clinicians are not. Who is your most trusted resource at this very moment? Who is the colleague or supervisor you can go to without hesitation to sort through the most challenging of actions and reactions in your work? List the name here:

____

How willing are you right now to contact this person and ask (if you haven't already) for his or her willingness to be available to you for any future crisis that emerges? To affirm this ongoing availability?

1	2	3	4	5
Not Willing		Somewhat Willing		Very Willing

If you're willing, contact this person now and notice what happens for you when you do, as well as what happens after. What does this suggest about your ability to manage the unmanageable? If you're not interested in contacting this person now, spend some time writing below about what, specifically, leads you away from doing so. Look not only at external, pragmatic barriers, but at the experiences you're having that might be downgrading your "will-o-meter" (including thoughts such as "I'm too busy reading now to pick up the phone—I'll do it later." . . . Thank your mind for that one!).

____

____

____

____

In addition to reaching out to a supportive colleague or supervisor, it's imperative that you have a specific plan for how you go about separating from the extremes of your work, and resetting yourself emotionally. Particularly after very intense interactions with clients, clinicians can be left spinning and may veer down reactive, impulsive routes of self-management. Many times after really tough exchanges, I've sat alone in my office reeling with the shock waves of emotion from what just occurred. The client's pain, anger, or shocking behavior has left me slumped in my chair, staring at the wall. The temptation is to go either deeply (and rigidly) inward (Quadrant D on the Process Grid) or snappishly outward (Quadrant C) with impulsive, acting-out sorts of behaviors. Harder to do is to truly listen (mindfully, and with dispassionate acceptance, to the throb of one's thoughts and affect), look to one's core guiding values, and leap in their direction. You don't need me to lecture you on relaxation skills or how taking truly rejuvenating vacation time is critical. All you need at the moment is to remind yourself of what, specifically, you're willing to commit to doing to take that leap in the direction of what matters in the wake of the most overwhelming of client actions. What concrete things will you do to keep yourself right-sided when things come out of left field at you? Think body, mind, spirit, relationship—all domains should be addressed.

- When I've been significantly affected by a client's actions (I'm noticing myself intensely drawn toward the left on the Interpersonal Process Grid), I commit to taking the following actions in the service of [list values] ______________________________. I will do the following:
  ____
  ____
  ____
  ____
  ____

Channeling Bruce Lee: Becoming a Therapeutic Martial Artist

The most skillful martial artists move with power, control, and grace. Despite the flailing rage coming at them, the true masters seem capable of rapid conversion of their attacker's intensity into their own quick, effective response. Though it may not be advisable to stand up from your chair and give your angry, volatile client an axe kick to the side of the head (tempting though it may be), it is nonetheless possible to learn to get more skillful at such "energy conversion" in our work.

The exercises below may seem a bit unusual, but give them a try. Some things are best realized through direct experience. You've been working throughout this book on opening your perspective. I'm asking you to (literally) open your arms wide to what happens (and what can be possible in the most challenging moments) when you do. Let's literally do some mindfulness in motion.

LEAN IN

These exercises are adapted from the work of aikido master George Leonard (1992). Find a willing partner, ideally a colleague who is also working to expand work with difficult clients.

- Stand normally with your partner standing behind you.
- Breathe normally and, as you exhale, tap your forehead lightly, drawing your attention there. As you do so, your partner should (without telling you exactly when) give you a shove from behind at your shoulder blades—not enough to send you flying, but enough to make you take a step forward.
- After this happens, stand upright again, and continue breathing.
- Now, on the exhale, tap your abdomen lightly, drawing your attention there. Again, your partner should suddenly shove you at the shoulder blades with the same degree of force. Do you notice any difference in what happens?

LEAN IN

Before your partner slides away expecting a retaliatory shoving match with you, ask him or her to again stand behind you.

- Stand as you were before, but now have your arms outstretched at your sides at about a 45-degree angle.
- When your arms are outstretched, your partner will again unexpectedly and silently step forward, and this time will grab your wrist tightly and pull down toward the ground (not enough to remove arms from sockets or topple you, but enough for you to feel definitively yanked—please be careful with this, and don't look to perform a professional wrestling move!).
- Focus on the sensations of the grab as much as possible without struggling against it. Allow the grab, and its energy, to fill your awareness.

- What thoughts and emotions emerge? Notice those as well. As your partner continues to hold you tightly, talk aloud, describing the sensations and thoughts as they arise.
- Now, lower your entire body by bending at the knees just a bit, doing so until you again feel centered. Even though your partner is still holding your wrist, do you notice any difference from the initial reactions?

Note your response to this exercise below. Give specific thought to whether the energy of this sudden attack from another person may have added itself to your own. Can you frame yourself as having been fueled by the exchange?

____

____

According to Leonard (1992) (and it's been true when I've tried it as well), most people are more balanced and less thrown by centering themselves (and their attention) lower in their bodies. As a metaphor, what does this suggest as to what happens when we're stuck in our heads (thoughts) as clinicians as a crisis emerges? What might happen if we learned to center in our experience of the crisis—feeling it, taking in its energy and converting it into effective responding? What if, in an actual crisis, you actually practiced your own centering action? For me, it's noticing the tension in my lower abdomen and consciously releasing my belly, allowing my attention and my breath to drop more fully into it, and bringing in more air on the next breath than my reactive reflexes were permitting. What might you do in the toughest moments to anchor yourself? To create an emotional, mental, and even physical center?

You know yourself. Take a moment and consider what action you might take to center yourself amid the tsunami of the moment. What aspect of body, breath, touch, sight, or movement might you anchor yourself to?

____

____

Teacher, author, and cofounder of the Insight Meditation Society Joseph Goldstein (1993) tells the story of a close friend (Sharon Salzberg, another noted meditation teacher) who was living in India. While riding in a rickshaw in Calcutta, Salzberg and a companion were attacked by a man in an alley. They managed to slip away from the attacker unharmed. Goldstein and Salzberg's teacher, Munindra-ji, upon hearing the account of the episode, replied, "With all the lovingkindness in your heart, you should have taken your umbrella and hit the man over the head" (p. 75).

Again, you're no punching bag. Through integrating the energy from a client's intense actions, you are doing much more than passively or masochistically absorbing negativity. Not only do we not help ourselves by allowing others to violate our boundaries, to attack us, we also are not helping them. When we passively take it from our clients, we are unintentionally reinforcing their destructive patterns. The compassionate response in some circumstances is a firm refusal, limit, blocking, or thwarting of the client's untoward actions. The firm response needs, however, to come from a place of compassion. This requires that you've fully anchored yourself in what is (listened and accepted what's occurring), taken in the energy of the moment, connected with guiding values, and then (with good timing) taken a leap. Do so with consistency and clients may slow their egregious behavior, and they may more readily receive your influence to move in a helpful direction. Do so and Bruce Lee would be proud.

Being Gandhi: A Primer in Peacemaking Skills

No one with any knowledge of history can doubt the bold genius of Mahatma Gandhi's assertive, courageous response to the oppressive British rule of India in the last century. From marches to the sea, to nonviolent demonstrations, to his personal hunger strikes, Gandhi wielded peace as an incredible, compassionate power. Without ever picking up a weapon, as we all know, Gandhi's leadership in action effectively toppled British rule and set India on the path to freedom. You may not lead national revolutions, but you can effect a nonviolent revolt within your own professional practice. With care and skill, you can respond to clients' most outlandish behavior in a manner that unties the knot that the client has thrown into your lap. "As I have all along believed that what is possible for one is possible for all, my experiments have not been conducted in the closed, but in the open" (Gandhi, 1962, p. 4). Gandhi would be the first to tell you that you need not be a world leader or a guru to manage really difficult circumstances. You need only be willing to persevere.

What follows is a menu of options for effective "leaping" after you've truly listened and looked at what the client is presenting in the moment and what directions are most important for the work. The list is by no means exhaustive, and many items will be familiar to you. I provide it here as a cue for you to consider what specific actions you can begin inserting into the moments in your clinical interactions when you have previously reacted—the times when you know you did not help the work move forward. Consult the list and consider it an opportunity to begin crafting your own playbook of sorts. Gandhi had his go-to strategies. You should have yours.

Potential Leaps Out of the Fire With Clients

1. "Broken record" (i.e., repeat) to clients a quick summary of what they're feeling behind their behavior (e.g., "You're really pissed right now").
2. Offer a specific time for a follow-up to discuss and problem solve after things have calmed down.
3. Acknowledge your role in the situation, or any error you've made.
4. Lean in toward the client as you soften your eyes, face, and posture. Communicate through gesture that you're not backing down, and yet you're not retaliating either.
5. Make a show of your slowed breathing and cadence of movement. As you slow, so might the client.
6. Acknowledge the truth in clients—either in the content of what they're saying or doing or, at the very least, in their emotions. Show them that you see what's right in them at that moment.
7. LEAD with appropriate limits on the client's boundary-violating behavior (as we discussed in Chapter 10). Directly, concisely, and firmly let the client know what you'll do or not do if the actions continue.
8. Ignore the bait (the emotional hooks clients toss at you) and be willing to wait and let the moment evolve toward something more

workable. You do not have to respond to everything the client says or does. Silent waiting is indeed a response.

9. Speak your mind. Let clients know how their behavior (and perhaps yours as well) is contributing to the stuckness of the moment in a way that allows them to see a genuine human being sitting across from them ("So as you're yelling and screaming at me, here I am over here thinking that if I say or do anything, you'll find a way to make me wrong. . . . I'm feeling a bit trapped and can't make a move even though you came here for me to help you").
10. Steer the moment. As the client's attack is mounting, step in proactively to shift the focus, interrupt, or direct what can and cannot happen (e.g., you might suddenly stand up from your chair, approach a board or easel, and begin writing an agenda for the remainder of the interaction—or write a message to the client that summarizes his stance, yours, and the need to move in a helpful direction). In doing this, you're using nonverbal behavior and verbal structure to rein in the interaction.
11. Strategic exit. You know the interaction is hopelessly gridlocked or heading in a more destructive direction and you assertively either direct the client to leave, or leave yourself (e.g., "I want to address this, but I won't continue the session when you're clearly impaired from using and can't control yourself. Either you leave now, and I will call to reschedule, or I will call security").
12. Be Robin Williams. Do something spontaneous and out of context that will interrupt and spark a possible shift in the interaction. Comedian Robin Williams is famous for his improvisational skills. Being careful not to mock or demean the client, you can do anything from standing up on your desk (as Robin Williams did in the movie *Dead Poets Society*), tossing out your best one-liner (the more tangential, the better), or letting loose with your own rendition of "Hey Diddle Diddle." If done with good timing, the client at best will pause and laugh. A medium response would be a question such as, "What's wrong with you?" (but at least the escalation halts temporarily). At worst, the client will be incensed—again, this is more likely if there's reactive sarcasm on your part, or making light of the client's perspective. If you're merely doing something out of con-

> text and surprising, this is less likely. I've used this strategy to effect on a number of occasions (particularly in therapy groups with behavior-challenged boys). What you're aiming for is a pause in the predictable and unworkable pattern. You're creating a juncture for diverting the interaction onto a more useful path.

Again, this list is a menu, not a prescription. Do some of these things in the wrong context at the wrong time and things can go from bad to malpractice suit. Here's where the mindful scans in Chapter 8's intervention timing discussion are critical. If you've truly connected with mindfulness to all that's emerging inside and outside you in the moment, and if you access guiding values, you are much more likely to respond with the right intervention that attunes to the client, de-escalates the situation, and prevents outright rupturing of the work.

LEAN IN

Center yourself as we've practiced. Cue up the anchors for your sample client. Visualize an interaction that was particularly challenging with this person. See yourself inserting one or more of the actions from the list above into the interaction. How do you see things shifting? Are things more or less workable?

Consider using a partner to role-play this interaction. Provide your partner with enough specifics about your client to replicate some of the content, tone, tempo, and intensity of the episode. Use the role-play as an opportunity to listen, look, and leap with assertive actions to manage the situation. Process the experience with your partner and get feedback as to the partner's perception of you and the impact of your behavior in order to assess the viability of your interventions.

Being Johnny Appleseed: Becoming a Therapeutic Seed-Sower

America, though young by global standards, has still managed to produce its own share of myths and legends. Frontier and wilderness legends like the Bigfoot creature or the axe-wielding Paul Bunyan capture the imagination. Some legends are inflations of historical figures—like young George Washington's honest owning-up when asked about cutting down the cherry tree, or Davy Crockett's adventures fighting at the Alamo. One of my favorites as a kid growing up in Ohio was Johnny Appleseed (born John Chapman in the late 18th century). The Appleseed legend centers around a man who traveled the frontier American Midwest (including places near where I was born) planting apple nurseries. Johnny Appleseed's fame came from the stories of his devotion to environmental conservation and his kind disposition.

As with all legends, there is clearly an inspirational halo around the person—an appeal to us real folks to trek in their direction. So it is for us as clinicians as we near the end of our own trek together. In this chapter we've discussed how to make moves in the hardest of moments with our clients. In these final practice activities of the chapter, we aspire to stretch our compassion muscle to the utmost, even in interactions when it feels impossible to do so. Though we may never fully achieve the Appleseed legendary ideal of kindness toward all, we are likely to get better at managing the worst situations from the effort. Here, we review (with slight adaptation) Chapter 6's presentation of the Tibetan meditation practice of *tonglen*, or, as I'm calling it here, "extreme orienting." Use it to tone your emotional physique in preparation for all the difficult interactions lying ahead of you in your clinical schedule.

LEAN IN

Center yourself as we've practiced. Make sure you're sitting in a location where you won't be disturbed. Though you're cultivating quiet and a distraction-free space, the goal is to practice in calm conditions enough that the technique will be more accessible amid the storms of actual interactions. As we did with *tonglen* practice in Chapter 6, we'll begin with a visualization of open space (whatever signifies vastness and expansiveness for you—sky, canyon, ocean, your cranium—whatever). Due to the level of complexity of the instructions, it may help to either have someone read them aloud to you as you practice or record yourself reading the instructions.

1. Center yourself in a sense of openness, and breathe into it—breathing in the openness on your inhalation, breathing out calm on the exhalation. Situate yourself in this space for a moment, just long

enough to separate from the emotional and mental residue of your activities just prior to sitting down to practice.

2. Shift your awareness toward visualization of a very close loved one. See that person vividly and concretely. Visualize his or her face if possible. Involve all your senses and notice what emerges. Connect to how it feels for you to conjure the person. Rest in this image and your experience of what emerges for a time.
3. Imagine your loved one in significant physical and/or emotional pain. As we've practiced before, on the in-breath, imagine you are filling your chest, your whole body, with this negativity. To make it more vivid, imagine your loved one's pain as something black, hot, or abrasive. Whatever negative sensory quality you might attach, imagine breathing it in. As you are taking this negative quality in, do it with a wish to take the pain on yourself, to fill yourself with it. Take it in with a sense of immense space within yourself to contain it.
4. On the out-breath, imagine sending release, ease, goodness, healing, or some other open, gentle, positive quality to your loved one. Attach a sensory component to the out-breath if possible (e.g., bright light, a specific bright color, cool air, warmth, a clear sky). As you send out this positive aspect, do so with a wish to give it away so that your loved one might be free of pain, and might have relaxation, ease, and so on. Focus on how it feels to take in this pain, and give your ease and release. How willing are you to continue doing so? In with the pain, out with peace.
5. After a minute or two of focusing on your loved one, shift your focus to a difficult client whose behavior has thrown you in some way. See the client vividly in your mind's eye. Conjure up your anchors. Breathe in the pain, the upset, the frustration you are feeling in reaction to your difficult client. On the in-breath, take in the full measure of this negative feeling and do so with the intention to fill yourself with it. Tell yourself: "There are many other clinicians who have felt this way." On the out-breaths, send yourself the positive release, the relaxation, the healing. Tell yourself: "May I be free of this. May I open myself even further."
6. After a short time focusing on yourself and your reactions to your cli-

ent, shift focus to the person of your client. Repeat the same procedure as above, bringing in the client's pain and upset on the in-breath and the wish that you might take on that pain and that you may give the client all the release, ease, and healing on the out-breath—that you intentionally take in the negativity and give your best qualities, your ability to sit in quiet and ease, so that the client might heal and change. While continuing to take in and send out on the medium of the breath, remind yourself of how many individuals are likely suffering as your client is. Also, remind yourself of how many caregivers such as you are struggling with reactions as they try to help.

Notice what shows up as you try to hold your client in this way—bringing in the pain and giving out your release. Try to observe your reactions and continue with the exchange of pain and release on the medium of your breath.

7. Shift your focus back to your loved one. Center yourself on that person until you can once again feel the connection with his or her perspective and difficulty. Continue the breath exchange as before. After a minute of this, return more quickly to visualization of your client. Notice any changes in your ability to take in the pain relative to your first attempt. Continue alternating this way between your loved one and your client, noticing whatever arises as you do.
8. End with visualization of openness and spaciousness. Realize how much space there is for all that you have experienced.

Note below your thoughts and reactions to having practiced cultivating compassion for your most challenging client. Are you willing to continue practicing in this manner? What might come of your efforts?

LEAN IN

Tibetan Buddhist nun and author Pema Chodron (2002) refers to practicing *tonglen* formally (as above) as well as on the spot—intentionally using the medium of the breath to take in others' and our own pain, and send out ease and healing in actual moments of difficulty. Remember, there's nothing magical about this technique, and it's not mere wishful thinking. You're actively cultivating compassionate openness and receptivity within yourself, changing the structure of your brain (as we discussed in Chapter 1), and increasing your odds for successfully managing the toughest situations with clients.

After practicing formal *tonglen* for some time (I'd give it at least a few weeks of daily practice), begin looking for opportunities to use it on the spot in your work. Identify your own personal markers of reactivity (i.e., any of the thoughts you tend to fuse with, specific emotional or physiological experiences that suggest defensive left-side clenching, or the larger-scale emotional patterns we discussed in Chapter 5). You can also look for markers in those with whom you're interacting (i.e., your clients) as well.

Begin with one or two markers that occur with some frequency and commit to implementing *tonglen* sending and taking whenever these occur. Bring in the other person's upset and distress, as well as your own, and send out relaxation on the tide of your breathing. Aim for quiet, quick implementation (maybe just a few breaths' worth) while staying in the moment of what is happening. Again, stick to just one or two markers at the start. To address too many simultaneously may be overwhelming and lead you to discard the practice. Specify your identified practice markers below:

Marker 1: ____

Marker 2: ____

Note in the space below what emerged for you in practicing *tonglen* in your actual interactions. What did you learn about your ability to hold your experience, as well as your ability to manage the interaction? Are you up for continuing to apply this technique to other markers of reactivity?

____

____

____

Johnny Appleseed liked to toss his apple seeds about in order to grow something better for those around him. Our clients can certainly act in morally repugnant, divisive, destructive, and abusive ways. We manage these interactions most effectively when we listen to the inevitability of the energy in them and in us, quickly and carefully discern the relevant values as guidance in the moment, and make our therapeutic (or self-protective) move. Like Johnny, by doing so you are planting seeds amid the context of your work with these individuals. I often remind my supervisees that we, as clinicians, may never witness the flowering of what we've planted. The clients may prematurely terminate, and yet something worthwhile may grow nonetheless. Sometimes the most helpful thing for us to do is to accept our small seedlike role along the client's path and let go of our desire for a Grand Canyon of consequence in their lives. Remember, with our most difficult client interactions, there will be a lot of garbage, but eventually (whether we're there to see it or not) flowers will come.

* * *

MAP CHECK

Take a moment and review what we've covered in this chapter. What was one aspect, one piece of content, that resonated with you—sparked your interest, curiosity, or even angst in some way?

____

Why did this matter to you? What makes this worth writing about? Worth your focus and effort? What is the gravity that this carries for you and your work?

____

What is one specific action you can take within the next 24 hours related to this issue that feels as though it would be important and has the potential to move you in the direction of what matters?

____

* * *

As we draw this chapter to a close, I encourage you to keep thinking and feeling your way toward a more compassionate perspective on yourself and your most challenging clients. We're not talking about the mere boundary testers or no-showers. We're talking about the folks who wake you up at night, perhaps even the ones who threaten to actually do so in a not-so-nice way. You must keep yourself safe and intact, and you must protect yourself and safeguard the effectiveness of the work whenever possible. You also must strive to soften while you stand your ground.

Read the following excerpts from a poem by Zen teacher Thich Nhat Hanh (1992). For this exercise, there's no prompt to lean in, and there are no lines to write on. There's no trying or recording, there's only an experience for you to have right now, and in other moments if you're willing.

Please Call Me by My True Names

The rhythm of my heart is the birth and death of all that are alive . . .
I am the frog swimming happily in the clear pond . . .
I am the grass-snake who . . . feeds itself on the frog . . .
I am the 12 year old girl, refugee on a small boat . . . raped by a sea pirate . . .
and I am the pirate, my heart not yet capable of loving and seeing . . .
Please call me by my true names, so I can wake up, and so the door of my heart can be left open.

≺ CHAPTER TWELVE ≻

The Road Ahead

CONSIDER THE following vignette. You are the therapist.

> "You are so pathetic!" yelled the adolescent son to his mother outside the shopping mall, within earshot of dozens of strangers. "I can't stand walking around in public with you." This boy then let loose with a sailor's string of vulgarity and verbal abuse on his mom. "You're ridiculous!" screamed the boy. "I hate you."

This scenario might not seem all that unusual—a teenager snapping at his parent in public. Many of us have seen it, or experienced it ourselves as parents. The difference here: The parent was fighting cancer, and was then undergoing chemotherapy and radiation treatments. The fact that this mom was wearing a scarf to cover her blotchy and balding scalp gave this boy little pause in his tirade.

Again, you are the clinician working with this family. Notice what thoughts and reactions show up as you imagine hearing about this boy's behavior toward his sick and imperiled mother.

"He seems to pick the worst times to do this to me," says the mom. "In the car, out at the grocery store. He knows when I have the least control," she continues. "It's humiliating. He needs to realize how he's affecting me—how these episodes are going to totally shut him out of society if he keeps it up. I can't do enough for him. I can't fill up the hole inside."

This boy, your client, knows that poking his mother with barbs such as "hate you," "worst mother ever," or "you don't really love me" will spark a struggle that might undo any limit or demand she's placed on him. You find yourself warming to the mother, and going downright cold on this kid who berates, belittles, and takes her for granted.

Imagine you've worked with the mother to cover up her emotional buttons, putting them as far out of reach as possible. You've perhaps taught her some of the same strategies we've practiced here—but you're struggling to practice them yourself with this boy. He often directs his anger and frustration at you.

"What do you know? You're just wanting to get paid."

He is indeed a difficult client. You've helped this mother visualize her own feelings and reactions. You've helped her to distance from her unhelpful thoughts about her son. It is extremely hard for her, but she has practiced noticing and allowing her emotional reactions to her son during sessions with you. She's working to develop healthy perspective regarding her thoughts and beliefs in reaction to him.

Imagine this particular parent later tells you of an episode on a street corner. Struggling with the effects of cancer treatment, she collapsed out of weakness and fell to the sidewalk.

"You are so pathetic," yelled her son. "I can't stand being out with you. You make me sick."

Instead of lashing out and reacting to her son's outlandish behavior with knee-jerk yelling and empty threats, she decided to take a deep breath, step back in her mind, and wait.

"It took about 5 minutes of me being there letting him rant, breathing, allowing, and letting people stare," she tells you. "But eventually he did stop, and then he did something really incredible—he broke down crying right in front of me." She looks at you and with some energy in her voice, continues, "He told me that he just gets so freaked out when he sees me struggling after I've had my chemo. That he worries about what will happen." Though there's a sadness on the mother's face, you also see a flicker of smiling. "I rarely see this side of him," she says. "And I never would have if I snapped at him like I wanted to."

Trusting Your New Path

The mother and son depicted here played frequent games of emotional tug-of-war. You, as the family's therapist, would likely find yourself tempted with such game playing as well. What message does it send our clients, especially our most difficult clients, when we do not pick up the ropes they toss us?

Take a moment and bring your own difficult client to mind. In the space below, write about what might happen if you, like the mother in this vignette, were able to consistently drop the ropes the client offers, or not pick them up in the first place. What might change in your work together?

You cannot hold others, your clients, in compassion if you're too busy gripping yourself tightly. It can be helpful to practice releasing your grip, mindfully noticing the sensations and experience of open and complete acceptance of what is. Compassion for others flows out of self-compassion. You will be more able to trust yourself to use the strategies presented in this book with more challenging clients, the ones who push at you or pull away, once you've learned to trust in your own good intentions and the intact, valid quality of your own experience. Without this trust, the skills will take root like seeds tossed on concrete.

LEAN IN: THE OPEN HAND

We all grip ourselves too tightly from time to time. Perhaps we scold ourselves for yet again giving in to some craving, some impulse to avoid, an urge to attack or defend within our personal or professional lives. Maybe we've fallen short of the promises made to others, including our clients. Maybe a client is pressing a point during a discussion and we find ourselves stiffening, preparing our counterattack. It might simply be that we've forgotten our car keys and now we'll be late for a session. Whatever it is, we all do it—we grip ourselves so tightly, and in the process, we close up. At least for a while, and for some of us, for years, we lose the ability to take in what life is offering. Worse yet, we deprive the world of what's best in us.

Open Hand is a way to practice an ongoing willingness to receive; to let go. Practiced regularly, it has the potential to become both a metaphor and a method for opening one's self.

To begin, sit in an upright, open posture. Take a few deep breaths. Feel your presence in the place you're sitting. Center yourself. When you're ready, close your eyes and focus your attention on the sensations of either your left or your right hand (either is fine). Tighten your hand into a fist and hold it fast for several seconds. Release your hand. Repeat this process a few times. Notice the difference between the tension and the feeling of release. Now, allow your hand to lie open on your lap. Bring your attention to the sensations arising there. Try not to simply think about your hand, but instead, sense the pulsing, the tingling, itching, whatever might be present in the moment. Continue focusing your mind on what your open hand senses.

Notice and allow the play of thoughts, emotion, and other sensations throughout your body. Allow them to come and go. Notice their appearance and their inevitable passing. Gently label these experiences and with kind intention bring yourself back to the sensations of your open hand. Feel the presence of openness there. Rest in this. There is no ownership in this experience, no gripping—just an easy flow between you and the world. Continue in this relaxed open way for as long as feels necessary.

After a time of focusing on this openness, try repeating phrases to yourself that capture a sense of receptivity and open trust in yourself as a clinician. Perhaps phrases such as these:

- May I trust in this openness.
- May I learn to let go of reactivity.
- May I notice my grip and trust in its release.
- May I treat myself with kindness when I do react and grip my experience of clients.

The exact words matter less than an authentic connection to the theme of openness, of choosing to let the clutched fingers of ego relax.

If you're willing, now take things one step further. Anticipate a time in the near future when you will likely close up with a client—when gripping and shutting off is a distinct possibility. Perhaps you've done so in similar situations many times. Maybe it seems an inevitable reflex. Nevertheless, if you're willing, allow yourself to experiment with this situation in a new way.

With your attention deeply resting in the sensations of your open hand, visualize yourself in this situation. Notice the early onset of tension, the tightening in your body, and the flash of thought and emotion that close you up and block you. Return to the sensation of openness in your hand. Rest in that presence and notice the swirl of old patterns of tightening around this open presence. Gently return, over and over, to the feeling of your open hand. Allow this open feeling to swell such that the clutching, the tense, rigid gripping of your old patterns, your reactions and angst in reaction to this client, seem to become smaller and smaller, until they disappear on their own. Continue in this way for as long as feels necessary or comfortable for you. Whatever happens in the play of your experience, come back to the here and now of literal and figurative openness.

When you are ready, open your eyes. Carry this open presence with you and know that you can return to it whenever need be.

Consider all that you've explored in this book about your emotional reactions, emotional and behavioral patterning, and how to use defusion and mindful, present-moment contact to manage these experiences. You've also taken a look at how you might set appropriate limits and boundaries with clients, authentically admit your errors, and use planful process intervention to respond to clients' difficult behavior. You've taken a hard look at the hardest reactions within yourself and gotten "APPALLed" enough to intervene. Perhaps you've worked a bit to improve your management of intervention timing in your work. We've walked quite a long way together (though we're likely both sitting right now).

LEAN IN

Take a few minutes and leaf through this book, reviewing all the discussion and activities we've covered. What among everything was the most meaningful component for you? What specific aspect resonated the most? What connected you with what matters most in your clinical work?

____

____

____

____

What does this say about your values as a clinician? What is the driving force for what you're about as a helper?

____

____

____

____

Letting Your Fingers Point the Way

It can be easy to lose touch with the reasons for opening yourself up to possibilities and change with your most difficult clients. When the stress of the work comes at us so relentlessly, it is tempting to draw our fingers up into tight fists. We clutch things we're afraid of losing, or we ready ourselves to strike back at perceived threats. The theme is rigidity and tension, a closing up that, at least temporarily, cuts us off from progress.

Inside this fist, inside the anger, the fear, the distress, are the reasons to release the grip and open once again. No matter how tightly you grip your fist, eventually your muscles will fatigue and you'll loosen. What if you could remember to loosen before sheer fatigue sets in or you're overwhelmed? What if you could choose more often to let go of the struggle with your reactions to certain clients, and even with this process of attempting to increase your resilience as a clinician, so that your hands are free to reach out to doing the best work possible?

LEAN IN

Look at the fingers of one of your hands. The thumb is your "intention"—your desire to open yourself to the core values that guide your work. Your thumb can reach out and touch the tips of each of the other fingers on the hand—these other four fingers are the "reasons," the shared values, for where the work is going that are coiled up and temporarily lost when pulled into a fist.

In a mere moment, your intending thumb can silently reach out and lightly touch each of these reasons, these values for pursuing the work with a particularly challenging client. With four quick taps, your hand can release with the memory of what you gain by letting go (adapted from David Wexler's [1991] four fingers activity).

Review your exploration and written responses in Chapter 2's discussion of your professional values, as well as Chapter 6's focus on orienting toward your difficult clients. For a particular client, and based on your exploration in this book, list below up to four valued directions for the work (either specific to the work with clients, or in general regarding your role as a clinician). In what direction is the work going despite all the difficulty along the way? Focus less on specific outcomes and more on ongoing processes or qualities that the work is meant to cultivate in you or the client. List your best "four fingers"—reasons for opening within the work—in the spaces below:

1. ______________________________
2. ______________________________
3. ______________________________
4. ______________________________

During a time of reflection or mindful checking in regarding your caseload, take a few minutes and assign each reason to a finger and, touching it with your thumb, hold it in the center of your awareness. Let any thoughts, sensations, images, or emotions arise and fall away. Stay focused on this reason, coming back to it as many times as necessary to enliven and elaborate it. Focus your attention on each reason until your awareness rests fully and completely within it for a time, and then move to the next finger.

Once you have established a clear connection to your reasons for opening to the work, you will be ready to bring these reasons to bear during actual interactions. In fact, nothing is more real than your reasons—it is the chaotic ebb and flow of daily life that is less real.

When, in the course of work with this client, or during a time when you're finding yourself gripping thoughts and reactions in your work, mindfully remember your four fingers. If you are willing, bring the intention of your thumb silently and gently to each of your four fingertips in slow succession. See what happens if you choose to fully connect, in the moment of reflexive tightening, with your reasons for what matters most in your work. Each time you meet with this client, or anytime you find yourself heading into a clinical interaction with less than ample enthusiasm, begin the interaction with a quick thumb-to-finger tap. Notice how quickly you can call up and access the values always lying underneath the surface. If you really give this practice a serious try, my bet is you'll never tap thumb to finger again without these values leaping forward for you.

The Mapmaker in You

Now is the time to put together a specific self-management plan based on the material we've covered. You're at a crossroads in your work because now you have an opportunity to turn your values into action. If you're up for it, you can take what you've learned about yourself and interactions with clients and put some strategies into practice within a larger plan for yourself that takes you in the direction of your values. Let's walk together through the following steps to create this plan.

Using the Interpersonal Process Grid (Figure 2.1), if a client is engaging you with aggressive behavior that falls into Quadrant C (externalizing, disconnection), in what quadrant does your typical (preworkbook) reaction fall? ______

What about if the client engages you with Quadrant D (internalizing, disconnection) behaviors indicative of withdrawal, or turning inward? What quadrant would you react from (in a knee-jerk, nonstrategic fashion)? ______

Thinking of your chosen client, what are the warning signs that this person is about to engage you with these left-sided behaviors? What aspects of the situation, what signals suggest that these behaviors are imminent? Are there any signals in your own body, your thoughts?

____
____
____

What are the likely pattern-based thoughts you anticipate having in reaction to noticing these warning signals? What thoughts are sticky, rigid, and fused?

____
____
____

Assuming you find these thoughts to be unworkable, what defusion or perspective-taking strategies might you apply for each? How might you have these thoughts more flexibly?

____
____
____

For the emotions arising in response to this client, what mindfulness strategies and practices might you employ? When and where will you practice mindful, present-moment contact with your clinical work?

____
____
____

What obstacles might you encounter to using these strategies consistently? What is your plan to address them?

____
____
____

What is your plan for proactively visualizing your client's perspective, for fostering compassion for your most difficult clients? How might you adopt a curious stance as to what it is about the client's inner life that generates the most problematic behavior? (i.e., his or her own scripting, life context, and emotional experience). What will you do, and how often?

___

___

___

Does any of the client's behavior meet the criteria for setting an appropriate limit? How might you frame the limit, and how would you deliver it? Might any behaviors be actively ignored? Are there self-limiting behaviors that might benefit from process intervention? How exactly might you respond to a specific pattern?

___

___

___

I encourage you to take what you've generated here, write it out, and keep it somewhere readily available to you where you work. Review and revise it often, and let colleagues know about your plan. The more effort you put into this sort of proactive planning, and the more you make it accessible, the more you'll be able to manage interactions as they're erupting in the moment without impulsive, from-the-hip solutions.

Adopting an Attitude of Impromptu Self-Training

Remember the finger cuffs metaphor? There is much we can gain from learning to lean into the difficulty we experience with our clients. Sometimes it is the only way to disentangle from tricky situations. We've discussed a number of cognitive, acceptance-based, and mindfulness strategies for doing so. The more you can adopt an impromptu stance—of learning to cue yourself to practice self-management strategies in the moment—the more you will develop the resilience for managing these difficult situations. Let's again review the 3 Ls of in-the-moment self-management.

- Listen . . . leaning into emotions and reactive thoughts . . . allowing them . . . a stance of curiosity regarding your experience . . . defusion and mindful, attentive awareness to simply listen to thoughts without picking them up . . . breathing with full awareness . . . listening for the echo of emotional patterns . . . listening to the energy arising in your body and mind and letting it fluctuate on its own in the few seconds while you're pausing . . . listening for evidence, for clues, of the full context of the situation.
- Look . . . mindfully breathing in and out . . . looking toward the guiding values of your work. . . . What matters most in this moment? . . . What direction is most important for things to go right now? . . . What right-sided moves are most consistent with where you and the client ultimately want this work to go? . . . What's the long view?
- Leap. . . . You've given yourself time to stop and look; you've listened to your thoughts and emotions without following them; now you can leap—take action in the direction of the values that guide the work. . . . Here you are proactively leading the relationship, whether it be with compassionate prizing, process intervention, or even a limit on the client's behavior. . . . What specifically are you doing on the right side of things?

LEAN IN

Think less of a particularly difficult client and focus on how you might work to implement your self-management plan during interactions with this person. What thoughts, feelings, sensations, and urges are you willing to have in order to put your plan into effect? What might arise that would benefit from listening, looking, and leaping on your part?

As you're practicing what we've covered, you may experience significant frustration or a sense that things aren't moving or changing for yourself as you'd hoped—the resilience you wanted isn't materializing. Can you permit these reactions as well?

____

____

____

____

What will you do about the strong, negative reactions that show up in the midst of your work with your most difficult clients? What if anger, resentment, disgust, desire, and so forth surge forward during your interactions with a client and your plan seems out of reach? In order to remember to use the 3 L steps, it may help to develop a simple, yet meaningful cue that will prompt you to move toward your negative reaction, allow it to exist and pass through you, and then also nudge you toward taking flexible action that is attuned to your client (and to yourself), and moves the work in the direction of shared values.

In visualizing your sample client's experience, what single word or image captures or best describes what you, from that person's perspective, think he or she needs the most when behaving in a particular difficult way? In other words, what is the real message the person's actions (or lack thereof) convey? What single word or image comes to mind? For example, for an irritable, belligerent man with chronic relationship problems, that one word might be *connection*, or *understanding*, or an image such as your client's spouse reaching out to take his hand.

What is your cue word or image for the client's perspective? What does the client need most in that context?

Now, considering your reactive tendencies (in terms of quadrants on the Interpersonal Process Grid), what single word best captures your own perspective? What is it you need most in those moments during and immediately following your client's left-sided behavior? It might be *security*, *calm*, *competence*, or *resilience*. Try not to simply describe your reaction, your own left-sided behavior. Think about what's behind it. What do you need? What meaningful word or image comes most readily to mind?

What is your cue for your perspective? Your needs in the context of the work?

These two words or images can serve as your prompts to get centered in your experience, to more fully orient toward your client even in the midst of strong emotion and not be so easily pulled into a tug-of-war interaction.

If the client snaps at you, or rejects your honest efforts to help, you can label the behaviors (the client's and yours) with what is emotionally central for each of you (i.e., bringing these cues to mind in response to noticing one of the warning signs you've listed above). As we discussed in Chapter 1, such labeling activates the less emotional, perspective-taking aspects of the brain. It provides you a window of opportunity—an opening for responding with more self and other-directed attunement.

"All you do is nod and umm and uhh me to death! When are you going to actually say something helpful?"

You sit back in your chair, surprised and a bit thrown by this sudden flaring from your client. You're thinking about how you've been trying for months to help the client take action to cope with depression. You've invested quite a bit of energy into this particular client. The client has often gotten angry in session, and often directs it at you.

Imagine you are the therapist in this situation. What might the warning signs be? What specific things might you notice about the client or yourself that would prompt you to take a step back in your mind?

____

____

____

Once you see the warning signs, it's time to *listen*—to stop, breathe, pause, and immediately bring your cue words or images to mind (which will help connect you with your own and your client's experience). Continuing to breathe mindfully, you might apply defusion, perspective taking, or full awareness of sensation in the moment. Then you should begin to *look* toward your values (perhaps with a thumb-to-finger tap to jar the value loose in your mind). The key is to create a small space for a proactive, attuned response (an appropriate *leap*) as opposed to a knee-jerk, left-sided reaction.

Take the situation above (or an actual situation from one of your own clients) and apply the 3 Ls (notice warning signs, call up cues, use breathing or mindful attention, apply defusion, notice your emotions, and prepare for appropriate, value-consistent action). In the space below, describe your experience of applying these steps.

____

____

Maintaining Your Momentum

What you will likely find is that, like any new skill—particularly one you're attempting to use in difficult circumstances—it will not come easily at first. You might find it hard to notice the warning signs. The knee-jerk reactions often come so quickly that you can't pull up your cues, or implement breathing and defusion strategies in time to avoid a tug-of-war. It can seem daunting, if not impossible.

In order to generate and keep up your momentum for developing your inner resilience and skills at relational and self-management, it's important to commit to some principles. Think of this as a shopping list of sorts—come back from the store without these items, and you're going to end up professionally malnourished when it comes to the harder, rougher edges of your clients.

1. Hold Up a Mirror to Yourself

Find ways to get samples of your in-session behavior (either through audio- or videotaping or through others' observations of your work). Maybe it will help to expand and revise how you write session notes so that you are providing at least a few concrete details of what you did during interactions. Sit with your observations—mindfully check in and ask yourself what you notice. How do you feel about the awareness and care you brought forth in your behavior?

2. Two's Company (Importance of Feedback)

An important step in implementing your self/session management plan is to consider the benefits of discussing and processing all of the material we've covered with a processing partner. This may be a supervisor, but there may be limits (based on the nature of the supervisory relationship) on how willing you'll be to fully reveal your negative experiences. If this is the case, select a colleague you trust who will keep your discussions confidential, and someone you believe will offer authentic insight and support.

The mere fact that you are going public with your professional growth efforts will help solidify your motivation and resolve.

Be sure to proactively structure your processing discussions with your partner. Ask if he or she is willing to give you specific feedback on how you are doing in developing and implementing your plan for managing the work with your clients. Ideally, the processing will be mutual, with you offering the same support and structured feedback on implementation of mindful, flexible use of strategies.

After the first meeting with a partner, what did you learn from the conversation about how to best manage your emotions and reactions to clients?

____

____

____

What impact did your conversation have on your commitment to the ongoing practice of your plan for managing your reactions?

____

____

____

3. Piggyback Others

Let go of any unworkable thoughts of inferiority and spend time observing and learning from other clinicians who happen to be a bit farther down the self-management and relational intervention path than you. Ask them questions and show gratitude for the examples they provide. Give them reasons to open to you so you can learn as much as possible. They (because they've worked on this stuff) will likely want to be accessible to you because they've learned that doing so helps them grow as well.

4. Keep Tabs

Either informally through your notes, or more formally (such as with a tally of your use of specific strategies and ratings of their effect), maintain ongoing data regarding your implementation of the strategies and techniques we've covered. Don't rely on your subjective sense of things alone.

Anchor your sense of progress in a more objective, reliable method whenever possible in order to see the small, yet detectable increments of progress that our inner radar often misses.

5. Practice (Duh)

It may sound ridiculously intuitive, but it's nonetheless important to emphasize practicing these strategies in both actual and imagined, anticipated difficult situations. The more you place yourself mentally in various situations where flooding and difficult left-sided reactions are likely, the more you can practice proactive right-sided responses. It may also help to start with "easier" difficult client situations. Starting with the most challenging client on your caseload might be overwhelming and sap your motivation for change (i.e., knock you right back into precontemplation). Don't do what I did my first day learning to ski and buy a lift ticket for the challenging slopes after only 30 minutes on the beginner's slope. Guess where I ended up? (Think ski patrol and you're pretty close.)

List three possible difficult situations you will likely face with clients in the coming weeks. Carving out a few minutes, allow yourself to imagine these situations vividly. Practice implementing the 3 Ls in order to manage your thoughts and emotions. Be sure to consider proactive leadership interventions you might use as well. If you're willing, repeat the practice until you are able to readily visualize yourself engaging in these behaviors in a solid, centered way, with less judgment, labeling, and emotional reactivity. Look for opportunities to try out these strategies in actual practice.

____

____

____

6. Listen to Your Mother (and Don't Bite Off More Than You Can Chew)

Take it slow and don't try to change too much too quickly. Focus on specific situations and specific clients, and take things step-by-step. If you're feeling overwhelmed and beginning to fuse with notions of giving up on this self-management business, cut yourself some slack and take a break. Come back to the material and your self-management plan later (or perhaps revise and downsize it).

7. Make It Worth Your While

If you are indeed regularly connecting with your values for this practice, this connection alone is likely to be sufficient incentive for you. Doing this hard work of professional growth will simply feel important and worthwhile—taking you where you want to go. In addition, though, you might consider rewarding yourself for your efforts—buy that book or a new office chair, or take that day off for a massage (highly recommended) as an acknowledgment of all you're doing for your clients (and for yourself).

8. Make and Keep Commitments to Yourself Regarding Practice

Clinical self-management work will require practice and commitment. There is no silver-bullet easy fix for these patterns. If you commit to practice, you will likely experience significant benefits over time. Your emotional, perspective-taking, sense of presence, and calm-in-the-storm equanimity, as well as your relational leadership muscles, will grow stronger.

Considering the values you've identified for your work, what is a specific, concrete goal for improving your management of clinical interactions that will move you in the direction of these values?

____

____

____

What is the smallest, most doable step to begin in this direction that you are willing to pause and take right now?

____

____

____

9. No Destination

Keep your focus on the fact that you'll never "get there." There will always be more skill to develop, more you can learn about sharpening your ability to manage the charged, angst-ridden aspects of your work. Take (good) continuing education courses (like mine!). Read a professional text (instead of that trashy beach novel). Sign up for advanced certification training. Create and implement a new intervention project within your work that expands things. Don't rest in routine, because it's when we're lulled by the repetitive droning of routine work that we're most thrown by the sudden clang of difficult interactions with clients. If we're used to choosing challenge and change, the stance of intentionality buffers, if not enlivens, us when the "stuff" hits the fan.

Of Dropped Ropes and Ripples on Water

When I was a boy, I loved to toss rocks into the large reservoir down the street from my house. Sometimes I skipped them on the surface, but if thin pieces of rock were unavailable, I opted for the big chunky ones that would make the biggest "kerr-plunk!" I remember standing and watching the water ripple out from the point of impact into the distance. Such rippling is what I believe we're all hoping for as therapists. We hope for a positive impact that will carry forward in the lives of our clients, and that will produce momentum in the lives of others we may never meet.

LEAN IN

Here's our final mindfulness activity—perhaps the most important. This is a version of a meditation I first heard psychologist, researcher, and author Jon Kabat-Zinn (2005) deliver. He refers to it as a pebble meditation. I like it because it reminds me of those days as a boy tossing rocks into the reservoir. It also helps me remember what's most important to me in my work.

Start by sitting in a centered, stable manner. With your eyes closed, visualize that you are standing next to a lake or pond. Hear and see the movement of water. Watch the play of light on its surface. You are tossing a rock into the water. Listen as it hits the water. As it makes contact, you're also listening for an answer to this question: Why am I doing this work? Why keep moving down this path of fully addressing my difficult interactions?

With each breath in and out, you're listening to whatever emerges in you. Don't push for answers; simply let them emerge as you follow the rock's descent down through the water. Track the rock as it slides into the depths of the lake, bubbles sliding around it, all manner of fish darting with ease out of its path. As the rock descends, so does your attention down into the deepest spots in your heart and mind. Let yourself be curious as to what is resting there. What do you notice? What's most important? Sit with this awareness of yourself, your work, and this journey we've begun for a bit. You've certainly come a long way, but for now, you're just noticing what is most resonant. What has depth, what ripples out the most about your endeavors as a helper?

Researchers (Cacioppo, Fowler, & Christakis, 2009; Neumann & Strack, 2000) have documented the "contagion" that can develop in people's moods and behavior within their social networks. Simply by being in relationship with others, by being associated, people's likelihood for experiencing certain significant mood states (such as loneliness and depression), as well as certain problem behaviors (such as smoking and overeating), increases dramatically. Moods and behaviors seem contagious—they can ripple out among people.

While much research on mood contagion remains to be done, what is known begs a question of us in clinical practice: Assuming we, as social animals, can "ripple out" and be contagious to one another with emotions, how do we want our emotions and in-session behavior to impact our clients? What sort of infectious agent do you want to be for your clients?

List below the emotions, the perspective, you hope to spread to your clients.

____

What obstacles can you envision that might inhibit your expression of these?

____

____

We are contagious to our clients (and they to us) whether we intend it or not. Remember, we are wired for social connection. The problem is that, because of our personal histories and the limitations of cognitive perspective, we often get locked into unhelpful patterns. We play tug-of-war instead of getting down in the dirt with our clients, allowing the smudges and stains of their experience, and acknowledging our own. My primary goal for this book has been to assist you in learning to step out of reaction and cultivate proactive responses that will likely have a significant positive influence on the helping relationship. You're probably little different than me—you hope to toss rocks into the water that will ripple out in a positive way. You can't do so if you're wasting time yanking at ropes along the water's edge.

Smiling at Road Kill

Some time ago, I was driving my normal route on my way to work in the morning, and as I moved down an exit ramp from the highway, I noticed a dead raccoon lying along the side of the road. I did what the vast majority of people do when they see a carcass along the shoulder of a busy street—I averted my eyes and focused my attention elsewhere. Who wants to stare at a dead and decaying animal? It's unpleasant and there are certainly better things to focus on.

Each morning, I passed this same spot. Amazingly, no one bothered to remove the carcass over a period of a couple of months (it seems others were averting their eyes as well). Each morning I caught a glimpse of it, and each morning I felt the familiar impulse to look away. Somehow though, I became aware of my impulse and I chose to really note the presence of these remains—to check in with them (crazy as that sounds). Over the days, weeks, and months, I watched them decay, transform, and ultimately disappear altogether. Now, tall grass stands in the place where this animal rested.

I can only imagine the fluttering of thoughts in your mind at present—just notice them for a moment (your mind: "Where the heck is all this talk about dead animals going?"). Don't snap the book shut now because we're wrapping things up. Trust me, I am going somewhere with this. . . .

Thich Nhat Hanh (2005) once said that "what you are *not* is the illusion of what you *are*" (italics mine). We like to think that we, as well-trained and highly experienced clinicians, are separate and distinct from our clients, particularly our more interpersonally challenging ones—the distasteful ones that lead us to want to turn away. They press buttons and they act out or withdraw in self-destructive ways. We are intact, whole, and doing correct, professional things. Well, as you might guess, I'm questioning this.

The raccoon that died along the side of the road I passed each day was actually not as distinct from me as I originally thought. Once I opened myself to noticing it, I realized that the road kill became the grass that released oxygen that I may have breathed in as I passed each morning. In addition, all this mindful breathing—more importantly, the willingness and intention to expand my perspective—seems to have opened me such that I was more willing to allow people to ease into traffic around me (without my foregoing, angst-ridden steering wheel pounding), perhaps easing their frustration and harried driving, perhaps leading to less pushing and pulling later in their day. My increased openness in thought and emotions (sparked by willingly noticing and leaning toward this simple dead animal) may have rippled out into my own work day—more allowing of whatever showed up in my interactions with all the difficult clients during a typical day of clinical work.

What was the line, the actual boundary between me and this dead raccoon? This reasoning may seem to be a stretch, but let yourself play with it a bit. As we end our time together, think about all we've discussed about the mutuality of clinical work, the inevitability of communication and emotional influence, and ask yourself: *Am I really separate and distinct from my more challenging clients?* Isn't it an error for me to consider them difficult when I've played a role in each and every interaction, particularly those in which we've played tug-of-war? How effective will I be if I continue to practice within an illusion of distinction and impenetrability with my clients? Our journey has been about learning to give up this illusion—to open ourselves as much as possible to influence and being influenced so that we can give up the sense of them as difficult, and create a "we" that works toward progress and change. There is no "difficult"—there is only what's there within and between you.

With our clients, "difficult" does not have to be a death knell for the work. As we discussed in Chapter 6, if we're willing to step back enough, we can see how the most outrageous, vexing clients actually created unexpected gains for us. If we, as clinicians, do this inner work to create perspective and manage our emotions and behavior, then we become more available to our clients. We develop our resilience to challenging patterns of interaction and we remain open to possibilities for attunement, connection, effective intervention, and the opportunities we could never have imagined in those hard moments.

If we, as clinicians, use a rope-dropping stance to manage our reactive thoughts and emotions during work with clients, we are doing so not out of a sense of acquiescing, agreeing with, or condoning their self-destructive patterns. We can prize our clients without picking up their behavior or attitudes and heralding them. By doing the inner work to address our reactions to clients, we lead the relationship forward. We can set appropriate limits and structures on the work and proactively intervene. We can act from a stance of attunement and interconnectedness.

Take a backward glance at where we've traveled in this exploration. Hopefully, you have learned about your clients and yourself. As we travel alongside our clients for the time we're together, our efforts to gain perspective and emotional presence will do much to make the journey not only bearable, but one of lasting meaning.

Remember—you *will* fail.

But also remember—you can keep dropping the rope. You can keep leaning in.

References

Aggs, C., & Bambling, M. (2010). Teaching mindfulness to psychotherapists in clinical practice: The mindful therapy programme. *Counselling and Psychotherapy Research, 10,* 278–286.

Antle, M. C., & Silver, R. (2009). Neural basis of timing and anticipatory behaviors. *European Journal of Neuroscience, 30,* 1643–1649.

Baer, R. A. (2003). Mindfulness training as a clinical intervention: A conceptual and empirical review. *Clinical Psychology: Science and Practice, 10,* 125–143.

Barkley, R. A. (1997). *Defiant children: A clinician's manual for assessment and parent training* (2nd ed.). New York: Guilford.

Barnett, J. E. (2011). Psychotherapist self-disclosure: Ethical and clinical considerations. *Psychotherapy, 48,* 315–321.

Barrett, M. S. (2001). Is psychotherapy more effective when therapists disclose information about themselves? *Journal of Consulting and Clinical Psychology, 69,* 597–603.

Berk, L. S., Tan, S. A., Fry, W. F., Napier, B. J., Lee, J. W., Hubbard, R. W., Lewis, J. E., & Eby, W. C. (1989). Neuroendocrine and stress hormone changes during mirthful laughter. *Amercian Journal of the Medical Sciences, 298,* 390–396.

Berne, E. (1964). *Games people play*. New York: Grove.

Boorstein, S. (1995). *It's easier than you think: The Buddhist way to happiness*. New York: HarperCollins.

Bowlby, J. (1958). The nature of the child's tie to his mother. *International Journal of Psychoanalysis, 39,* 350–373.

Brazelton, T. B., & Greenspan, S. L. (2000). *The irreducible needs of children: What every child must have to grow, learn and flourish*. New York: Perseus.

Brendtro, L., Mitchell, M., & McCall, H. (2009). *Deep brain learning:*

Pathways to potential with challenging youth. Albion, MI: Starr Commonwealth.

Brisch, K. H. (2002). *Treating attachment disorders: From theory to therapy*. New York: Guilford.

Bruce, N. G., Manber, R., Shapiro, S. L., & Constantino, M. J. (2010). Psychotherapist mindfulness and the psychotherapy process. *Psychotherapy: Theory, Research, Practice and Training, 47*, 83–97.

Buber, M. (1958). *I and thou*. New York: Scribner's.

Cacioppo, J., Fowler, J., & Christakis, N. (2009). Alone in the crowd: The structure and spread of loneliness in a large social network. *Journal of Personality and Social Psychology, 97*, 977–991.

Cappas, N. M., Andres-Hyman, R., & Davidson, L. (2005). What psychotherapists can begin to learn from neuroscience: Seven principles of brain-based psychotherapy. *Psychotherapy, 42*, 374–383.

Carter, C. S. (2009). The ups and downs of emotion regulation. *Biological Psychiatry, 65*, 359–360.

Cheng, Y., Chen, C., Ching-Po, L., Kun-Hsien, C., & Decety, J. (2010). Love hurts: An fMRI study. *Neuroimage, 51*, 923–929.

Chiesa, A., & Serretti, A. (2009). Mindfulness-based stress reduction for stress management in healthy people: A review and meta-analysis. *Journal of Alternative and Complementary Medicine, 15*(5), 593–600.

Chodron, P. (1994). *Start where you are: A guide to compassionate living.* Boston: Shambhala.

Chodron, P. (2002). *Comfortable with uncertainty*. Boston: Shambhala.

Christensen, A. (1990). Gender and social structure in the demand/withdraw pattern of marital conflict. *Journal of Personality and Social Psychology, 59*, 73–81.

Christopher, J. C., & Maris, J. A. (2010). Integrating mindfulness as self-care into counseling and psychotherapy training. *Counselling and Psychotherapy Research, 10*(2), 114–125.

Conrad, D., & Kellar-Guenther, Y. (2006). Compassion fatigue, burnout and compassion satisfaction among Colorado child protection workers. *Child Abuse and Neglect, 30*, 1071–1080.

Corballis, M. C., & Beale, I. L. (1983). *The ambivalent mind: The neuropsychology of left and right*. Chicago: Nelson-Hall.

Creswell, J. D., Way, B. M., Eisenberger, N. I., & Lieberman, M. D. (2007). Neural correlates of dispositional mindfulness during affect labeling. *Psychosomatic Medicine, 69*, 560–565.

Crits-Christoph, P., Connolly, M. B., Crits-Christoph, K., Narducci, J., Schamberger, M., & Gallop, R. (2006). Can therapists be trained to improve their alliances? A preliminary study of alliance-fostering psychotherapy. *Psychotherapy Research, 16*, 268–281.

Croskerry, P. (2003). The importance of cognitive errors in diagnosis and strategies to minimize them. *Academic Medicine, 78*, 775–780.

Csikzentmihalyi, M. (1997). *Finding flow: The psychology of engagement with everyday life*. New York: Basic Books.

Dalai Lama. (1999). *Ethics for the new millenium*. New York: Riverhead.

Dalai Lama, & Cutler, H. (1998). *The art of happiness*. New York: Riverhead.

Daly, K. D., & Mallinckrodt, B. (2009). Experienced therapists' approach to psychotherapy for adults with attachment avoidance or attachment anxiety. *Journal of Counseling Psychology, 56*, 549–563.

Daniels, D. N., & Price, V. (2009). *The essential enneagram: The definitive personality test and self-discovery guide*. San Francisco: Harper.

Darley, J., & Batson, C. (1973). From Jerusalem to Jericho: A study of situational and dispositional variables in helping behavior. *Journal of Personality and Social Psychology, 27*, 100–108.

Davidson, R. J., Kabat-Zinn, J., Schumacher, J., Rosenkranz, M., Muller, D., Santorelli, S., et al. (2003). Alterations in brain and immune function produced by mindfulness meditation. *Psychosomatic Medicine, 65*(4), 564–570.

DePaulo, B. M. (1992). Nonverbal behavior and self-presentation. *Psychological Bulletin, 111*, 203–243.

Duffy, A., & Momirov, J. (2000). Family violence: Issues and advances at the end of the twentieth century. In N. Mandell & A. Duffy (Eds.), *Canadian Families* (2nd ed.). Toronto: Harcourt Brace Canada.

Efklides, A. (2008). Metacognition: Defining its facets and levels of functioning in relation to self-regulation and co-regulation. *European Psychologist, 13*, 277–287.

Emerson, R. W. (1841). Self-reliance. *Essays: First series*. Boston: James Munroe.

Figley, C. (1995). *Compassion fatigue: Coping with secondary traumatic stress disorder in those who treat the traumatized*. New York: Brunner/Mazel.

Fisher, H. (2004). *Why we love*. New York: Henry Holt.

Flavell, J. H. (1979). Metacognition and cognitive monitoring: A new area of cognitive developmental inquiry. *American Psychologist, 34*, 906–911.

Foreman, S. A., & Marmar, C. R. (1985). Therapist actions that address initially poor therapeutic alliances in psychotherapy. *American Journal of Psychiatry, 142*, 922–926.

Freud, S. (1959a). Future prospects of psychoanalytic psychotherapy. In J. Strachey (Ed. & Trans.), *The standard edition of the complete psychological works of Sigmund Freud* (Vol. 11, pp. 139–151). London: Hogarth. (Original work published 1910)

Freud, S. (1959b). The dynamics of transference. In J. Riviere (Ed. & Trans.), *Collected papers of Sigmund Freud* (Vol. 2, pp. 312–322). (Original work published 1912)

Freudenberger, H. J. (1985). *Women's burnout: How to spot it, how to reverse it, and how to prevent it*. Garden City, NY: Doubleday.

Froh, J. J., Sefick, W. J., & Emmons, R. A. (2008). Counting blessings in early adolescents: An experimental study of gratitude and subjective well-being. *Journal of School Psychology, 46*, 213–233.

Gallagher, H. L., & Frith, C. D. (2003). Functional imaging of "theory of mind." *Trends in Cognitive Science, 7*, 77–83.

Gandhi, M. (1962). *The essential Gandhi: An anthology of his writings on his life, work and ideas* (L. Fischer, Ed.). New York: Vintage.

Gelso, C., & Hayes, J. (2007). *Countertransference and the therapist's inner experience: Perils and possibilities.* Mahwah, NJ: Erlbaum.

Gilbert, D., & Malone, P. (1995). The correspondence bias. *Psychological Bulletin, 117*, 21–38.

Goldstein, J. (1993). *Insight meditation: The practice of freedom*. Boston: Shambhala.

Goleman, D. (2006). *Social intelligence: The revolutionary new science of human relationships*. New York: Bantam.

Gordon, A. M., Impett, E. A., Kogan, A., Oveis, C., & Keltner, D. (2012). To have and to hold: Gratitude promotes relationship maintenance in intimate bonds. *Journal of Personality and Social Psychology, 103*(2), 257–274.

Gottman, J. M. (1999). *The marriage clinic: A scientifically based marital therapy*. New York: Norton.

Gottman, J. M. (2002). *The relationship cure*. New York: Three Rivers Press.

Gottman, J. M., Katz, L. F., & Hooven, C. (1996). Parental meta-emotion philosophy and the emotional life of families: Theoretical models and preliminary data. *Journal of Family Psychology, 3*, 243–268.

Graham, E. E. (1995). The involvement of sense of humor in the development of social relationships. *Communication Reports, 8*, 158–169.

Grepmair, L., Mitterlehner, F., & Nickel, M. (2008). Promotion of mindfulness in psychotherapists in training. *Psychiatry Research, 158*(2), 265.

Gunaratana, B. (2002). *Mindfulness in plain English*. Somerville, MA: Wisdom.

Gutheil, T. G., & Gabbard, G. O. (1993). The concept of boundaries in clinical practice: Theoretical and risk-management dimensions. *American Journal of Psychiatry, 150*, 188–196.

Guy, J. D., Poelstra, P. L., & Stark, M. J. (1988). Personal distress and therapeutic effectiveness. *Professional Psychology: Research and Practice, 20*, 48–50.

Hanh, T. N. (1992). *Peace is every step*. New York: Bantam.

Hanh, T. N. (2001). *Essential writings*. Maryknoll, NY: Orbis Books.

Hanh, T. N. (2005). *Meditation and psychotherapy*. Louisville, CO: Sounds True.

Hanson, R. (2009). *Buddha's brain: The practical neuroscience of happiness, love and wisdom*. Oakland, CA: New Harbinger.

Harlow, H. F. (1958). The nature of love. *American Psychologist, 13*, 673–685.

Harris, R. (2009). *ACT made simple: A quick-start guide to ACT basics and beyond*. Oakland, CA: New Harbinger.

Harris, S. (2009). *Communicating with distressed constituents: A legislator's guide*. Sacramento: California Psychological Association.

Harrison, R. L., & Westwood, M. J. (2009). Preventing vicarious traumatization of mental health therapists: Identifying protective practices. *Psychotherapy: Research, Practice and Training, 49*, 203–219.

Hayes, J. A., Gelso, C. J., & Hummel, A. M. (2011). Managing countertransference. *Psychotherapy, 48*, 88–97.

Hayes, J., McCracken, J., McClanahan, M., Hill, C., Harp, J., & Carozzoni, P. (1998). Therapist perspectives on countertransference: Qualitative data in search of a theory. *Journal of Counseling Psychology, 45*, 468–482.

Hayes, J., Riker, J., & Ingram, K. (1997). Countertransference behavior and management in brief counseling: A field study. *Psychotherapy Research, 7*, 145–153.

Hayes, S. C., Bond, F. W., Barnes-Holmes, D., & Austin, J. (2006). *Acceptance and mindfulness at work*. Binghamton, NY: Haworth.

Hayes, S. C., & Smith, S. (2005). *Get out of your mind and into your life: The new acceptance and commitment therapy*. Oakland, CA: New Harbinger.

Hayes, S. C., Stroshahl, K., & Wilson, K. G. (1999). *Acceptance and commitment therapy: An experiential approach to behavior change*. New York: Guilford.

Herron, R. E. (2011). The science of health promotion: Changes in physician costs among high-cost transcendental meditation practitioners compared with high-cost nonpractitioners over 5 years. *American Journal of Health Promotion, 26*, 56–60.

Hofmann, S. G., Sawyer, A. T., Witt, A. A., & Oh, D. (2010). The effect of mindfulness-based therapy on anxiety and depression: A meta-analytic review. *Journal of Consulting and Clinical Psychology, 78*(2), 169–183.

Holroyd, J., & Brodsky, A. (1977). Psychologists' attitudes and practices regarding erotic and nonerotic physical contact with clients. *American Psychologist, 32*, 843–849.

Holzel, B. K., Carmody, J., Vangel, M., Congleton, C., Yerramsetti, S. M., Gard, T., & Lazar, S. W. (2011). Mindfulness practice leads to increases in regional brain gray matter density. *Psychiatry Research: Neuroimaging, 191*, 36–43.

Holzel, B. K., Lazar, S. W., Gard, T., Schuman-Olivier, Z., Vago, D. R., & Ott, U. (2011). How does mindfulness meditation work? Proposing mechanisms of action from a conceptual and neural perspective. *Perspectives on Psychological Science, 6,* 537–559.

Iacoboni, M. (2008). *Mirroring people: The science of empathy and how we connect with others.* New York: Picador.

Jung, C. (1963a). *Memories, dreams and reflections.* New York: Random House.

Jung, C. (1963b). *The psychology of the transference.* New York: Routledge.

Kabat-Zinn, J. (1994). *Wherever you go, there you are: Mindfulness meditations in everyday life.* New York: Hyperion.

Kabat-Zinn, J. (2005). *Pebbles and pearls: Meditations with Jon Kabat-Zinn.* Louisville, CO: Sounds True.

Kagan, J., & Snidman, N. (2004). *The long shadow of temperament.* Cambridge, MA: Harvard University Press.

Kamei, T., Kumano, H., & Masumura, S. (1997). Changes of immunoregulatory cells associated with physiological stress and humor. *Perceptual and Motor Skills, 3,* 1296–1298.

Kazdin, A. E. (1997). Parent management training: Evidence, outcomes and issues. *Journal of the American Academy of Child and Adolescent Psychiatry, 36,* 1349–1356.

Kazdin, A. E. (2005). *Parent management training.* Oxford: Oxford University Press.

Kazdin, A. E., & Weisz, J. R. (2003). *Evidence-based psychotherapies for children and adolescents.* New York: Guilford.

Kinsbourne, M., & Cook, J. (1971). Generalized and lateralized effects of concurrent verbalization on a unimanual skill. *Quarterly Journal of Experimental Psychology, 23,* 341–345.

Kirk, U., Downar, J., & Montague, P. R. (2011). Interoception drives increased rational decision-making in meditators playing the ultimate game. *Frontiers in Neuroscience, 5,* 1–11.

Kivlighan, D. M., & Shaughnessy, P. (2008). Patterns of working alliance development: A typology of client's working alliance ratings. *Journal of Counseling Psychology, 47,* 362–371.

Kleespies, P. (2008). *Behavioral emergencies: An evidence-based resource for evaluating and managing risk of suicide, violence and victimization*. Washington, DC: American Psychological Association.

Kopp, S. (1977). *Back to one: A practical guide for psychotherapists*. Palo Alto, CA: Science and Behavior Books.

Kottler, J. A. (1993). *On being a therapist*. San Francisco: Jossey-Bass.

Kramer, G. (2007). *Insight dialogue: The interpersonal path to freedom*. Boston: Shambhala.

Krause, N. (2006). Gratitude toward God, stress, and health in late life. *Research on Aging, 28*, 163–183.

Kreiman, G., Koch, C., & Fried, I. (2000). Imagery neurons in the human brain. *Nature, 408*, 357–361.

Ladany, N., O'Brien, K. M., Hill, C. E., Melincoff, D. S., Knox, S., & Peterson, D. A. (1997). Sexual attraction toward clients, use of supervision, and prior training: A qualitative study of predoctoral psychology interns. *Journal of Counseling Psychology, 44*, 413–424.

Larson, D. (1980). Therapeutic schools, styles, and schoolism: A national survey. *Journal of Humanistic Psychology, 20*, 3–20.

Leahy, R. L. (2003). *Cognitive therapy techniques*. New York: Guilford.

Lefcourt, H. M., Davidson, K., Shepherd, R., & Phillips, M. (1995). Perspective-taking humor: Accounting for stress moderation. *Journal of Social and Clinical Psychology, 14*, 373–391.

Leonard, G. (1992). *Mastery: The keys to success and long-term fulfillment*. New York: Plume.

Levenson, H. (1995). *Time-limited dynamic psychotherapy: A guide to clinical practice*. New York: Basic Books.

Levenson, R. W., & Ruef, A. M. (1992). Empathy: A physiological substrate. *Journal of Personality and Social Psychology, 63*, 234–246.

Lewis, T., Amini, F., & Lannon, R. (2000). *A general theory of love*. New York: Random House.

Liebling, B. A., & Shaver, P. (1973). Evaluation, self-awareness and task performance. *Journal of Experimental Social Psychology, 4*, 297–306.

Luders, E., Kurth, F., Mayer, E. A., Toga, A. W., Narr, K. L., & Gaser, C. (2012). The unique brain anatomy of meditation practitioners: Alterations in cortical gyrification. *Frontiers in Human Neuroscience, 6*, 34.

Luoma, J. B., Hayes, S. C., & Walser, R. D. (2007). *Learning ACT: An ac-*

ceptance and commitment therapy skills training manual for therapists. Oakland, CA: New Harbinger.

Lyubomirsky, S., & Nolen-Hoeksema, S. (1995). Effects of self-focused rumination on negative thinking and interpersonal problem solving. *Journal of Personality and Social Psychology*, *69*, 176–190.

Mahoney, M. J. (1991). *Human change processes*. New York: Basic Books.

Marci, C. D., Moran, E. K., & Orr, S. P. (2004). Physiologic evidence for the interpersonal role of laughter during psychotherapy. *Journal of Nervous and Mental Disease, 192*, 689–695.

Martin, C., Godfrey, M., Meekums, B., & Madill, A. (2011). Managing boundaries under pressure: A qualitative study of therapists' experiences of sexual attraction in therapy. *Counselling and Psychotherapy Research, 11*, 248–256.

Martin, D. J., Garske, J. P., & Davis, M. K. (2000). Relation of the therapeutic alliance with outcome and other variables: A meta-analytic review. *Journal of Consulting and Clinical Psychology*, *68*, 438–450.

Martin, R. A., & Dobbin, J. P. (1988). Sense of humor, hassles and immunoglobulin A: Evidence for a stress-moderating effect of humor. *International Journal of Psychiatry in Medicine, 18*, 93–105.

Martin, R. A., & Lefcourt, H. M. (1983). Sense of humor as a moderator of the relation between stressors and moods. *Journal of Personality and Social Psychology*, *54*, 520–525.

McCollum, E. E., & Gehart, D. R. (2010). Using mindfulness meditation to teach beginning therapists therapeutic presence: A qualitative study. *Journal of Marital and Family Therapy*, *36*(3), 347–360.

Mikulincer, M., & Shaver, P. R., & Pereg, D. (2003). Attachment theory and affect regulation: The dynamics, development, and cognitive consequences of attachment-related strategies. *Motivation and Emotion, 27*, 77–102.

Muran, J. C., & Barber, J. P. (Eds.) (2010). *The therapeutic alliance: An evidence-based guide to practice*. New York: Guilford.

Neff, K. D. (2003). Self-compassion: An alternative conceptualization of a healthy attitude toward oneself. *Self and Identity*, *2*, 85–101.

Neumann, R., & Strack, F. (2000). Mood contagion: The automatic transfer of mood between persons. *Journal of Personality and Social Psychology, 79*, 211–223.

Nezu, A. M., Nezu, C. M., & Blissett, S. E. (1988). Sense of humor as a moderator of the relation between stressful events and psychological distress: A prospective analysis. *Journal of Personality and Social Psychology, 54*, 520–525.

Ochsner, K. N., & Gross, J. J. (2008). Cognitive emotion regulation: Insights from social cognitive and affective neuroscience. *Current Directions in Psychological Science, 17*, 153–168.

Orlinsky, D. E., & Ronnestad, M. H. (2005). *How psychotherapists develop: A study of therapeutic work and professional growth*. Washington, DC: American Psychological Association.

O'Sullivan, L., & Ryan, V. (2009). Therapeutic limits from an attachment perspective. *Clinical Child Psychology and Psychiatry, 14*, 215–235.

Patsiopoulos, A. T., & Buchanan, M. J. (2011). The practice of self-compassion in counseling: A narrative inquiry. *Professional Psychology: Research and Practice, 42*, 301–307.

Payer, D. E., Baicy, K., Lieberman, M. D., & London, E. D. (2012). Overlapping neural substrates between intentional and incidental down-regulation of negative emotions. *Emotion, 12*, 229–235.

Pirsig, R. (1974). *Zen and the art of motorcycle maintenance*. New York: Bantam.

Pope, K. S., Keith-Spiegel, P., & Tabachnick, B. G. (1986). Sexual attraction to clients: The human therapist and the (sometimes) inhuman training system. *American Psychologist, 41*, 147–158.

Prochaska, J. O., & DiClemente, C. C. (1982). Transtheoretical therapy: Toward a more integrative model of change. *Psychotherapy: Theory, Research and Practice, 20*, 161–173.

Prochaska, J. O., & Norcross, J. C. (1994). *Systems of psychotherapy: A transtheoretical analysis* (3rd ed.). Pacific Grove, CA: Brooks/Cole.

Proust, M. (1925). The sweet cheat gone. *Remembrance of Things Past* (vol. 11, chapter 1). Hertfordshire, UK: Wordsworth Editions.

Ramachandra, V., Depalma, N., & Lisiewski, S. (2009). The role of mirror neurons in processing vocal emotions: Evidence from psychophysiological data. *International Journal of Neuroscience, 119*, 681–691.

Razmarin, E., Muran, J. C., Safran, J., Gorman, B., Nagy, J., & Winston, A. (2008). Subjective and intersubjective analyses of the therapeutic alliance in a brief relational therapy. *American Journal of Psychotherapy, 62,* 313–328.

Rodgers, N. (2011). Intimate boundaries: Therapists' perception and experience of erotic transference within the therapeutic relationship. *Counseling and Psychotherapy Research, 11,* 266–274.

Rodolfa, E., Hall, T., Holms, V., Davena, A., Komatz, D., Antunez, M., & Hall, A. (1994). The management of sexual feelings in therapy. *Professional Psychology: Research and Practice, 25,* 168–172.

Rogers, C. R. (1961). *On becoming a person.* Boston: Houghton Mifflin.

Rothschild, B. (2006). *Help for the helper: The psychophysiology of compassion fatigue and vicarious trauma.* New York: Norton.

Ruiz, J. M., Matthews, K. A., Scheier, M., & Schulz, R. (2006). Does who you marry matter for your health? Influence of patients' and spouses' personality on their partners' psychological well-being following coronary artery bypass surgery. *Journal of Personality and Social Psychology, 91,* 255–267.

Safran, J., & Muran, C. (2000). *Negotiating the therapeutic alliance: A relational treatment guide.* New York: Guilford.

Sandell, R., Ronnas, P., & Schubert, J. (1992). Feeling like a good psychotherapist—or a bad one: Critical incidents in psychotherapists' experiences. *Psychoanalytic Quarterly, 6,* 213–229.

Schneider, W. J., Cavell, T., & Hughes, J. (2003). A sense of containment: Potential moderator of the relation between parenting practices and children's externalizing behaviors. *Development and Psychopathology, 15,* 95–117.

Seigel, D. J. (2010). *The mindful therapist: A clinician's guide to mindsight and neural integration.* New York: Norton.

Seligman, M. (1975). *Helplessness: On depression, development, and death.* San Francisco: Freeman.

Shapiro, S. L., & Carlson, L. E. (2009). *The art and science of mindfulness: Integrating mindfulness into psychology and the helping professions.* Washington, DC: American Psychological Association.

Simpson, J. W., Collins, A., Tran, S., & Haydon, K. (2007). Attachment and the experience and expression of emotion in romantic relationships: A developmental perspective. *Journal of Personality and Social Psychology, 92*, 355–367.

Smith, K. J., Subich, L. M., & Kalonder, C. (1995). The transtheoretical model's stages and processes of change and their relation to premature termination. *Journal of Counseling Psychology, 42*, 34–39.

Stamm, B. H. (1999). *Secondary traumatic stress: Self-care issues for clinicians, researchers and educators*. Lutherville, MD: Sidran.

Stiles, W. B., Glick, M. J., Osatuke, K., Hardy, G. E., Shapiro, D. A., Agnew-Davies, R., Rees, A., & Barkman, M. (2004). Patterns of alliance development and the rupture-repair hypothesis: Are productive relationships U-shaped or V-shaped? *Journal of Counseling Psychology, 51*, 81–92.

Storaasli, R. D., Kruashaar, B., Wilson, K., & Emrick, C. (2007). Convention, tradition, and the new wave: Assessing clinician identity in behavior therapy. *Behavior Therapist, 30*, 149–155.

Strauss, J. L., Hayes, A. M., Newman, C. F., Brown, G. K., Barber, J. P., Laurenceau, J. P., & Beck, A. T. (2006). Early alliance, alliance ruptures, and symptom change in a nonrandomized trial of cognitive therapy for avoidant and obsessive-compulsive personality disorders. *Journal of Consulting and Clinical Psychology, 74*, 337–345.

Surrey, J. (2005). Relational psychotherapy, relational mindfulness. In C. K. Germer, R.D. Siegel, & P.R. Fulton (Eds.), *Mindfulness and psychotherapy*. New York: Guilford.

Sweet, M., & Johnson, C. (1990). Enhancing empathy: The interpersonal implications of a Buddhist meditation technique. *Psychotherapy, 27*, 19–29.

Trungpa, C. (2003). *Training the mind and cultivating loving-kindness*. Boston: Shambhala.

Valdesolo, P., Ouyang, J., & DeSteno, D. (2010). The rhythm of joint action: Synchrony promotes cooperative ability. *Journal of Experimental Social Psychology, 46*, 693–695.

Vasquez, M. J. T. (2009). Sometimes a taco is just a taco! *Professional Psychology: Research and Practice, 38*, 406–408.

Wachtel, P. (2008). *Relational theory and the practice of psychotherapy*. New York: Guilford.

Wexler, D. B. (1991). *The PRISM workbook: A program for innovative self-management*. New York: Norton.

Wicks, R. (2008). *The resilient clinician*. New York: Oxford University Press.

Wilson, K. G. (2008). *Mindfulness for two: An acceptance and commitment therapy approach to mindfulness in psychotherapy*. Oakland, CA: New Harbinger.

Yalom, I. D. (1995). *The theory and practice of group psychotherapy* (4th ed.). New York: Basic Books.

Yoon, K. L., & Joormann, J. (2012). Is timing everything? Investigating the impact of rumination and distraction on interpersonal problem solving. *Cognitive Therapy and Research, 36*, 165–172.

Index

In this index, *f* stands for figure.

1366918

Fraser Wilson

BBC. 5 session